Federal taxes and
management
decisions

Federal taxes and management decisions

RAY M. SOMMERFELD
College of Business Administration
The University of Texas at Austin

1974

RICHARD D. IRWIN, INC. Homewood, Illinois 60430
Irwin-Dorsey International, London, England WC2H 9NJ
Irwin-Dorsey Limited, Georgetown, Ontario L7G 4B3

First Printing, January 1974

ISBN 0-256-01592-9
Library of Congress Catalog Card No. 73–91361
Printed in the United States of America

To Andrea and Kristin

Preface

THIS TEXT is written for all students who need to be able to recognize the important tax consequences that are apt to attach to many common business transactions. This group includes most students of business administration enrolled in general management programs, especially those in M.B.A. programs. It may also include that majority of accounting and law students who do not intend to become tax specialists.

Federal Taxes and Management Decisions is pragmatic. It attempts to demonstrate to the student how substantially different tax liabilities sometimes attach to nearly identical economic events and thus enable him to recognize that tax rules do in fact substantially alter human behavior at the individual and the business entity level, at least for those who understand the rules. The book constantly emphasizes practical results, giving little or no consideration to the intellectual, social, or political considerations inherent in those results.

From the standpoint of instructors, most of us are so deeply steeped in the tradition of teaching tax problems and solutions—rather than the recognition of tax opportunities and pitfalls—that we think of examinations only in terms of short problems and an occasional essay question on very specific tax provisions. For example, we ask the student to explain why a particular tax provision exists or we ask him to expound upon the economic consequences of a given provision. In a course on tax recognition, the student's task is simply to identify the problems and opportunities that are hidden in common business transactions and need to be investigated more thoroughly by a tax expert. If the student can explain even roughly why he thinks the critical factors need further investigation, he has done his job as a future business manager. Illustrative cases have been included at the end of this book to suggest the type of examination and discuss questions that can be successfully utilized by the instructor in a tax recognition course.

In addition to using case-type examinations, the author would urge all adopters of this text to consider seriously the need for supplemental reading materials selected from the periodical business literature. By illustrating how a general notion discussed in the text has been used by known people in recognized corporations makes the entire study much more fascinating. Professors who adopt this text in classroom quantities can obtain from the publisher a suggested list of supplemental readings as well as brief solutions to the cases at the end of the text.

The chapters of this text are generally topical in nature and can, therefore, be read and understood independently. The only major exceptions are chapters 2, 3, and 5, and they should be read before any subsequent materials if the book is to be used as a primary text. Chapter 2 provides a broad review of some basic income tax propositions that are fundamental to the remainder of the book; hopefully it will also clarify some common misconceptions. Chapter 3 explains which entities are required to report and pay taxes on their incomes. It also explains how the income earned by other entities is attributed to one of the taxable entities and the important differences in the tax rate schedules that are applied to each of the taxable entities. Chapter 5 reviews the basic rules which determine the tax treatment of capital gains and losses. Unfortunately those rules are unusually intricate and many a reader will be tempted to conclude that it would not be worth the time required to really comprehend that material. Such a conclusion would be most unfortunate because capital gains and losses represent by far the most important single income-tax-saving opportunity available today and, before anyone can really appreciate those opportunities, it is necessary that he understand the basic rules.

All other chapters—except the last two which deal with related problems—represent self contained discussions of important tax saving opportunities in specific though common business decisions. Chapter 13 describes some of the more common tax traps. It is as important for the potential entrepreneur to be aware of a tax trap as it is for him to be aware of common tax saving opportunities. The final chapter describes the several events which collectively constitute the taxing process of taxing—the filing of returns, the audit selection procedures, the accompanying administrative reviews by the IRS, and possible litigation alternatives.

Chapter 13 also deals with the common problem of identifying qualified taxpayer assistance. In a very important sense, the tax responsibilities of the future business managers to whom this book is addressed end just where the tax expert's begin. It is assumed that no one would directly apply the ideas suggested here until a tax expert had been consulted. Hopefully, the book may help the student distinguish between real tax experts and those who are only marginally qualified.

Finally, the reader should understand that the book is in no sense comprehensive. The provisions selected for discussion are those which contain the most significance in the most common transactions. In general these are income tax provisions although a lesser emphasis is placed, in some chapters, on estate and gift tax considerations. The reason for this concentration of attention is explained by the fact that the federal income tax dominates the tax structure of the United States. By comparison relatively little can be done by the taxpayer to modify his non-income tax liabilities. The only major exception involves the federal estate and gift taxes which, as noted, are discussed in this text.

The author would like to take this opportunity to thank the many students who have contributed so importantly to his own education. Their patience and assistance in bringing this project to fruition is deeply appreciated.

Austin, Texas   RAY M. SOMMERFELD
December 1973

Contents

I

An introduction

Just how did 112 Americans with annual incomes in excess of $200,000 legally avoid the payment of any federal income tax in 1970? Well, the Treasury Department now says that the correct number is 106, not 112 as originally reported. They explain the 106 cases as follows. In seven cases the primary answer was a large foreign tax credit; because these taxpayers paid large foreign taxes, they do not have to pay U.S. taxes on the same income. In 12 cases the major factor was an unusually large state and local tax deduction. Because these 12 report income on a cash basis, the state and local taxes which they paid in 1970 on even larger incomes earned in 1969 were sufficient to relieve them of further federal tax liability in 1970. Another 12 are explained in terms of large charitable contribution deductions. In 55 cases the primary explanation was a large interest expense deduction—a result which will be less likely in years after 1971 for reasons explained later. In the final 20 cases the Treasury Department says the explanation must be found in unusually large miscellaneous deductions for security losses; accounting, bookkeeping, and professional fees; investment counsel; and management fees. One of these 20 offset $400,000 in gambling income with gambling losses.

Except for the group of 55 with the large interest expense deduction, this detailed analysis of 106 income tax returns is of minimal importance to tax planning in general. An equally detailed study of the way in which several thousand other high income taxpayers actually reduced their effective tax rate to much less than the apparent

1

tax rate schedules imply would be vastly more informative. For many reasons, no such detailed study exists. We know with certainty, however, that if such a study were made it would include most of the tax planning ideas considered here.

This book is intended to help you understand just how tax reduction was possible for these 106 people and why it may or may not be possible for you. In all candor, however, you should understand that the probabilities of being able to reduce your own tax liability to zero really are very limited and not terribly important. What is far more important is the fact that there are things that you may be able to do that will reduce your tax liability substantially even though they will not reduce it to zero. Headlines and political interest may focus only on the few wealthy individuals who reduce their income tax to nothing; fortunately real economic success is not so demanding.

Before we go further the reader also should understand that this book has relatively little immediate impact for the nonpropertied, salaried employee of a large corporation. The only and honest reason for neglecting this person is the cold fact that little can be done to save him significant amounts of taxes. Our income tax bears most heavily upon the wage and salary earner simply because he has so few options available and the tax laws have taken the necessary precautions to block most of those. Self-employed individuals and, more especially, persons with substantial amounts of property have available an almost endless number of alternatives and, because of the magnitude of these options, many important opportunities for tax saving remain. Our concern will be with those opportunities.

THE MORALITY OF IT ALL

No socially sensitive reader can escape subtle doubts about the morality of finding more and better ways to reduce his own tax liability when those taxes supposedly are collected and then expended for the greatest common good. These doubts, however, might be resolved on at least two grounds. First, tax avoidance has been found by the courts to be wholly legal. Perhaps the most celebrated statement on this point was delivered in 1947 in the case of *Commissioner* v. *Newman* where, in a dissenting opinion, Justice Learned Hand wrote: "Over and over again courts have said that there is nothing sinister in so arranging one's affairs as to keep taxes as low as possible. Everybody does so, rich or poor, and all do right, for nobody owes any public duty to pay more than the law demands: taxes are enforced exactions, not voluntary contributions. To demand more in the name of morals is mere cant."[1] Even though Justice Hand's words are from a dissenting opinion and, therefore, of no legal value as precedent, the statement is widely quoted as authoritative. Other legal opinions have reached the same conclusion, only they have stated it in less colorful language.

Granting the legality of tax avoidance does not necessarily lead to the conclusion that it is in the country's best interest that knowledge of tax loopholes be even more widely disseminated. In response, however, there is even less to be said in favor of restricting the knowledge of tax loopholes to any select few. All validated observations made in the past support the conclusion that the rich have been substantially more successful in their tax avoidance than have the poor. Nothing in this book is going to change that result because, as explained earlier, it is the mere ownership of property that gives the taxpayer the large number of alternatives which make substantial tax savings possible. To the limited extent that greater utilization of existing tax loopholes is facilitated by this book, it is hoped that it will serve to diffuse the benefits among a larger number of less wealthy people. If the results finally are deemed to be socially unacceptable by the masses, the widest possible dispersion of knowledge about the loopholes can only hasten the corrective political mechanism.

BASIC TERMINOLOGY

Taxation, like every other discipline, relies upon some basic terminology to convey fundamental ideas. In tax planning, the understanding of a few common terms is essential. Among the most critical words and phrases are the following: exclusion, deduction, tax base, tax rate, and tax credit. Virtually every successful plan to save taxes is based on the manipulation of one or more of these variables. Because the concepts behind these words and phrases are so critical to tax saving opportunities, it seems advisable to clarify their meaning before we turn our attention to more specific details.

Exclusion

In tax parlance the word *exclusion* is used to refer to any item that, in ordinary English usage, would be considered part of a more

---

[1] *Commissioner* v. *Newman,* 159 F. 2d 848 (2d Cir., 1947).

general class of items or events that has been made the basis for a tax but which has been specifically removed from the tax base by law. For example, the sales tax imposed by most of the states in the United States is technically imposed on all retail sales. At the same time virtually all of the state legislatures have decided to exclude from the sales tax base all sales of foodstuffs for off-premise consumption. Thus, the retail sales of food items in a grocery store constitute an exclusion from the more general retail sales tax base.

In tax planning one of the simplest and most effective methods of tax minimization involves the maximization of exclusions. As you might suspect, the list of exclusions typically is very brief and, therefore, the amount of tax-planning potential in this area is rather limited. Relative to the federal income tax, one very major exclusion does exist. The federal government does not tax the interest earned by a taxpayer who invests his capital in a state or local government's bonds. Consequently, any taxpayer can reduce his federal income tax liability to zero simply by switching his investment portfolio from corporate stocks and securities to state and local government bonds. The major economic cost which attaches to this simple tax-saving plan is the reduced earnings that usually result because of the tax exempt feature. That is, state and local government bonds typically pay lower rates of interest than bonds of equivalent risk precisely because high-tax-bracket investors are willing to accept lower rates of interest which go tax free in preference to higher rates of interest which produce a lower after-tax return on their investment. To illustrate, the taxpayer in a 50 percent marginal tax bracket is better off investing in 6 percent state bonds than in 10 percent commercial paper because his after-tax return remains at 6 percent in the former instance but is reduced to 5 percent in the latter case. A taxpayer in the 30 percent marginal tax bracket would not, of course, reach the same conclusion.

Deductions

In tax literature the word *deduction* is used to refer to any item that the law authorizes as a reduction of a gross quantity to a net quantity designated as a tax base. Because both exclusions and deductions serve to reduce the net tax base, it is very easy to confuse the two concepts. For purposes of interpreting and applying certain tax rules, however, it is important that a clear distinction be maintained. As a simple illustration of this difference, consider the need of two taxpayers to file a federal income tax return. Taxpayer A earns $50,000 in interest on State of California bonds but incurs no authorized expenses in connection with that income. Taxpayer B earns $50,000 in rents from an apartment house and incurs $50,000 in deductions for depreciation, property taxes, interest, maintenance costs, etc. The law provides that a single taxpayer generally must file an income tax return if his gross income exceeds $2,050. Application of this filing requirement provision means that Taxpayer A need *not* file a return but that Taxpayer B must. A has a gross income of zero because his income can be excluded from the gross tax base by definition. B has a gross income of $50,000 since his expenses are only deductions from the gross tax base. Neither A nor B, of course, will pay income tax if this is their only source of income, since both will have a net tax base of zero.

Obviously, taxes can be minimized to the extent that deductions can be maximized. The first step in maximizing deductions consists of learning which items are deductible simply to avoid overlooking one or more authorized deductions. Sometimes maximizing deductions may also require the rearrangement of one's business affairs and the creation of a particular form of business organization. The tax-saving value of a deduction is also directly related to the marginal tax bracket of the taxpayer incurring it. Thus a taxpayer in the 70 percent marginal tax bracket will save $7,000 in income taxes for every additional $10,000 in deductions that he may claim; a taxpayer in the 22 percent marginal tax bracket would save only $2,200 in taxes from an equivalent deduction. Therefore it is important that the taxpayer insure, to the extent possible, that his authorized deductions are incurred at the most advantageous time—for example, in an unusually high income year—or by the most advantageous taxpayer—for example, by an individual rather than a corporation under certain circumstances.

Tax base

The term *tax base* refers simply to the net quantity on which any particular tax is levied. For purposes of income taxation that net quantity is called *taxable income;* for estate taxation, *taxable estate;* and for gift taxation, *taxable gifts.* The key word in each instance is the adjective taxable. What it connotes, of course, is that the residual quantity is the dollar value which remains after the taxpayer has given adequate consideration to all pertinent definitional problems, exclusions, and deductions. Careful attention to these three items makes possible the minimization of any tax base.

A taxpayer may be able to further minimize his tax liability by making certain that he has spread the tax base over the maximum number of taxable entities. Because the tax rates utilized in income, estate, and gift taxation are all progressive rates—that is, the marginal tax rates get higher as the tax base increases in amount—it is generally to the taxpayer's benefit to split a tax base among a number of taxable entities so that each reporting unit may begin by applying the rates at the lowest possible level rather than allowing a single entity to report the entire tax base and thus be forced to apply higher and higher marginal tax rates to the same aggregate amount of tax base.

Tax rate

A *tax rate* is a specified percentage, or series of percentages in the case of a progressive tax, which the law stipulates as the appropriate multiplier in the determination of a gross tax liability. Stated another way, any tax liability is calculated by multiplying the tax base by the statutory tax rate(s). For example, a state legislature may stipulate that it will utilize a 5 percent tax rate in determining the retail sales tax liability in a particular year. In that event anyone who purchases a $100 item that is subject to the retail sales tax will pay a sales tax of $5 on his purchase ($100 × 5%).

In income taxation, Congress has specified four different rate schedules for individual taxpayers—one each for single persons, heads of households, married persons filing jointly, and married persons filing separately—and another totally different rate structure for corporate taxpayers. Obviously, then, a taxpayer with a given amount of income automatically will change his tax liability any time that he rearranges his affairs so that a different rate schedule will be applied to that given amount of income. Perhaps the most obvious rearrangement is marriage: a single individual earning a taxable income of $50,000 can reduce his tax liability from $20,190 to $17,060 per year simply by getting married to a person who has no taxable income to report. This illustration also demonstrates clearly the importance and complexity of the nontax considerations which often must be weighed before rushing headlong into perfectly legal tax planning ideas.

Congress also has designated that certain special "kinds" of income shall be eligible for special tax rates. For individual taxpayers income can be classified in one of three ways; as earned income, certain capital gain income, or other income. The special rates that are available for special kinds of income differ for different taxpayers. Furthermore, each special rate necessitates a special definition of exactly which income items shall be eligible for that special rate and which items of income shall be excluded from the special privileges. Several tax-saving opportunities exist because individuals may be able to achieve a reclassification of their income from a less privileged to a more privileged class.

Tax credit

A *tax credit* is any specially authorized reduction in a gross tax liability. Note that tax credits are fundamentally different from deductions and exclusions even though all three items are subtracted at one point or another in the tax calculation procedure. A $500 tax credit reduces a gross tax liability by the full $500; a $500 deduction will reduce a tax liability by some smaller amount, the specific reduction being determined by the marginal tax rate of the taxpayer authorized to claim the deduction. Once again the list of tax credits is typically small. For the entrepreneur the most important tax credit is the investment credit. The income tax law presently authorizes a variable tax credit based on purchases of specified assets. By a careful selection of assets, by giving attention to the determination of that asset's estimated life, and by carefully timing its disposition, a taxpayer can substantially modify his tax liability by changing the dollar amount of the investment credit to which he is entitled.

To summarize the basic terminology introduced in this chapter, we might construct the following simple computational diagram to illustrate the various steps followed in the tax determination process.

Specification of a general class of items or events
made the basis for a tax by legislative action
less *exclusions*

equals the gross tax base
less *deductions*

equals the *net tax base*
times the specified *tax rate(s)*

equals the gross tax liability
less *tax credits*

equals the net tax payable to the government

As the reader considers the various tax saving propositions detailed in the remaining chapters, he should attempt to categorize each one in the context of this computational diagram. In other words, he should ask himself exactly why that particular tax saving is made possible. He will very often discover that the answer depends upon the combined effect of two or more variables; for example, by a timely maximization of deductions, the taxpayer may be able to modify the effective tax rate in a most favorable manner. The reason for attempting to place each idea in this perspective is simply that by the act of analyzing each illustration carefully, the reader will become attuned to the often simple differences which constitute a common thread among all tax-saving opportunities. The sooner the reader can identify these common threads, the sooner he will be able to apply the same basic idea to his own particular situation.

2

The income concept: General
rules and common
misconceptions

PERHAPS the most accurate but least useful definition of taxable income is that attributed to unnamed skeptics who have suggested that taxable income is what the Code says it is and nothing more pretentious. The Code is a document of approximately eighteen hundred pages replete with general rules, exceptions, exceptions to exceptions, slight modifications, and vague definitions. The Treasury Regulations, which interpret the Code, exceed four thousand pages of comparable material. To decry the complexity of the Code does little, however, to aid in understanding it. This chapter will attempt to simplify and restate some of the more important general rules used to measure income for tax purposes. These general rules tend to be harsh in their application. The reader should not, however, give up hope too early. Most of the remaining chapters of this book explain how taxpayers may be able to mitigate the generally harsh criteria established in this chapter.

Virtually all readers of this book have had some exposure to the income concept. If nothing else, most of them will have filed their own tax returns at one time or another. Other readers will have examined or even prepared an income statement for a business enterprise. Notwithstanding those experiences, this chapter will review some basic elements of the income concept as it is applied in federal income tax matters. Primary attention will be given to the basic concepts that are most frequently misunderstood or misapplied in particular circumstances. The chapter is divided into two major sections. The

9

first section deals with gross income, or the positive element in income determination. The second section deals with tax deductions, or the negative element in income determination. Taxable income is, of course, the arithmetic difference between the aggregate number used to represent gross income and the aggregate number used to represent deductions.

GROSS INCOME

Before we even attempt to define gross income, the reader should get accustomed to the first basic rule of federal income taxation. That is, *all income is taxable income unless the taxpayer can find good authority for excluding it*. To help the reader interpret this basic rule as it applies to gross income, the next several pages will be used to consider some of the more important corollary rules which are used to implement the basic rule in specific circumstances. These corollary rules explain the importance of the realization criterion; the insignificance of the form of payment; the unimportance of the direct or indirect status of a benefit received; and the relative significance of accounting methods, statutory exclusions, and assignment of income principles.

The realization criterion

Stated in its simplest form, the realization criterion says that mere appreciation in value will not be considered to constitute taxable income. Alternatively, it says that income will not be recognized for tax purposes until it has been realized. The reader must be careful to avoid misinterpretation of the alternative definition; the realization criterion does *not* say that a taxpayer must have an increase in cash, or even an increase in current assets, before he has taxable income. Income generally is associated with an increase in net wealth and most increases in wealth, unless attributable to mere appreciation in value or to a statutory exclusion, do constitute taxable income. However, an increase in wealth in the current year is not essential to the presence of taxable income. To illustrate this conclusion, assume that a taxpayer purchased common stocks 15 years ago and that these stocks steadily increased in value for the first nine years and that the value of the shares then remained constant for the next six years.

In the first nine years of ownership, the taxpayer would not report any taxable income even though the stocks may have appreciated from their cost of $10,000 to a value of $100,000. In the next five years the taxpayer would not perceive that he had any income, excluding the possibility of dividends, because his stock value failed to increase further. If, however, in the fifteenth year the taxpayer exchanged those stocks for a plot of land, for other stocks or bonds, or for almost any other property, the taxpayer would be deemed to have realized the $90,000 income that had previously gone unrecognized. Even though this taxpayer had realized no increase in net wealth during the last six years prior to the exchange, and even though the property the taxpayer took in exchange for the stock was relatively unmarketable, he would have to recognize the entire $90,000 taxable income in the one year in which the exchange was made. That conclusion is the essence of the realization concept.

Virtually any change in the form or the substance of a property or property right is sufficient to constitute realization for income tax purposes. To the frequent surprise of a taxpayer, income may be realized when others forgive his outstanding debts; when he wins a prize in a contest; when he embezzles funds; when he incorporates his extant business; when he divides property with an ex-wife in a divorce action; or when he finds a treasure trove on his property. Because realization is such a pervasive concept, and because the income tax is a concomitant facet of realization, a taxpayer should always consult with an advisor on the potential tax consequences which may attach to any intended action that could modify the form or the substance of any of the taxpayer's property rights.

Accounting methods

The subject of accounting methods will be considered in greater depth in Chapter 12. At this early juncture we need only note that the Code technically provides that taxable income shall be computed on the same basis of accounting as the taxpayer uses in maintaining his regular set of books. This provision, unfortunately, is often as misleading as it is helpful when applied to the notion of gross income. Most noncorporate taxpayers operate on a cash basis of accounting and this fact sometimes causes them to conclude that they need not report any taxable income unless and until they receive cash. This conclusion is not justified in many circumstances. A taxpayer on a cash basis of accounting will utilize a cash-receipts test to determine the proper year of reporting such routine items of income as wages, salary, interest, dividends, and rents. He will not, however, apply the same cash-receipts test to such nonrecurring transactions as the sale of an investment or the sale of his home. In all nonroutine transactions the tax authorities will apply a *cash-equivalence* rule and treat the taxpayer as if he had received cash equal in amount to the value of the noncash property received on the disposition. Return momentarily to the earlier illustration in which a taxpayer exchanged stocks worth $100,000 for, say, a plot of speculative desert land, even if that taxpayer were ordinarily a cash-basis taxpayer; the authorities would insist that the land received must have been worth $100,000 and tax him accordingly. Tax administrators generally will assume that a taxpayer would not enter into an exchange unless he thought he received equivalent value. Hence, they tend to value the most easily valued property and assume the value equivalence for the other item exchanged. Special rules will be applied to transactions between related taxpayers where there is reason to believe that an exchange was not made at arm's length.

Constructive receipt

A taxpayer on the cash method of accounting occasionally will attempt to postpone the recognition of even routine taxable income by refusing to exercise his domination over funds received. A taxpayer might, for example, defer picking up his paycheck until January 2; he might refuse to open an envelope known to contain a dividend check until the first day of a new year; or he might not withdraw or record interest that had accumulated on a savings account in the current year. In each of these situations the tax rules would find that the income in question was taxable in the current year because it had been constructively received. Whenever a taxpayer has the authority to exercise control over the income, he has constructively received it regardless of when he actually exercises his power of domination.

The tax authorities occasionally stretch the concept of constructive receipt well beyond the boundaries of common sense. For example, employees of many state agencies are required by law to participate in a state retirement program. Frequently this participation requires a "contribution" from the employee which can be regained and enjoyed only upon (1) quitting the job, (2) retiring, or (3) dying. A reasonable person might well argue that such an employee does not have constructive receipt over the withheld portion of his salary until he quits, retires, or dies. The tax authorities disagree and the courts sustain their contention that the full salary, including any amounts withheld, is fully taxable when earned. The rationale for their conclusion apparently rests upon the belief that the taxpayer does receive an indirect benefit immediately (the knowledge that he is covered by a retirement program) and that the value of that benefit is equal to the amount withheld from his salary.

Form of payment

As previously observed, the asset form in which a taxpayer receives his income is wholly immaterial to the income tax consequence. A wage is equally taxable if it is paid in the form of a case of good scotch, a book, or cash. Noncash payments necessitate the determination of a fair market value which may create administrative problems in obtaining agreement between the taxpayer and the Internal Revenue Service (IRS) agent. The taxpayer typically will undervalue the asset received and the IRS agent will overvalue it. Both parties realize that a reasonable estimate usually can be agreed upon during the administrative or judicial proceedings which accompany a tax dispute.

The author has known numerous instances in which taxpayers erroneously believed that they had cleverly avoided the income tax by taking their rewards in noncash forms. Three illustrations may be helpful. In one instance, a university professor took pride in the fact that he always elected to receive his honorarium for speeches in the form of personally selected books which he added to his library. In the second instance, a dentist exchanged services with his laundryman neighbor. That is, the dentist kept the teeth of the laundryman and his family in good repair in exchange for free laundry and dry cleaning services for the dentist and his family. The third instance involved a new corporate venture in which the young entrepreneurs took their compensation in the form of corporate stocks. Legally the professor, the dentist, and the entrepreneurs all realized taxable income in an amount equal to the fair market value of the goods or services that they received. In each instance the taxpayer erroneously failed to report the income that he had received and in each instance the error went undetected by the IRS. The chance of the IRS uncovering such an error is admittedly remote. Nevertheless, the reader should understand clearly that each of these intended tax-saving plans could be considered fraudulent and each of the taxpayers could end up in a federal penitentiary for tax evasion. Any tax advisor who either condones or recommends tax planning of this variety is grossly incompetent, as well as a party to fraud, and should be dismissed immediately.

Indirect benefits

The relative insignificance in tax matters of the form of payment extends also to the direct or indirect status of any benefit received. A taxpayer must recognize as part of his own taxable income any receipts which he earned but which he arranged to be paid directly to another person. Suppose, for example, that a physician were to direct a patient to pay his fee directly to the physician's grandchild. Even though the physician never received any cash for the service rendered, he would be taxed fully on the amount paid to his grandchild by the patient. The tax rules would determine the tax liability just as if the physician had received the fee and immediately made a gift of it to his grandchild.

The application of the indirect benefit concept is sometimes more difficult to apply than the previous illustration would suggest. Corporate employers often expend rather large sums of money for the apparent benefit of the corporation's employees. The corporation may purchase, for example, life, health, and accident insurance policies; recreational facilities; pension plans; and other perquisites, all for the benefit of the employees. Whether or not the indirect benefits from these corporate purchases will be taxed to the employee depends upon a host of special rules. In general it is safest to assume that all benefits received, directly and indirectly, do constitute gross income. In Chapter 6, we will learn why and how employee benefits in particular may be one of the most promising ways for many taxpayers to achieve substantial tax savings in a wholly legal fashion.

Illegal gains

Profits obtained from illegal activities are just as taxable as those earned from more legitimate activities. As a matter of fact, income tax evasion has been made the basis for legal prosecution in instances where the government seemed to be unable to obtain a conviction on other grounds. In recognition of this fact, some underworld characters take unusual precautions to maintain an excellent set of financial records. In the absence of good records, the IRS is authorized to use relatively crude methods of estimating a taxpayer's income and, just to be safe, these estimates are often on the high side. To illustrate, the income of a house of prostitution has been estimated on the basis of a commercial laundry's records, apparently after an IRS special agent had determined the modus operandi of the house. In any legal dispute over a tax liability, the burden of proving the IRS estimates wrong usually rests with the taxpayer. Without records the taxpayer is hard pressed to defeat the commissioner's estimates of gross income.

Although well beyond the scope of this book, and beyond the expertise of the author, the concurrent legal problems created by the need to report illegal gains for income tax purposes appear to be substantial. To what extent the Justice Department should be given access to tax files for other than tax litigation purposes represents an interesting question. The danger of self-incrimination is obvious. Any taxpayer receiving illegal gains—whether it be from the sale of narcotics, gambling, extortion, embezzlement, or air piracy—should realize that he badly needs a good tax *attorney* as well as a good criminal lawyer.

The word attorney was italicized in the prior sentence for good reason. In Chapter 1 the need for a good tax *advisor* was emphasized. Most qualified tax advisors are either lawyers or certified public accountants. To date the concept of privileged communication has not been extended under federal law to the C.P.A. It is extremely important, therefore, that income tax records from *criminal* activities be handled initially by an attorney. The attorney can engage a C.P.A. on behalf of his client if appropriate and thereby extend his privileged communication to the accountant's workpapers.

Source of payment

Even well-educated taxpayers occasionally get the notion that certain receipts will not be taxed if they are paid by a very particular kind of taxpayer. A prominent university professor, for example, believed that he was correct in not reporting his summer compensation for income tax purposes because it had been paid to him by a tax-exempt research organization. As a matter of fact, the taxable status of the organization making a payment is seldom of significance in determining the tax consequences of the payment to the recipient. In the case of this professor, a portion of the money received could be excluded under some very special rules for fellowship grants but not simply because they were paid by a tax-exempt organization.

Other taxpayers have been amazed to learn that income paid by a foreign entity and received in a foreign country may be subject to the U.S. income tax. We have what is known as a global income tax. That means simply that U.S. citizens and resident aliens, including all domestic corporations, are generally subject to the U.S. income tax regardless of where their income is earned, paid, or received. Nonresident aliens—that is, citizens of another country who are not physically in the U.S. and who may never have been here—are also subject to the U.S. income tax but only on their income from U.S. sources. Needless to say, the rules applicable to the taxation of multinational transactions are doubly complex. Often a single income stream is subject to taxation by more than one country which necessitates a series of tax treaties and other tax credit provisions to avoid double taxation. The Code does provide for a limited exclusion of income earned abroad by individual taxpayers under prescribed conditions. The more important aspects of multinational transactions will be discussed later in this book. Suffice it to observe here that the source of an income payment generally is not pertinent to the determination of tax consequences to the recipient.

Assignment of income

The most difficult tax problem sometimes is not in determining whether or not a particular receipt constitutes gross income but, rather, in identifying whose income it is. Because the detailed discussion of taxable entities is deferred to Chapter 3, this discussion of assignment of income problems will necessarily be very brief. Income ordinarily derives from one or some combination of three events: (1) the rendering of a service; (2) the disposition of a property; or (3) the payment by one person for the use of another's property. For some analytical purposes, we combine the latter two notions into a single class and say that income is derived either from services or from property (or capital).

Initially it seems clear that income derived from the rendering of a service must be reported by the person rendering that service; and that income derived from property must be reported by the person who owns (or holds legal title to) that property. One need not venture far into the world of business to discover how useless that concept is for determining tax consequences. Applied literally, it would say that every employee should report the gross value of his services notwithstanding the fact that he personally may receive only some fractional share of that value. A study of taxation would further prove that our concepts of property and services are amazingly ill-defined. Much of the intrigue of tax planning comes from the sometimes deliberate confusion of those ill-defined concepts.

To illustrate this tax confusion briefly, consider the income earned by an entertainer or an athlete. If this individual goes about the conduct of his business simply and solely as an individual, there is not much doubt that any fees which he receives for services rendered will be attributed and taxed to him personally. If this same individual incorporates his talent, and then technically his corporation negotiates for his appearance contracts, is the income which is received by the corporation taxable to it or to the person as an individual?

Or take another example. If an individual spends his time writing music or tinkering with mechanical devices, and if he subsequently obtains a copyright for his musical score or a patent for his gadget, is the income he receives attributable to a service (his writing music or tinkering with mechanical devices) or to a property (a copyright or a patent)?

Finally, consider the taxpayer who clipped a series of interest coupons from his bonds and made a gift of those coupons, but not of the bonds, to his son. Is the interest paid to the son, at the maturity date of the interest coupons, taxable to the son as the owner of the coupons or to the father as the owner of the bonds from which the coupons were clipped?

These three brief illustrations suggest both the breadth of opportunity for tax planning and the need for expert assistance. The answers to the questions are not always clear cut. As you will discover later in this book, the corporate veil is sometimes, but not always, pierced so that the income earned by a corporation may or may not be attributed and taxed to the individual owner. Gains from the sale of patents get a favorable tax treatment, as a capital gain from a property disposition, whereas gains from the sale of a copyright are taxed in the same way as income earned directly by an individual. Income from property may be transferred to another taxpayer without transferring the basic property but only if several special conditions are met. All of these problems are discussed later in more depth.

Exclusions

Our final consideration pertinent to the gross income concept will consist of a brief review of the items of economic income that simply are not deemed to constitute gross income for tax purposes. The vast majority of these exclusions are statutory in origin. Before we turn our attention to the statutory exclusions, however, we might note in passing the few exclusions that exist by judicial or administrative interpretation. As a class, virtually no items of imputed income are deemed to constitute gross income. Economists in particular like to point out the reality of such items of imputed income as owner-occupied homes, home-produced and consumed foods, and the services of the housewife. Even though the value of these items could be imputed, and even though not taxing them may create an inequity between home owners and renters, between farmer-gardeners and city dwellers, and between housewives and career wives, the U.S. income tax never has been extended to items of imputed income on the grounds that such an extension would be administratively very difficult to implement.

Administrative interpretation has also excluded from the tax base such payments as social security and unemployment benefits (unless received from the social security system of a foreign country) and public assistance payments. Tax administrators apparently believe that it would not constitute desirable government policy to tax away part of the payments made by welfare agencies designed to help people deemed to be in particular need.

Most statutory exclusions are contained in Code sections 101 through 123. Even a cursory reading of the section titles will suggest how narrow in application some of the exclusions really are. Because this book is intended as a layman's introduction to tax planning, rather than as a complete treatise on tax rules, many of these items will not be discussed. Consideration of the exclusions of more general interest to tax planning is deferred to subsequent chapters for pedagogical reasons. For example, the discussion of all exclusions requiring that the recipient be an employee is deferred to Chapter 6, where they can be treated as part of the larger problem of compensation considerations. Before we begin a discussion of the remaining items of general interest, it may be desirable for the reader simply to review the titles of the sections that create the statutory exclusions. These titles are:

Sec. 101. Certain death payments.
Sec. 102. Gifts and inheritances.
Sec. 103. Interest on certain governmental obligations.
Sec. 104. Compensation for injuries or sickness.
Sec. 105. Amounts received under accident and health plans.
Sec. 106. Contributions by employer to accident and health plans.
Sec. 107. Rental value of parsonages.
Sec. 108. Income from discharge of indebtedness.
Sec. 109. Improvements by lessee or lessor's property.
Sec. 110. Income taxes paid by lessee corporation.
Sec. 111. Recovery of bad debts, prior taxes, and delinquency amounts.
Sec. 112. Certain combat pay of members of the Armed Forces.
Sec. 113. Mustering-out payments for members of the Armed Forces.
Sec. 114. Sports programs conducted for the American National Red Cross.
Sec. 115. Income of States, municipalities, etc.
Sec. 116. Partial exclusion of dividends received by individuals.
Sec. 117. Scholarships and fellowship grants.
Sec. 118. Contributions to the capital of a corporation.
Sec. 119. Meals or lodging furnished for convenience of employer.
Sec. 120. (Repealed)
Sec. 121. Gain from sale or exchange of residence of individual who has attained age 65.
Sec. 122. Certain reduced uniformed services retirement pay.
Sec. 123. Amounts received under insurance contracts for certain living expenses.

Other statutory exclusions are scattered throughout the Code in such diverse sections as:

Sec. 37. Retirement income. (Technically this provision is worded as a tax credit rather than as an exclusion, but it has the same effect as an exclusion.)
Sec. 74(b). Prizes and awards. (The exception, which is tantamount to an exclusion, is contained in subsection (b).)
Sec. 79(a). Group-term life insurance purchased for employees.
Sec. 621. Payments to encourage exploration, development, and mining for defense purposes.

Simply reading this list will make a person aware of the many special provisions that must be considered in solving a real tax problem. We will now consider in greater detail the statutory exclusions for prizes, gifts and bequests, state and local bond interest, and scholarship and fellowship grants.

Prizes. Subsection 74(b) provides an exception to the general rule that gross income includes any amounts received as a prize or award. That general rule is stated in subsection (a). The exception reads as follows:

> Gross income does not include amounts received as prizes and awards made primarily in recognition of religious, charitable, scientific, educational, artistic, literary, or civic achievement, but only if—
>
> (1)   the recipient was selected without any action on his part to enter the contest or proceeding; and
>
> (2)   the recipient is not required to render substantial future services as a condition to receiving the prize or award.

The general rule of subsection 74(a) clearly makes taxable such awards as door prizes, raffles, and television quiz show bounty. Equally clearly, the exception in subsection 74(b) excludes from gross income the stipend attached to a Pulitzer Prize or a Nobel Award. As our introduction to the vast wasteland of statutory interpretation, however, let us consider a real problem which lies somewhere between the more obvious extremes. Paul Hornung was given an automobile, by a publishing company, because of his prowess on the football field. Could the value of this automobile be excluded by Hornung under the authority of subsection 74(b)? In other words, would such an award be considered to be an ". . . award . . . in recognition of . . . artistic . . . achievement"? The court said "No." Apparently the court concluded that playing football—even the way Paul Hornung played it—is not an artistic achievement within the meaning of the Code. Could it, then, be excluded as a gift?

Gifts and inheritances. Section 102 provides that "gross income does not include the value of property acquired by gift, bequest, devise, or inheritance." The major problem involved in interpretation of this brief section is the difficulty of distinguishing on any operational basis between transfers that are truly gratuitous and those made for other reasons. In Paul Hornung's case, the court believed that the transfer was not gratuitous, but that it was made with the hope that it either had provided or would provide better sports stories and, therefore, greater magazine sales.

In general, if the recipient has rendered, or will render, any service to the apparent donor, the tax authorities find that the transfer is not gratuitous and, therefore, that any amount received constitutes gross income. Under this interpretation ordinary tips given to waitresses, bellhops, and other service personnel are includable in gross income. So are traditional gifts to clergymen following weddings and other religious ceremonies. A more delicate problem of statutory interpretation was presented to the court in the cases of *Greta Starks* and *Everett Brizendine*. To state the essential fact of those two cases succinctly, each involved a "kept" woman. The delicate tax question involved the need to distinguish between a gift and compensation for services rendered. By examining "all of the facts and circumstances," a favorite phrase of our courts, one case resulted in ordinary income and the other in a tax-free gift.

Relative to inheritances, the reader should be cautioned to observe the difference between a basic bequest and income which may accrue on that bequest. Only the former generally can be excluded from gross income. For example, a taxpayer generally can exclude from taxable income any amount that he receives as the beneficiary of a life insurance policy purchased by another individual prior to his death. The income derived from the inheritance, however, is as taxable to the heir as income derived from property that he has personally accumulated. Only the basic bequest or inheritance can be excluded because of Section 102. A widow may also be entitled under Section 101(d) to an exclusion for interest earned on life insurance proceeds left with the insurance company to be paid as an annuity. With that exception, however, virtually all other income earned on inherited property will be taxed to the heir.

State and local bond interest. As explained in Chapter 1, any interest derived from bonds issued by a state or local government is generally excluded from gross income for federal income tax purposes. Upper-bracket taxpayers consequently find it financially advantageous to invest large sums in state and local government bonds. The governments issuing these bonds are able to float them at lower rates of interest because of the tax shelter they provide the purchaser. Tax reformers have contended for a number of years that this exclusion should be ended because the results are highly inequitable in that they benefit most the wealthiest segment of our society. The tax reformers usually cite estimates to support the contention that the federal government could increase its *net* tax revenues even if it were to grant direct subsidies to the state and local governments in an amount sufficient to compensate them for any increase in interest costs. Whether or not the estimates are realistic, Congress thus far has refused to terminate this statutory exclusion both because of some genuine concern for the greater bureaucracy that would attend a direct subsidy and because of pressures brought by governors, mayors, and investment bankers.

Scholarship and fellowship grants. Section 117 excludes from gross income amounts received by an individual as a scholarship or fellowship grant. The amount that can be excluded depends on whether or not the recipient is a degree candidate. The exclusion extends also to amounts received for travel, research, clerical assistance, and equipment which are incident to the scholarship or fellowship grant.

Implementation of this exclusion is again made difficult by the definitional imprecision common to the terms "scholarship" and "fellowship grant." In any instance where a specific service is required of the grantee, the tax authorities are inclined to argue that the grant is compensation for services rendered, and therefore included in gross income. For example, the stipends paid to medical residents and interns, teaching and laboratory assistants, and other graduate students who render a service to their educational institution are often found to constitute taxable income rather than an exclusion. The difficulty in statutory interpretation is compounded by the fact that the work experience is an important and integral part of the student's education and for this reason the stipend reasonably could be considered to be a scholarship even though a service is rendered. Perhaps the most

unfortunate aspect of this exclusion is the fact that it is being administered rather differently in various sections of the country.

Exclusions and deductions both serve to reduce the size of the income tax base and, therefore, the tax liability. The list of possible
income tax deductions is considerably longer than the list of statutory
exclusions. Deduction rules are additionally confused by frequent limitations and options. The remainder of this chapter is devoted to an
elaboration of the general rules common to the deductions authorized
in the computation of taxable income.

DEDUCTIONS

Deductions may be defined only as those items that collectively
constitute the difference between the quantity called gross income and
the quantity called taxable income. The basic rule applicable to deductions is just the opposite of that stated earlier for gross income: that
is, *nothing is deductible unless the taxpayer can find good authority
for deducting it.* Even momentary reflection on the general proposition
just stated should cause the reader some concern because income, by
definition, is generally thought to be a net concept. In accounting,
income is usually defined as the difference between properly matched
revenues and expenses. A tax on income, therefore, seems implicitly
to provide for an automatic deduction of all properly matched expenses. Technically this is not true for income tax purposes. The Code
does include a provision (Section 162) which authorizes the deduction
of all ordinary and necessary expenses paid or incurred in carrying
on any trade or business. Nevertheless, some items that are deductible
in computing financial accounting income are not deductible in computing taxable income, and a few items that are not deductible in
computing financial accounting income are deductible in the computation of taxable income. Especially as used in the income taxation
of an individual, the word "deduction" is a much broader, more
legalistic word than is the word "expense."

In addition to the provision authorizing the deduction of all ordinary and necessary business expenses, the Code authorizes many other
more restrictive deductions. These include an optional standard deduction, for individual taxpayers only; a personal and dependent exemption deduction; a deduction for interest, taxes, losses, bad debts, depreciation, and charitable contributions; research and experimental
expenditures; soil and water conservation expenditures; a dividend-

received deduction, for corporate taxpayers only; and many other special deductions. Very special deductions are granted some industries such as railroads, the extractive industries, exempt organizations, banks, and insurance companies. As noted earlier, the details of all tax provisions cannot be examined in this book. Only the more important deductions for tax planning purposes will be considered here. The important thing for the reader to remember at this point is that unless an expenditure fits the definition of an ordinary and necessary expense incurred in a trade or business, it generally cannot be deducted without very specific authorization in the Code to the contrary.

The rules applicable to tax deductions are complicated by the need to distinguish carefully between expenditures incurred in a trade, business, or profession; expenditures incurred in an income-producing venture that can not be deemed to constitute a trade or business, either because of its special nature or because of its limited size; and expenditures of a purely personal nature. The first of these three classes of expenditures is usually deductible without limit; the second is probably deductible, but sometimes only in an amount not to exceed the income produced; and the last is not deductible at all unless a very specific provision to the contrary authorizes its deduction, notwithstanding its purely personal character.

The difficulty of distinguishing between a trade or business and an income-producing venture is well demonstrated by many hobbies. The breeding of animals, the racing of horses and automobiles, the restoration of antiques, and even farming may be a primary source of recreation for a harried taxpayer. The same activities usually produce some gross income. Because the rule applicable to gross income says that all receipts must be included in gross income, it seems only fair that the related expenses should be tax deductible. On the other hand, since most purely personal expenditures are not deductible, it seems equally unfair to authorize the deduction of expenses related to certain hobbies and not to others just because some occasionally produce gross income. Thus the tax authorities frequently are faced with the need to determine whether or not a particular activity constitutes a full-fledged trade or business or something else. To assist in making this decision, the Code was recently amended to include a statutory presumption, subject to rebuttal by the taxpayer, that any activity which does not produce a net income in any two of five consecutive years will be deemed to constitute a hobby. Expenses related to a hobby may be deductible, but only to the extent that gross income is reported. If we assume for the time being that we can distinguish between hobbies and real trades or businesses, we can proceed to examine more carefully the general rules applicable to trade and business expenses.

Deductions and expenses compared

The basic criteria which must be considered before assuming that an expenditure directly related to a trade or business can be fully deducted can be separated into three positive and three negative tests. That is, an expenditure incurred in a trade, business, or profession generally will be deductible if:

1. It is "ordinary," which has been interpreted to mean that it is common to other taxpayers who find themselves in similar circumstances.
2. It is "necessary," which has been interpreted to mean that it is helpful to the conduct of the taxpayer's trade or business.
3. It is "reasonable in amount," which has been interpreted to mean that any other taxpayer would pay an equivalent sum for an equivalent good or service.
4. It is *not* a personal expense.
5. It is *not* a capital expenditure.
6. It does *not* relate to tax-exempt income.

Unlike taxation, accounting has no explicit rule that says that an expense must be reasonable in amount. This difference occasionally accounts for reported differences between financial accounting income and taxable income, especially in closely held corporations. Owners of these corporations often overstate their own salaries, as well as the salaries paid to other members of their immediate family, for tax reasons which will become clearer in the next two chapters. Whenever this happens the authorities may find that what purported to be a salary must be treated as if it were a dividend, a gift, or some other distribution, and taxed accordingly. The reasonableness criterion in the recent past has been applied in the opposite direction as well. A salary paid to Victor Borge by his own corporation was found to be unreasonably small with the unpleasant consequence that the corporation ended up being treated as one engaged in a hobby rather than in a *bona fide* business. Mr. Borge, the famous pianist-comic, probably did not find it funny that this meant paying a personal income tax on the extra salary attributed to him, in addition to finding that the expenses incurred by his rock-cornish-hen (farm) corporation were nondeductible.

The rule that precludes the deduction of expenses related to the production of tax-exempt income also may explain some differences between the income reported by financial accounting and by taxation. Businesses very often insure the lives of the owners to guarantee the availability of a sufficient amount of cash to purchase any deceased owner's share of the business from his estate. As noted earlier, the insurance proceeds received following the death of an owner would be excluded from gross income by Section 102. Consequently, the premiums paid to obtain the insurance are not deductible by businesses for tax purposes in the years preceding the owner's death. Accounting, on the other hand, generally reports some portion or all of the insurance premium as an expense of doing business. Accounting may also report some portion of the insurance proceeds as income.

Some deductions are subject to limitations for tax purposes. For example, charitable contributions made by corporations are limited to 5 percent of the corporation's adjusted taxable income; percentage depletion is limited to 50 percent of the net income from the depletable property; and corporate capital losses are deductible only to the extent of capital gains in any one year. Because there is no financial accounting convention that similarly limits any of these items, the amounts deducted for financial accounting purposes in any given year may vary substantially from those deducted for income tax purposes. The major differences between these two figures, however, are attributable to tax provisions which have been written into the Code for economic, national defense, or social reasons.

Economic policy considerations. During the past two decades Congress has enacted several major tax provisions relating to deductions with the apparent intention that the result should be conducive to the achievement of economic growth, the maintenance of·reasonable price stability, and/or the reduction of unemployment. Still other tax measures have been justified on the grounds that they are essential to the maintenance of a strong national defense. When these policy considerations are deemed sufficiently important, the implications of the tax provision on the traditional conventions used to measure income are not given much weight. Thus it is not unusual to discover that, in instances where economic or defense considerations are primary, tax rules differ substantially from accounting rules for essentially identical expense items.

Among the list of accounting and tax differences that can be attributed to economic motivation are the following: rapid depreciation allowances, first-year depreciation allowances, percentage depletion, and the investment credit. Three of these four produce tax deductions larger than the usual measure of the comparable expense for financial accounting purposes. The fourth provides a direct tax credit. Recent changes in the tax rates have also been motivated by these same economic considerations. Some of the tax provisions motivated by economic objectives will be considered in subsequent chapters because they represent important opportunities to achieve major tax savings through careful planning.

Social policy considerations. Other tax provisions that seem peculiar in light of accounting conventions may also be explainable whenever the primary objective of the provision related in some way to a social objective. Sociological factors such as family size, blindness, old age, marital status, or condition of health have little or nothing to do with problems of income measurement for financial accounting purposes. Income is simply the difference between gross revenues and the expenses incurred to produce those revenues. Special problems peculiar to a person earning an income may influence his disposition of income, but these problems in no way influence the size of the income measure. For tax purposes, sociological factors are often important to the procedure used to measure the size of the income stream. Congress tries, sometimes in an occult manner, to recognize the fact that equal financial accounting incomes need not represent equal tax-paying abilities. To achieve a degree of social equity, the Code recognizes some of the differences in the ability-to-pay taxes by allowing special deductions for large families, for blind taxpayers, for persons over 65, for those who incur large medical expenses, and for a host of other social considerations. In a few instances, these provisions intended to achieve a higher degree of interpersonal tax equity can be used for an unintended taxpayer's benefit.

Accounting methods

We observed earlier in this chapter that the Code provides that taxable income shall be computed on the same method of accounting as the taxpayer uses in maintaining his regular books. The cash-basis method of accounting for expenses produces relatively few problems pertinent to tax deductions since both financial and tax accounting require that no deduction be made until cash is actually paid. The accrual method of accounting, however, presents more serious problems in application. That method of accounting is based on the notion that expenses should be deducted in the same year that the revenue which they produce is reported. Accountants refer to this notion as the matching concept. Application of that concept often necessitates the estimation of expenses in advance of the time that they are actually known with certainty. The expense associated with a guarantee or warranty, for example, is typically not known with precision until several years after the sale of the guaranteed product. Good financial accounting requires that such expenses be estimated in advance and that they be deducted in the same year in which the gross revenue from the sale is reported. With major exceptions for the estimation of depreciation of fixed assets and for doubtful accounts, the Code generally forbids the deduction of any expense for tax purposes until the amount of that expense is fixed by more objective evidence than statistical estimates based on historical records.

The absence of a strict matching concept in taxation, especially for taxpayers reporting their income on a cash method of accounting, explains a number of important tax-saving opportunities. These opportunities are expanded when the deduction item is treated in one way and the related gross income item is reported in another, more favored way. To illustrate this important difference, consider the tax-saving potential associated with the immediate deduction of interest expense for borrowed funds which are invested in a way that will yield only a long-term capital gain at some time in the future. For reasons which will become clearer in the next few chapters, this means that the cost associated with the borrowing may be shared by the government on a 70 to 30 basis—that is, an individual in a 70 percent marginal tax bracket will discover that the government effectively pays 70 percent of his interest expense, through the reduction of his tax liability, if the interest can be deducted from ordinary income—whereas the fruit of his investment may be shared with the government on a 25 to 75 basis—that is, the government may demand as little as 25 percent of the profit back in income tax if the profit from the investment can be categorized as a capital gain. Adding to the taxpayer's delight is the fact that the interest may be deducted when paid whereas the capital gain tax may be deferred until it is realized. This particular opportunity to achieve tax savings was so widely abused that Congress put some limitations on the deduction of "excess investment interest" for years beginning after 1971. The new statutory limitation is so generous, however, it will affect only a very few persons. This opportunity to achieve major tax savings because of the absence of a strict matching concept in taxation is still very much alive and remaining opportunities will be illustrated throughout the book.

Losses

The proper tax treatment of losses is often confusing. In this introductory chapter we can do little more than get acquainted with some of the more important general distinctions pertinent to the tax treatment of losses. Additional details of some of these distinctions will be discussed later, while other details will have to remain outside the confines of this work. To begin, we might distinguish between (1) the loss attributable to a specific transaction and a specific property, and (2) the loss more generally associated with the nonprofitable conduct of a trade or business, considering all of the many transactions common to that business.

The correct tax treatment of a loss derived from a specific transaction and a specific property is primarily determined by the purpose for which the property was held. If it was held for the production of income in an ordinary trade or business, any loss associated with the disposition of the property generally will be fully deductible for tax purposes. If the property was held solely as an investment, any loss associated with the disposition of the investment generally will be deductible but will be subject to special limitations applicable only to capital losses. If the property was held solely for personal purposes, any loss associated with the disposition of the property generally will not be deductible unless the disposition is attributable to a casualty or a theft. According to these diverse rules the loss on the sale of a machine used in a business would be fully deductible; the loss associated with the sale of a common stock would be deductible only as a capital loss; and the loss associated with the sale of a personal residence would not be deductible (even though a gain on the sale of that same residence would be taxable). But note that the loss associated with the destruction of a personal residence by fire would be deductible as a casualty.

The general loss associated with the nonprofitable conduct of a business, considering the effect of all transactions common to that business, is called a net operating loss. If the authorized deductions exceed the gross income, the negative difference between the two sums effectively eliminates any tax for the current year. The question remains, however: What if anything can be done with that excess to offset taxable income in other years? The answer is that, after making several possible adjustments to the amount of this difference, the taxpayer may carry the loss back three years and treat it as a newly discovered deduction to be subtracted from the gross income reported in that year. If the taxpayer reported a taxable income in that year and paid a tax, the new deduction will create a refund of some or all of the tax he previously paid. This refund even includes interest for the interim years at six percent. If the adjusted loss of the current year is larger than the taxable income of the third prior year, the taxpayer treats any remaining loss as a deduction in the second prior year; if that is still insufficient to absorb the loss, the taxpayer proceeds to offset it against the income of the immediately preceding year. Finally, if that is still insufficient to absorb the total net operating loss, the taxpayer is allowed to carry the remaining loss forward and offset it against any gross income earned in the next five years.

Special problems are created when one taxable entity tries to utilize another entity's net operating loss. Thus if Corporation A acquires all of the stock or assets of Corporation B, and if Corporation B had an unused net operating loss carried forward, special rules must be applied to determine whether or not the surviving corporation is entitled to the losses originally incurred by Corporation B. Before these special rules were enacted, there was a brisk business in our country for worthless corporate shells because they provided valuable tax deductions for the acquiring taxpayer. The tax effect was to make the most worthless corporation the most valuable one! For the same reason, unlucky persons with accumulated net operating losses might make an excellent marriage prospect, financially speaking, for the more fortunate taxpayer who has need of some big tax deductions.

In summary, the reader should remember two very important rules of income taxation. First, remember that all income is deemed to constitute taxable income unless you (or your tax advisor) can find good authority for excluding it. Second, remember that nothing is deductible in the computation of taxable income unless you (or that same advisor) can find good authority for deducting it. In the remaining chapters we will discover how many taxpayers mitigate the apparently harsh results of these two rules.

3
Taxable entities

THE CODE technically acknowledges the existence of only three taxable entities. They are the individual, the corporation, and the fiduciary. All taxable income recognized in a single year must be attributed to some individual, corporation, or fiduciary. This means, of course, that the taxable income recognized by other entities—for example, that recognized by a sole proprietorship, a partnership, or a joint venture—must be allocated annually to one of the three entities that are acknowledged for tax purposes. In some cases the Code may require a nontaxable entity to file a return, but this return is for information purposes only and it does not, of itself, create an income tax liability.

THE INDIVIDUAL TAXPAYER

Theoretically every living person is a separate and distinct taxable entity. Age is of no significance: a two-year-old child who "models" baby clothes or "acts" in a television production is legally responsible for the payment of taxes and is as much a taxable entity as is each of the child's parents. In the case of the incapacitated or very young children, the law provides, of course, that the parent or guardian may be equally liable for the filing of the child's return and the payment of his tax liability. The important point is that the individual, rather than the family unit, is the taxable entity. As a practical matter, the technical point just stated is, at best, a half truth.

31

The married couple

The Code has provided since 1948 for something known as the "joint return" of married persons. The effect of the joint return provision is to decrease the effective tax rate for literally millions of married persons. The reason for initiation of the joint return in 1948 was to establish some reasonable degree of federal income tax equity as between those taxpayers who lived in community property states and those taxpayers who lived in the other states. The inequity of the situation that existed prior to 1948 can be demonstrated easily by the use of a simple graph. If there were only one progressive income tax rate schedule (as there was prior to 1948), and if the joint income earned by a married couple in a community property state could be treated for federal tax purposes as if it were earned equally by each of the partners to the marriage (which was and is the general result of those state laws), then the tax saving attributable to a married couple residing in a community property state, as compared to the married couple residing in a common law state, could be represented by the cross-hatched area in Figure 3–1. To reduce this inequality and

FIGURE 3–1

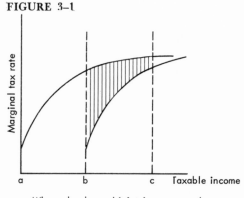

Where ab = bc and joint income equals ac

to stop what started to be a national movement by all of the states to adopt community property laws, Congress made provision in 1948 for the joint return of married persons. The important effect of this change was to do exactly what the community property laws had done earlier for others. That is, it effectively assumed that the income earned by any married person was earned one-half by each spouse and then permitted the federal income tax computation to be made accordingly. In order to simplify the administration of the law—by avoiding the assumed division of each spouse's income and subsequently the addition of the two independently determined income taxes—the IRS created a second tax rate schedule which could be applied only once to the combined incomes of the married couple. To achieve the Congressional objective, this new rate schedule necessarily was designed so that the marginal tax brackets were exactly twice as wide as those applied to income earned by single persons. In other words, if the first $500 of taxable income of a single person were to be taxed at the marginal rate of 14 percent, then the first $1,000 (2 × $500) of taxable income of the married couple had to be taxed at 14 percent.

The head of household

As a consequence of the introduction of the joint return, the basic entity for individual income tax purposes after 1948 remained the individual only for single persons; most married persons filed as a husband-wife team. In the mid-1950s Congress decided to add a third category of individual-entity taxpayers by creating a "head-of-household" status. The thought behind the creation of this third subcase of the individual entity was that some persons were really more like married persons than they were like single persons and that, under these circumstances, they ought to be entitled to some of the tax advantages that attached to the married state. The basic idea was that if a single person—in most instances, a person who was once married but was no longer in that status—retained the responsibility of supporting one or more dependent relatives, even though he were no longer married, then he should be entitled to some tax relief. The relief decided upon took the form of a new rate schedule whose brackets and marginal tax rates were arranged in such a manner as to give this person approximately one-half of the tax advantage of being married.

Single persons

Although the joint return and the head of household rates reduced the tax inequities which had existed between married persons living in different states and, to a lesser degree, between married persons and heads of households, these same tax innovations magnified the tax inequity between single and married individuals. In 1970, the tax on a $32,000 taxable income earned by a married couple was $8,660, whereas the tax on the same income earned by a single person was $12,210, a difference of $3,550 (or an increase of 41 percent) per year. Sufficient pressures again were brought on Congress and in 1971 a new, fourth tax rate schedule was introduced for single individuals only. This new schedule was constructed in such a manner that the tax paid by a single person on any amount of taxable income would never be more than 120 percent of the tax paid by the married couple on the same amount of taxable income. At the same time the rates applicable to heads of households also were adjusted downward so that they remained approximately midway between the single and the joint return rates. In order to avoid a return to the community property problem which existed 22 years earlier, Congress required that married persons filing separate returns use a rate schedule which is not the same as that applicable to single persons. The rates generally are higher for married persons filing separately than for single persons earning the same taxable income.

The most interesting consequence of this latest revision is to introduce a new tax inequity for married persons who independently earn a substantial and approximately equal taxable income. This result has been dubbed a tax on marriage. The real inequity which results can be illustrated simply. Using the current tax rate schedules, which appear at the end of this chapter, we can determine that the tax paid by a single person on a $22,000 taxable income is $5,990. If two persons each earning a $22,000 taxable income were to marry, their joint tax liability would increase to $14,060 which is $2,080 more annually than they were paying separately before saying "I do." How and when Congress will solve this last inequity remains to be seen. Since the number of married couples with working wives is relatively small, the chance for a prompt solution is politically reduced. On the other hand, if a few of these couples get a divorce and live openly "in sin" to gain a tax advantage, and if the communications media find their problem newsworthy, another solution may be found to this problem also.

A graphic presentation of three of the four tax rate schedules currently applicable to individual taxpayers is contained in Figure 3–2. Schedule Z, for heads of households, was omitted from Figure 3–2 simply because it makes reading the graph difficult. The tax rate function for these persons lies generally between the one shown for Sched-

FIGURE 3–2
1973 Tax rate schedules X and Y

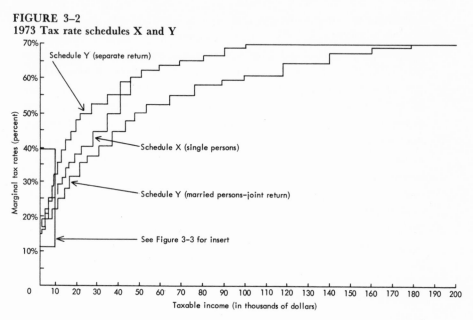

ule Y (joint) and Schedule X (single), but it frequently overlaps one or the other. Because of the problems of overlap at the lower income levels, a separate graph, Figure 3–3, has also been included to illustrate more clearly the movement of the three functions graphed at taxable incomes up to $10,000. Two very important aspects of the federal income taxation of individual taxpayers should be evident from even the most cursory examination of these two figures. *First, observe that the tax rates applicable to individual taxpayers are highly progressive. Second, observe that most of the progression takes place in the first $50,000 of taxable income.* That is, the marginal tax rates move rapidly from 14 percent to 50 or 60 percent in the first $50,000 of taxable income. The increase for the second $50,000 of taxable income is only 10 percent, from 50 to 60 percent for Schedule Y (joint), and from 60 to 70 percent for Schedule X (single). The progression for the third $50,000 is still smaller; in fact, there is no further progression for the single individual. *These two important facts explain why some tax saving ideas are especially meaningful in the relatively lower income brackets.* A single movement of $10,000 in taxable income down from the $40,000-to-$50,000 bracket to the zero-to-$10,000 brackets can mean sizable tax savings precisely because of the degree of progression in the marginal rates at these relatively low income levels.

FIGURE 3-3
1973 Tax rate schedules X and Y (for first $10,000 of taxable income only)

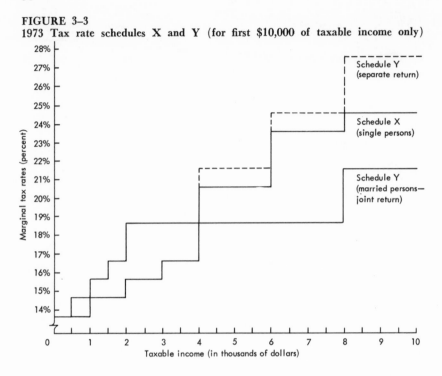

Definitional problems

Before returning to our major concern—that is, the importance of the basic taxable entity to tax planning ideas—a final word of caution is in order. The precise definitions necessary to determine whether or not a particular taxpayer is eligible to use rate Schedules X, Y, or Z are not as straightforward as the common words used to describe them would seem to imply. For example, a taxpayer married to a nonresident alien, such as Mrs. Jacqueline Kennedy Onassis, must calculate her tax liability using Schedule X (for single taxpayers) although she is legally married for virtually all other purposes. On the other hand, a person may be eligible to use Schedule Z (for married taxpayers) even though his spouse died a year or two earlier. This latter opportunity exists whenever the taxpayer can qualify for status as a *surviving spouse,* another technical income tax term requiring more than simply outliving the person to whom you were once married. Similarly status as head of household is determined by some very specific, and sometimes apparently inequitable, criteria. In keeping with the objectives of this book, no details of the pertinent definitions will be examined here. The taxpayer having a personal interest in such definitional problems ought to consult the current tax return instructional booklet, a reliable tax reference work, or a competent tax advisor.

Planning opportunities

To return now to the fundamental discussion of the individual as a separate taxpaying entity, we discover that a family unit may be able to lower its aggregate tax liability by dividing up the total income earned between a maximum number of family members. Just as the husband-wife team found it advantageous, prior to the days of the joint return, to split income between themselves, so also we find today that many wealthy individuals transfer property to minor children, to grandchildren, or to elderly relatives in order to relieve themselves of the higher tax liability that would attach to the same income stream had it been retained by the donor. Notice that this generally requires the transfer of an income-producing property. It cannot be accomplished through the transfer of only the income which stems from a property, and it is almost impossible to accomplish with income from personal services. In other words, a father generally could *not* for income tax purposes give his son either part of his salary or the interest income which he derives from selected corporate bonds unless, in the latter instance, the father is willing to actually transfer ownership of the bonds to the son. In reality, a less-than-complete transfer of property can achieve the desired income tax objective. If the father creates a trust with those bonds, and if that trust satisfies certain rules (the most important one being that the father cannot revoke the trust and regain the bonds in less than ten years), then the father can effectively transfer the income derived from the property from himself and to a designated person. The details of these and other tax saving opportunities which involve the careful selection of the entity to be taxed will be considered presently. Before looking at the opportunities, we must consider some of the general rules applicable to the other two taxable entities.

THE CORPORATE TAXPAYER

The corporation, like the individual, is recognized as one of the basic entities for income tax purposes. This fact creates about as many tax opportunities as it does tax traps. Most of the traps that it creates revolve around the obvious fact that a corporation is nothing but a legal fiction that is responsible ultimately to the persons who own the shares of stock which represent the corporate entity; when a small group of persons, or even a single individual, owns all of the shares it become exceedingly difficult to distinguish between personal and corporate interests.

Legal entities

The propriety of taxing a purely legal entity seems, at first blush, to be questionable. Legal entities, after all, cannot enjoy the incomes they earn because consumption is a purely human opportunity. Corporations and other legal entities can reinvest incomes they earn, and they can transform resources into (hopefully) more valuable forms, but they cannot destroy or consume these resources if they want to survive. Why then should these entities be taxed? Many people delight in pointing out the fact that the taxation of income earned by an entity necessarily means that a single income stream faces double income taxation. In the case of the corporation, it must first be taxed as part of the corporation's taxable income and later as part of the stockholders' taxable incomes when whatever is left after corporate income tax is distributed as a dividend. This double tax observation is generally applicable to the large publicly held corporation, but the smaller closely held corporation finds it quite easy to circumvent much of the double tax.

Among the alternatives to the double tax idea are the option of ignoring the corporate entity and allocating all corporate income immediately and directly to the stockholders whether or not the corporation distributes any of its earnings. This alternative is administratively impossible for large, publicly held corporations since ownership of these corporations changes on a daily basis and income simply cannot be measured that frequently. In addition, this alternative could create major hardships were the corporation to earn a large income and distribute none of it; a stockholder, under these conditions, could discover that he had a large tax liability with very limited funds to pay the income tax. Another extreme alternative would permit an entity's income to remain untaxed until it was distributed to the owners. If applied to a corporation, this would result in vast hoarding of corporate earnings and in widespread tax evasion. After all, anyone can create a corporation for $500 or less and even persons of very modest means would find that cost immaterial if there were no tax on corporate income until that income was distributed. Although other, intermediate positions can be designed to overcome most of the objections stated to each of these alternatives, none of them have ever gained much Congressional support. Options currently available to the small closely held corporation are explained later in this chapter.

To note that the corporation is recognized as a separate taxable entity, just as the individual, is to tell only half the story. The tax rate structure applicable to a corporation's taxable income is significantly different from the tax rate structure applied to the individual's income. In the absence of any complications, a corporate entity pays a normal tax equal to 22 percent of all its taxable income plus a surtax equal to 26 percent of its taxable income in excess of $25,000. Consequently, the large corporation pays, for all practical purposes, an income tax equal to 48 percent of its taxable income whereas the small corporation typically pays an income tax equal to approximately 22 percent of its taxable income. Except for the one major step, or bracket, the corporate tax is not graduated like the personal income tax. Figure 3–4 illustrates the essential features of this corporate tax rate structure.

FIGURE 3–4

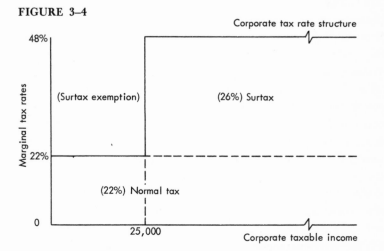

The reader should begin immediately to see possible corporate tax-saving ideas with only the two fundamental facts just stated. If each corporation is recognized as a separate taxable entity, and if the corporate tax rate structure contains only one major progressive bracket, it should be possible for the owners of middle-sized firms to split their business ventures in a most tax advantageous way. Suppose, for example, that a businessman owned a venture which provided him with a $100,000 annual taxable income. If this businessman elected to incorporate his business venture, should he attempt to form four corporations of approximately equal size or should he put the entire operation into a single corporate shell? Considering only tax factors and ignoring for the moment any possible complications in making this choice, it should be immediately evident that major tax savings would attach to the four-corporation alternative. That is, the corporate income tax on four equal incomes of $25,000, earned by separate legal entities, would appear to be $22,000 (4 × 22% of $25,000) while the corporate income tax on a single income of $100,000 would appear to be $41,500 (22% × $100,000 plus 26% × $75,000), an increase of $19,500 (or almost 89 percent) per year! Ventures earning more than $100,000 in taxable income could, of course, increase their tax saving even more by creating an appropriately larger number of corporate entities.

Economic realities

The simple tax-planning opportunity noted in the preceding paragraph has been widely observed and utilized in the U.S. for decades. The practical consequence has been that literally thousands of small corporations have been formed, where a few otherwise would have sufficed, primarily to achieve the substantial tax benefits that have been available. It is not at all uncommon to discover even today that one person is president and chairman of the board of not one corporation, but of ten or more corporations, all of which are closely related in operation and none of which is very large. This fact in all likelihood will be modified significantly in the very near future due to rather drastic changes in the Tax Reform Act of 1969.

The critical change introduced in the 1969 Act provides that, after December 31, 1974, controlled groups of corporations will be treated for many tax purposes as if they were a single taxable entity! In effect, economic realities once again won out over legal fictions when tax avoidance reached epidemic proportions. The definition of a controlled group of corporations was expanded concurrently so that virtually all corporations which were created for tax avoidance reasons (as well as some others) will be caught in the new web. The new definition of controlled corporations encompasses both brother-sister and parent-subsidiary ownership arrangements. The differences between these two can be illustrated simply, as shown in Figures 3–5 and 3–6. Figure

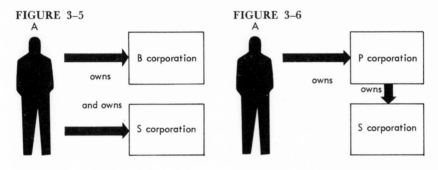

FIGURE 3–5

FIGURE 3–6

3–5 represents a brother-sister ownership arrangement; Figure 3–6, a parent-subsidiary arrangement. If we assume in Figure 3–5 that person A owns all of the stock of both B and S corporations, and if we assume in Figure 3–6 that person A owns all of the stock of P corporation and P owns all of the stock of S corporation, then it is very easy to see why it may be more appropriate to tax the corporations on the basis of economic realities rather than on legal fictions. To do otherwise permits widespread tax avoidance possibilities.

When Congress elected to close this blatant tax loophole, it did so with a vengeance and in the process may have engaged in some unnecessary statutory overkill which will create many tax problems in the future. Problems will arise in the interpretation and application of the new controlled corporation definition. That definition now provides that any group of corporations will be considered to be a controlled group if five or fewer persons (individuals, estates, or trusts) own (1) 80 percent of the stock of the corporations, and (2) 50 percent of the value of the stock considering ". . . the stock ownership of each person only to the extent such stock ownership is identical with respect to each such corporation." Tax advisors will worry for years about just what that definition means. For our purposes, we can ignore the multiple subtleties that confound tax advisors' minds and safely assume that any group of corporations 80 percent owned by five or fewer persons will constitute a controlled group. Incidentally, the five-or-fewer test is further complicated by a maze of constructive ownership rules. These rules provide that, when making percentage ownership tests, every person is deemed to own not only those shares recorded directly in his name, but also those shares owned by his wife, parents, children, grandchildren, and other relatives, and by other corporations, partnerships, and other entities in which he owns an interest. Needless to say, only the tax expert, and possibly a magician, can determine in some situations just which corporations are to be included in a particular controlled group.

The new tax rules do not become fully operative until January 1, 1975. Because that date is not remote and because the interim rules are relatively complex and of only limited tax-planning value, we will concern ourselves with only the post-1974 situation. At that time a controlled group of corporations will be eligible for only one $25,000 surtax exemption and only one $100,000 accumulated earnings tax credit (a feature which will be explained later). In other words, if a businessman divided a business venture which produced $100,000 annually in taxable income into four separate and equal corporations, after 1974 he would discover that those four corporations would pay an annual corporate income tax of $41,500 (22% × $100,000 + 26% × $75,000), not of $22,000 (4 × 22% of $25,000). For this reason, the golden era of multiple corporations has just about ended. Some valid nontax reasons for multiple corporations remain, and even a few tax reasons can be found to support their existence, but these are limited situations compared to the past. For most tax purposes, the future will favor a reduction in the number of corporate entities or, alternatively, in the filing of a single consolidated corporate tax return by the affiliated group (parent-subsidiary type) of controlled corporations. Some of the most important tax reasons for selecting a particular form of business operation are discussed in Chapter 4. Before looking at those reasons, we must consider briefly the third and last form of taxable entity.

THE FIDUCIARY TAXPAYER

The estate and the trust are the two common forms of the fiduciary taxpayer. The estate fills a necessary gap following the death of an individual taxpayer. A person's death marks the end of his final income tax period; on this final return of a decedent, taxable income is reported from the date of his last accounting, usually December 31 of the prior year, to the date of his death. Years may pass, however, before the assets of the decedent are distributed to the heirs or devisees.

The estate must report and pay tax on any taxable income earned on these assets in the interim period. Once the deceased taxpayer's assets have been fully distributed the estate ceases to exist and the new owners begin to report on their own tax returns the income earned on the property transferred to them.

A trust is a legal relationship in which one person, called a trustee, holds title to property for the benefit or use of another person, called a beneficiary. The trust may be testamentary (created by a will) or *inter vivos* (created among living persons by a legal document other than a will). The latter trust will be recognized as a separate taxable entity only if it is not revocable and if the term of the trust is for a period of ten years or longer or for the life of a designated beneficiary. If these or other requirements are not satisfied, the income will continue to be taxed to the grantor (the person who created the trust through the transfer of property). If all requirements are satisfied the trust becomes a separate taxable entity but only to the extent that it does not distribute income to the beneficiaries.

The fact that the trustee may be given an option over the distribution of income makes the trust a particularly viable vehicle for tax planning. If conditions are favorable—for example, if the income beneficiary is in a low tax bracket because of his age or because of an unusually large tax loss incurred from some other source—the trustee can proceed with an income distribution and avoid or minimize the income tax liability of the trust itself. If conditions are not favorable to a distribution, the trustee may be given the authority to retain the taxable income in which case the trust pays the income tax utilizing the same tax rate schedule as ordinarily applies to married persons filing separate returns. In summary, the trust is, for income tax purposes, something of a half-entity; it is recognized as a taxable entity only if and to the extent that it does not distribute its taxable income to the beneficiaries.

OTHER ENTITIES

For financial accounting purposes, many entities are recognized in addition to the individual, the corporation, and the fiduciary. For example, a sole proprietorship is typically treated as an entity, separate and distinct from its owner. For income tax purposes, however, the income of a sole proprietorship simply becomes one of several schedules that collectively constitute the aggregate income picture for the owner.

Except for the physical separation of financial data on Schedule C, Form 1040, the income of the proprietorship is commingled with the owner's gross income and deductions from other sources such as interest, rents, and dividends.

Partnerships

Although a partnership is required to file an annual tax return, Form 1065, this return serves only to indicate to the Internal Revenue Service the amount and kind of income, deduction, and credit that the individual partners ought to be reporting on their individual tax returns as their share of the income from the partnership venture. Again, each partner's share of the partnership's income is commingled with his income from all other sources on his individual Form 1040. If the partnership elects to retain all of a sizable taxable income, a partner may find himself owing a large tax liability with only limited resources to pay it. Under the reverse financial circumstances, a partner may discover that his share of a partnership's losses can be offset against his income from other business ventures and, therefore, be of real tax advantage to him.

Hybrid organizations

To posit that a partnership is not recognized as a separate taxable entity while a corporation is so recognized begs a very important question: what, exactly, is a corporation? Suffice it to note here that just because a business has been incorporated in compliance with state law does not of itself guarantee the recognition of this entity as a corporation for federal tax purposes. Most corporate entities organized in compliance with state law admittedly will be recognized as such for tax purposes, but they need not be so recognized in unusual circumstances. In other situations, businesses that are formally organized as a partnership may discover that for tax purposes they are treated as a corporate entity. And, occasionally, what is legally formed as a business trust may be taxed as a corporation. The judicial decisions in this relatively limited area seem to turn upon the presence or absence of such corporate characteristics as continuity of life, centralization of management, transferability of ownership, limited liability, and purpose of organization. The courts have carefully avoided delineation of which, how many, or what combination of corporate characteristics are sufficient to create or to destroy the business association which will be taxed as a corporation. The decisions proceed on an ad hoc basis and the reader must always be alert to avoid an inadvertent arrangement that could lead to an undesirable classification in a questionable situation.

Subchapter S corporations

More importantly, the reader ought to understand that it may be legally possible to organize a business venture as a corporation and then to elect to tax the organization in a manner similar to that of a partnership, assuming that the conditions for making this election can be satisfied. This provision is contained in Subchapter S of the Code; consequently, such corporations are frequently referred to as Subchapter S corporations. They are alternatively called small business corporations, which is unfortunate for two reasons. First, the qualifying criteria pertinent to this option say nothing about the dollar size of the firm's net worth, sales volume, or number of employees. Second, other special kinds of corporations are also known as small business investment corporations (SBICs) and small business corporations (if their stock has been qualified under Code Section 1244, a special rule to be considered later). The use of very similar or even identical terminology for essentially different kinds of organizations only tends to confuse the uninitiated. Until 1966, it was legally possible for a business to operate as a sole proprietorship or as a partnership but to elect, under Subchapter R, to be taxed as if it were a corporation. This option was terminated and all prior elections expired on January 1, 1969.

Before a corporation can elect Subchapter S treatment it must meet all of the qualifications set out in the Code. Among the more important of these qualifications are the following:

1. There can be no more than ten shareholders and each must consent to the election;
2. Only individuals can hold stock in the electing corporation (that is, there can be no corporate or partnership shareholders);
3. There can be only one class of stock;
4. All shareholders must be either U.S. citizens or resident aliens;
5. Not more than 80 percent of the firm's gross receipts may come from sources outside the United States; and

6. Not more than 20 percent of the firm's gross receipts may come from interest, dividends, rents, royalties, annuities, and gains from the sale or exchange of securities.

The first four of these criteria must be satisfied before a firm can make a valid election; failure to meet any of the six during a year will automatically terminate an otherwise valid election.

In addition to the taxable entities already discussed in this chapter, numerous other special tax situations exist that bear upon the entity problem. The Regulated Investment Company, the Real Estate Investment Trust, the Domestic International Sales Corporation (or DISC), and the Western Hemisphere Trade Corporation (or WHTC) are four such special cases. Rather than belabor these special cases here, we will conclude this chapter with a brief discussion relating the tax formula introduced in Chapters 1 and 2 to the basic entity concepts introduced in this chapter.

ENTITIES AND THE TAXABLE INCOME CONCEPT

The calculation of taxable income proceeds on a slightly different basis for corporations than it does for individuals and fiduciaries. The differences in question are sometimes of importance to the achievement of success in tax avoidance ideas. Consequently, these differences will be examined briefly in the remaining pages of this chapter. To introduce the important differences, let us expand the general formula used to determine the federal income tax liability as it was presented on page 7.

Special corporate considerations

Relative to the corporate entity, only one additional comment is deemed necessary at this point. Among the "special deductions" (those available only to the corporate entity) is a dividend-received deduction. A corporation generally can deduct, in the calculation of its taxable income, 85 percent of the dividends it receives during a year from other domestic corporate entities. In the case of controlled groups of corporations, 100 percent of the dividends received from other corporations in the same controlled group may be deducted. The reason for this special corporate deduction is relatively obvious if we reconsider a point made earlier in this chapter: income earned in the first instance by a corporate entity may be subject to a double tax. If

FIGURE 3–7

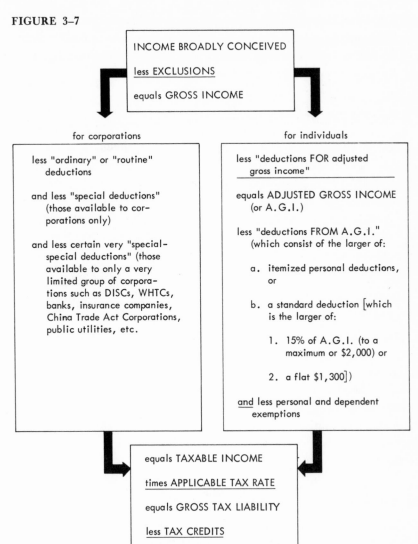

INCOME BROADLY CONCEIVED

less EXCLUSIONS

equals GROSS INCOME

for corporations

less "ordinary" or "routine" deductions

and less "special deductions" (those available to corporations only)

and less certain very "special-special deductions" (those available to only a very limited group of corporations such as DISCs, WHTCs, banks, insurance companies, China Trade Act Corporations, public utilities, etc.

for individuals

less "deductions FOR adjusted gross income"

equals ADJUSTED GROSS INCOME (or A.G.I.)

less "deductions FROM A.G.I." (which consist of the larger of:

a. itemized personal deductions, or

b. a standard deduction [which is the larger of:

1. 15% of A.G.I. (to a maximum or $2,000) or

2. a flat $1,300])

and less personal and dependent exemptions

equals TAXABLE INCOME

times APPLICABLE TAX RATE

equals GROSS TAX LIABILITY

less TAX CREDITS

equals NET TAX PAYABLE

one corporation owns another corporation's stock, does that mean that a single income stream will be subject to a triple tax? In the absence of a dividend received deduction, or of a special exclusion rule available to the corporate entity, that would be the unhappy circumstance. In the absence of such a provision, corporate ownership of another corporation's stock would be of dubious value since the tax consequence would make such relationships prohibitively expensive. To avoid this serious intervention in multicorporate ownership arrangements common to a modern economy, Congress elected to grant the dividend-received deduction to corporate entities.

Special considerations for individual taxpayers

A few additional comments relevant to the deductions available to individual taxpayers seem appropriate. First, note that every individual's tax deductions must be divided between deductions *for* adjusted gross income (AGI) and deductions *from* AGI. In the former category, no options are available and, therefore, the only question is one of definition. Which deductions are properly classified as deductions for AGI? In the latter category the taxpayer must make an election: he must elect between itemized personal deductions and a standard deduction, which is itself an option. Thus, relative to the individual's deductions from AGI, we encounter two kinds of problems: the definitional ones and the maximizing ones.

Deductions for AGI. Deductions for AGI are, generally speaking, the taxpayer's deductions which relate to his trade or business income. Unfortunately, like most general rules, this one is replete with exceptions and a satisfactory definition would require a time-consuming investigation of Code Section 62. In lieu of such an investigation, try to understand the following restatement of the more important limits which apply to deductions *for* adjusted gross income:

1. All deductions that can be classified as
    a. *Non-employee* trade or business expenses (for example, all routine business expenses associated with operation of a sole proprietorship);
    b. Expenses associated with the production of rents and royalties, whether or not that activity constitutes a "trade or business";
2. Only certain expenses incurred as an *employee,* including
    a. All expenses of travel away from home;
    b. All transportation expenses (which classification *excludes* both the cost of travel away from home and the nondeductible personal cost of commuting from home to work);
    c. Any reimbursed business expenses, but only to the extent of the reimbursement; and

   d. All expenses associated with activities conducted as an outside salesman;
3. The long-term capital gain deduction (explained in Chapter 4);
4. Certain losses from the sale or exchange of trade, business, investment, or "non-business" assets (not including personal assets);
5. The moving expense deduction; and
6. A few miscellaneous items.

Any legitimate income tax deduction not within one of the above classifications must be a deduction *from* the adjusted gross income of the individual taxpayer.

Deductions from AGI. An individual taxpayer's deductions from AGI can be subdivided into two major groups: the $750 personal and dependent exemption deductions and all other deductions. As noted earlier, the latter group is an option: that is, the taxpayer is entitled to the *larger* of a standard deduction or his other itemized or personal deductions. The standard deduction will never be less than $1,300, called a low income allowance, but may be a larger amount (not to exceed $2,000) based on an arbitrary 15 percent of adjusted gross income. Special limitations on the standard deductions are applicable to married persons filing a separate return. Note that no dollar limit is applicable to itemized deductions.

For most individual taxpayers, the important personal or itemized deductions are the medical expense deduction, the charitable contribution deduction, the interest expense deduction, and the deduction for certain taxes. To the extent that these items can be manipulated individually in successful tax avoidance, they will be discussed later. However, one very simple tax-avoidance idea ought to be noted here since it depends upon aggregate deductions from AGI.

It is not unusual to discover that a salaried individual taxpayer, in the lower income brackets, finds that his legitimate itemized deductions are typically about equal to a standard deduction. This individual often concludes that claiming the standard deduction is the wiser alternative because it permits him to forget record keeping and costs him little if anything in additional taxes. Actually this individual may be missing the only opportunity for tax planning available to him. Because the cash basis taxpayer has a great deal of control over the timing of his expenditures, he can often accelerate or postpone the incurrence of a tax deductible item. To minimize his tax liability, a taxpayer may elect a standard deduction only in alternate years.

In the year in which he itemizes his deductions, he can accelerate all charitable contributions, incur and pay his larger medical and dental expenses (for example, he could schedule his physical examination late in December each year to facilitate payment in December or in January as best suits his tax plan), and pay and possibly even prepay interest and property taxes. In the year in which this taxpayer claims a standard deduction, he should delay (at least in the last four months of the year) the payment of any medical or dental bills, the making of any charitable contributions, and the payment of any taxes or interest. These expenditures could be paid early in the following year, which would be another itemizing year. By this simple application of careful timing, the salaried taxpayer may be able to increase his aggregate deductions and minimize his net tax liability over several years.

We should also note that to whatever extent a taxpayer can legally classify his deductions as deductions for AGI, it may pay him to do so. This is true to the extent that he reduces the remaining deductions to the point where claiming a standard deduction becomes advantageous. That is, if a taxpayer could legally arrange to incur all of his deductible expenses as deductions for AGI he would gain to the extent that he could also claim a standard deduction in lieu of his other itemized deductions. Obviously, this reclassification of deductions is not at the option of the taxpayer and the definitional problems are substantial. Suffice it to note here that the self-employed taxpayer engaged in a trade or business is frequently at an advantage in this regard when compared to his employed counterpart.

1973 Tax rate schedule X (for *single* taxpayers not qualifying for rates in Schedule Y or Z)

If taxable income is		The amount of the gross tax liability is			
Over	But not over	A basic amount	Plus	A marginal rate times	The amount over
$ 0	$ 500	$ 0	+	14%	$ 0
500	1,000	70	+	15%	500
1,000	1,500	145	+	16%	1,000
1,500	2,000	225	+	17%	1,500
2,000	4,000	310	+	19%	2,000
4,000	6,000	690	+	21%	4,000
6,000	8,000	1,110	+	24%	6,000
8,000	10,000	1,590	+	25%	8,000
10,000	12,000	2,090	+	27%	10,000
12,000	14,000	2,630	+	29%	12,000
14,000	16,000	3,210	+	31%	14,000
16,000	18,000	3,830	+	34%	16,000
18,000	20,000	4,510	+	36%	18,000
20,000	22,000	5,230	+	38%	20,000
22,000	26,000	5,990	+	40%	22,000
26,000	32,000	7,590	+	45%	26,000
32,000	38,000	10,290	+	50%	32,000
38,000	44,000	13,290	+	55%	38,000
44,000	50,000	16,590	+	60%	44,000
50,000	60,000	20,190	+	62%	50,000
60,000	70,000	26,390	+	64%	60,000
70,000	80,000	32,790	+	66%	70,000
80,000	90,000	39,390	+	68%	80,000
90,000	100,000	46,190	+	69%	90,000
100,000	. . .	53,090	+	70%	100,000

52

1973 Tax rate schedule Y (for *married* taxpayers filing *joint* returns and certain widows and widowers)

If taxable income is		The amount of the gross tax liability is			
Over	But not over	A basic amount	Plus	A marginal rate times	The amount over
$ 0	$ 1,000	$ 0	+	14%	$ 0
1,000	2,000	140	+	15%	1,000
2,000	3,000	290	+	16%	2,000
3,000	4,000	450	+	17%	3,000
4,000	8,000	620	+	19%	4,000
8,000	12,000	1,380	+	22%	8,000
12,000	16,000	2,260	+	25%	12,000
16,000	20,000	3,260	+	28%	16,000
20,000	24,000	4,380	+	32%	20,000
24,000	28,000	5,660	+	36%	24,000
28,000	32,000	7,100	+	39%	28,000
32,000	36,000	8,660	+	42%	32,000
36,000	40,000	10,340	+	45%	36,000
40,000	44,000	12,140	+	48%	40,000
44,000	52,000	14,060	+	50%	44,000
52,000	64,000	18,060	+	53%	52,000
64,000	76,000	24,420	+	55%	64,000
76,000	88,000	31,020	+	58%	76,000
88,000	100,000	37,980	+	60%	88,000
100,000	120,000	45,180	+	62%	100,000
120,000	140,000	57,580	+	64%	120,000
140,000	160,000	70,380	+	66%	140,000
160,000	180,000	83,580	+	68%	160,000
180,000	200,000	97,180	+	69%	180,000
200,000	...	110,980	+	70%	200,000

1973 Tax rate schedule Y (for *married* taxpayers filing *separate* returns)

If taxable income is		The amount of the gross tax liability is			
Over	But not over	A basic amount	Plus	A marginal rate times	The amount over
$ 0	$ 500	$ 0	+	14%	$ 0
500	1,000	70	+	15%	500
1,000	1,500	145	+	16%	1,000
1,500	2,000	225	+	17%	1,500
2,000	4,000	310	+	19%	2,000
4,000	6,000	690	+	22%	4,000
6,000	8,000	1,130	+	25%	6,000
8,000	10,000	1,630	+	28%	8,000
10,000	12,000	2,190	+	32%	10,000
12,000	14,000	2,830	+	36%	12,000
14,000	16,000	3,550	+	39%	14,000
16,000	18,000	4,330	+	42%	16,000
18,000	20,000	5,170	+	45%	18,000
20,000	22,000	6,070	+	48%	20,000
22,000	26,000	7,030	+	50%	22,000
26,000	32,000	9,030	+	53%	26,000
32,000	38,000	12,210	+	55%	32,000
38,000	44,000	15,510	+	58%	38,000
44,000	50,000	18,990	+	60%	44,000
50,000	60,000	22,590	+	62%	50,000
60,000	70,000	28,790	+	64%	60,000
70,000	80,000	35,190	+	66%	70,000
80,000	90,000	41,790	+	68%	80,000
90,000	100,000	48,590	+	69%	90,000
100,000	. . .	55,490	+	70%	100,000

1973 Tax rate schedule Z (for unmarried or legally separated taxpayers who qualify as *heads of household*)

If taxable income is		The amount of the gross tax liability is			
Over	But not over	A basic amount	Plus	A marginal rate times	The amount over
$ 0	$ 1,000	$ 0	+	14%	$ 0
1,000	2,000	140	+	16%	1,000
2,000	4,000	300	+	18%	2,000
4,000	6,000	660	+	19%	4,000
6,000	8,000	1,040	+	22%	6,000
8,000	10,000	1,480	+	23%	8,000
10,000	12,000	1,940	+	25%	10,000
12,000	14,000	2,440	+	27%	12,000
14,000	16,000	2,980	+	28%	14,000
16,000	18,000	3,540	+	31%	16,000
18,000	20,000	4,160	+	32%	18,000
20,000	22,000	4,800	+	35%	20,000
22,000	24,000	5,500	+	36%	22,000
24,000	26,000	6,220	+	38%	24,000
26,000	28,000	6,980	+	41%	26,000
28,000	32,000	7,800	+	42%	28,000
32,000	36,000	9,480	+	45%	32,000
36,000	38,000	11,280	+	48%	36,000
38,000	40,000	12,240	+	51%	38,000
40,000	44,000	13,260	+	52%	40,000
44,000	50,000	15,340	+	55%	44,000
50,000	52,000	18,640	+	56%	50,000
52,000	64,000	19,760	+	58%	52,000
64,000	70,000	26,720	+	59%	64,000
70,000	76,000	30,260	+	61%	70,000
76,000	80,000	33,920	+	62%	76,000
80,000	88,000	36,400	+	63%	80,000
88,000	100,000	41,440	+	64%	88,000
100,000	120,000	49,120	+	66%	100,000
120,000	140,000	62,320	+	67%	120,000
140,000	160,000	75,720	+	68%	140,000
160,000	180,000	89,320	+	69%	160,000
180,000	. . .	103,120	+	70%	180,000

4

Tax aspects of selecting a
business form

Successful tax planning is dependent upon a timely selection of the most advantageous alternative. The tax problem is not unlike the problem of transporting one's self or some other object from, say, New York City to Chicago. There are almost an infinite number of alternatives for both problems. Considering the transportation problem, we could begin with such obvious alternatives as flying, driving, taking a bus, riding a bicycle, walking, or even going by ship (up the Atlantic and up the St. Lawrence seaway). Upon further investigation each of those alternatives yields many further choices. For example, if we elect to fly, will it be by commercial or private plane? By jet, prop-jet, or propeller-driven aircraft? First class, day coach, economy, or night coach fare? On United, American, TWA, or some other airline? A morning, afternoon, or evening flight? Do we want to go directly or stop over? If we stop over, should we go via Boston, Philadelphia, Miami, Dallas, Los Angeles, San Francisco, or Seattle?

Planning a trip, fortunately, is typically not all that complicated because we have some general constraints which grossly simplify our decision. For example, we may want to go the fastest, most direct, and cheapest way that will get us to our destination by 10 A.M. and allow us to leave from a specified airport. Alternatively, we may want to drive and take the "most scenic route," allowing a maximum of eight days en route. In tax problems, as in transportation problems, these constraints often dictate a specific answer. In other cases, they allow us greater though limited leeway. Fortunately, the number of

55

overriding tax constraints is sufficiently small that we can deal adequately with them in this book. The myriad of possible tax details can be left to the volumes which are written for the professional tax advisors.

THE BASIC TAX CONSTRAINTS

Most business-oriented persons are at one time or another introduced to the nontax advantages and disadvantages of the various forms of business organizations. They learn, for example, that the corporate form of organization provides numerous opportunities for raising large sums of capital; limits the financial liability of the owner to the amount invested in the corporate stock (in most instances); provides for unrestricted transferability of the ownership interest; and makes possible an unlimited life of the business entity. The same person knows that the sole proprietorship and partnership are much easier to create but that these business forms also provide for the unlimited liability of the owners; that they may be terminated in numerous ways, sometimes at a most disadvantageous moment; and that the transferability of ownership may be restricted.

In many situations these nontax considerations are of paramount importance in the selection of a business form for a particular enterprise. However, in an equally large number of small to medium-sized business ventures, this is not the case, particularly if the venture is owned by a small number of individuals. Under these circumstances, tax considerations commonly play a dominant role in the business-form selection process. Unfortunately, some businesses are formed and operated without the owners giving adequate consideration to the pertinent tax considerations. This chapter is concerned with precisely those considerations. Some basic tax planning ideas will be introduced here; concomitant details are considered in subsequent chapters. Consequently, it might be advisable to read this chapter twice; once now, and again on completion of the book. Hopefully on the second reading, the significance of many items that may seem remote after the first reading will have become obvious.

Maximum reinvestment of income

Many businesses, especially new ventures, want to maximize the capital available for reinvestment in the business. The amount of income that is available for reinvestment is closely related to the taxation of the earnings stream. Obviously a person can reinvest only after-tax profits. As a consequence, it is particularly important to consider the tax rate that will be applied to a given income stream if the after-tax income and the reinvestment potential are to be maximized. As noted in Chapter 3, the marginal tax rates applied to individual taxable income currently range from a low of 14 percent to a high of 70 percent. The marginal tax rates applied to corporate taxable incomes are either 22 percent or 48 percent. It is apparent, therefore, that one of the prime criteria in the selection of a business form is the aggregate income of the owner of the business. If he earns a sufficiently large income to subject him to a tax bracket that exceeds 22 percent or 48 percent, as the case may be, he may very well elect to arrange his business affairs in such a way that a corporate entity (or entities) may be used to shield income from the higher personal tax rates. Observe that this consideration becomes a pertinent factor at relatively low levels of income: the single taxpayer is subject to a *marginal* tax rate of more than 22 percent on all taxable income in excess of $6,000 per year; the married taxpayer filing a joint return pays 22 percent or more when his taxable income exceeds $8,000 annually. The 48 percent marginal corporate tax bracket becomes preferable when taxable income exceeds $32,000 for the single individual and $44,000 for the married person filing jointly. Hence, it is possible to maximize the income available for reinvestment by splitting an income between a corporation and an individual even at relatively modest incomes. As an overriding practical constraint, of course, the diversion of any income into a corporate entity for reinvestment presupposes the fact that the individual has sufficient income accruing to him personally to satisfy his personal financial needs.

Some readers will have serious misgivings about the point just made. That is, they may have observed that income earned by the corporate entity must sooner or later be taxed twice and, therefore, a better comparison might match the two taxes (corporate plus personal), in the case of the incorporated business, to the single tax in the case of the unincorporated one. On further examination, however, the reader will find that this double tax problem is just about as much myth as it is reality for the small, closely held corporation.

First, note that the owner of a closely held business can avoid any double tax on much of his corporation's income by the use of any of several simple expedients. For example, he may pay himself a salary for the service he performs in the corporate employ. This salary, so long as it is reasonable in amount, is deductible by the corporation in the calculation of taxable income. Consequently, the salary is taxed only once to the individual owner as personal compensation. Small corporations may reduce their taxable income to zero, virtually at the owner's discretion, by a simple adjustment of the owner-employee's salary. If the salary reaches the unreasonable range, and the corporation desires to reduce its taxable income still more, it may rent property from the owner and pay him a reasonable rent; pay interest on money borrowed from him; or pay a royalty for the corporation's use of the owner's patent or copyright. Any reasonable amounts paid for these items become a corporate tax deduction at the same time that they create additional gross income for the owner. As illustrated, the closely held corporation may be able to distribute a substantial portion of its income to the owner(s) without incurring a double tax. The only time a double tax is incurred is when the corporation accumulates the income and subsequently distributes it to the owner *as a dividend.* Dividends paid are *not* deductible by the corporation in the determination of the corporate taxable income even though the dividends received by the individual stockholder are fully taxable as ordinary income. Admittedly, individual stockholders are authorized to exclude $100 in dividends annually, but this does not provide them with any great opportunity for large tax savings.

To summarize, we might think of every person as having direct or indirect command over an annual stream of income which can be represented by the size of an arrow. If that income is derived from anything other than a salary paid by a noncontrolled corporation, the owner typically has a great deal of discretion over how this income stream should be diffused among business organizations and how, therefore, it will be taxed. His problem can be depicted as shown in Figure 4–1. This person would be in a high marginal income tax bracket because of the size of his annual income stream. If he wants to maximize his reinvestment potential, he might consider the distribution shown in Figure 4–2 desirable. If this owner had selected any form of business organization other than a corporation, he would have been treated as if he had received the $200,000 directly and would have paid an individual income tax of $110,980 (assuming that he was married and filed a joint return with his wife). This alternative leaves the owner with only $89,020 for consumption spending plus reinvestment in a business. Given the arrangement suggested in the second

FIGURE 4–1

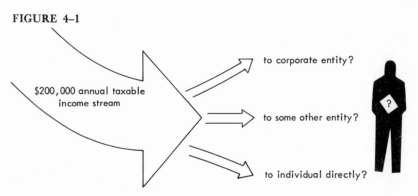

diagram, the corporation would pay an income tax of $68,380 and the owner would pay an income tax of $14,060. By this simple re-arrangement of his business affairs, this taxpayer has reduced his total income tax liability by $28,540 per year and thereby increased his annual opportunity to reinvest in a business by that same amount. To quantify the importance of this difference we need but observe that an annual tax saving of this size, reinvested at a 5 percent after-tax rate of return, accumulates to something like $3.4 *million* over a 40 year period! Given this fact, is it any wonder that more than 1.7 million corporate income tax returns are filed annually in the United States even though less than 4,000 corporations account for two-thirds of all corporate taxable income?

Perhaps an early word of caution is in order. The owner of every closely held corporation must take care to avoid the incurrence of an accumulated earnings tax. This income-related tax was instituted

FIGURE 4–2

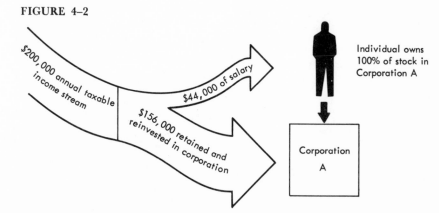

by Congress to control the abuse of the corporate tax rate shelter—a fancy name for the tax avoidance opportunity just explained. That is, Congress did not want wealthy individuals transferring most of their income-earning assets into a corporate shell *solely* for the purpose of avoiding higher personal income tax rates. To control this abuse, Congress instituted the Accumulated Earnings Tax which applies to all *unreasonable* accumulations of income (in excess of a $100,000 exemption). The details of this penalty tax are discussed much later in this book. Suffice it to note here that only unreasonable accumulations are taxed and that, generally, accumulations of corporate income are not found to be unreasonable so long as the owner puts them to good use rather than permitting them to lie relatively idle or simply reinvesting them in high-grade securities.

Retention of special income characteristics

A second important tax factor pertinent to selecting a business form concerns the desirability of retaining certain tax characteristics that are attributed to select "kinds" of income. The notion of exclusions was introduced in Chapter 1 and explained further in Chapter 2. What was not noted, however, was that the designation of certain income as exempt income may be lost when this income is commingled with other income in a corporate entity. That is, if a corporation earns interest on state or local government bonds, it, like the individual, need not report this interest as part of its taxable income for the year. Suppose, however, that after earning this interest, the corporate board voted to distribute this same income as additional salary to an employee or as a dividend to the stockholders. Would the cash distributed retain its tax-exempt characteristic? No. So long as the distributing corporation had either current earnings and profits or earnings and profits accumulated after March 1, 1913, the distribution would be taxed as ordinary income if distributed as a dividend; even if it had no such earnings, any distribution as a salary would be subject to tax by the employee receiving it. There is nothing that the corporate board could do by way of isolating or separating this income from other corporate income to make it retain its tax-free characteristics.

The rule just stated is not restricted to tax-exempt income. It applies equally to other tax-advantaged forms of income such as long-term capital gain. Suppose, for example, that a small corporation realizes a large amount of long-term capital gain in a particular year. Although the corporation can claim the tax benefits extended to long-term capital gains, the corporate board can do nothing to pass this tax advantage along to the owners if and when they choose to distribute the gain.

Based on even this limited discussion it is apparent that whenever a business venture earns a significant amount of tax-favored income it is generally desirable to have that business venture organized in such a form that the tax laws will treat it as a conduit rather than as a separate entity. This result generally is possible if the venture is organized as a sole proprietorship, a partnership, or a Subchapter S corporation. It is not possible when the business venture is incorporated unless the Subchapter S option can be exercised, and even then special limits become applicable in some instances.

Utilization of net operating losses

Net operating losses present a tax situation very similar to the tax-favored income items mentioned in the preceding paragraphs. That is, it is generally desirable for a business venture that incurs a loss to be organized as a tax conduit rather than as a separate taxable entity. This is true because the owner can often use the operating loss from one venture to offset taxable income from another venture on his individual tax return. If the loss is incurred in a separate corporate entity, the owner cannot pass the loss through the entity and utilize it on his personal tax return. In that case, the loss can be used only to offset prior or subsequent income of the corporation, as suggested on pages 29 and 30.

Business entities that either frequently or continually incur tax losses usually are organized as sole proprietorships, partnerships, or as Subchapter S corporations so that the owners can take maximum advantage of the tax loss on their personal tax returns. This consideration is also pertinent in the formation of a new business venture since it is commonplace for new ventures to incur losses during the first several years of operation. The Subchapter S corporation may be particularly useful in this instance since the new corporation that subsequently becomes profitable may elect to terminate the Subchapter S election at a most advantageous time.

The conclusion suggesting that loss operations are best organized in noncorporate forms presumes, of course, that the individual owner(s) would be in a higher marginal tax bracket than the corporation. If this presumption is not valid, an opposite conclusion is correct. In other words, if a net operating loss can be carried back by a corporation and offset against its own taxable income of prior years which was taxed at 48 percent, this alternative is preferable any time that the owner will have to utilize that same net operating loss in offsetting his own taxable income which was taxed at a marginal rate of less than 48 percent.

A second aspect of net operating losses is also pertinent to the business-form question. The owner of corporate stock generally gets no personal tax advantage from his corporation's losses until he elects to sell some or all of his shares. At that time, his shares presumably will be worth less because of the losses incurred by the corporation. If the stockholder does sell his shares at a loss, he will discover that such a loss is a capital loss and, as such, is restricted in the amount deductible in a particular year. As a general rule, the shareholder cannot deduct more than $1,000 per year in capital losses against his ordinary income. Admittedly, he may use capital losses to offset capital gains without limit, but most taxpayers would prefer to deduct losses against ordinary income and recognize the larger amount of capital gain since that gain carries significant tax advantages with it. As explained above, the owner of a sole proprietorship or partnership interest is not faced with the necessity of disposing of part or all of his interest in a business before he reaps the tax benefit of the loss incurred by the business; in addition, such an owner gets that loss as an ordinary loss rather than as a capital loss in most instances.

Employee status

The owner of a sole proprietorship or a partnership interest is generally not an employee of his own firm for tax purposes. The owner of a corporate entity may, however, be an employee of his own corporation. This difference constitutes another major factor that is pertinent to selecting from among alternative business forms. Generally speaking, significant tax advantages are available to an employee that are not available to a self-employed individual. In a limited number of cases, however, it may be to a particular taxpayer's advantage to avoid employee status.

Among the tax advantages granted an employee but denied to the self-employed person are stock option plans; tax-free group-life, health, and wage-continuation insurance plans; certain death benefits; and the chance to receive meals, lodging, and recreational facilities without increasing taxable income. In addition the tax advantages hidden in the deferred compensation plans that may be granted to employees, including pension and profit sharing opportunities, typically are more generous than are the tax benefits available under similar plans granted to self-employed individuals.

In a closely held corporation, these employee benefits may provide a best-of-all-possible tax worlds. This happy result occurs whenever the corporate entity is permitted a tax deduction for an item that need not be reported as gross income by the owner-employee recipient. In effect, the owner's left pocket (the corporation) has obtained a tax deduction for an item that his right pocket (the individual owner) may treat as an exclusion. A next-best alternative is to get the corporation an immediate tax deduction for an item of gross income that the individual owner need not report for a number of years and then, perhaps, only as a capital gain.

A corporate owner-employee also may be in a position to take advantage of an entertainment allowance, travel opportunities, or a company car. Because these items are difficult to separate from personal expenses that frequently would not constitute a deductible item if incurred directly by a taxpayer at his own expense, the IRS pays particular attention to audit returns that indicate possible misuse in this manner. The remaining opportunities are, however, sufficiently great that Chapter 6 is entirely devoted to this topic.

The major tax disadvantage that may attach to classification as an employee stems from the deduction problem discussed in Chapter 3. An employee is more restricted than is the self-employed person in deducting items *for* adjusted gross income. Many trade or business expenses incurred by an employee must be categorized as deductions *from* adjusted gross income. Since the itemization of deductions from AGI precludes the possibility of the taxpayer electing to claim a standard deduction, the employee in a very few instances may find that he would prefer to be self-employed. On the whole, however, the majority of the tax advantages rest with the *owner-employee* status that can be achieved only through incorporation.

Earned income

One new change in the tax rules introduced by the Tax Reform Act of 1969 may provide the single most important reason for selecting the corporate form of business organization in the near future. That change was the introduction of a new *maximum* tax on *earned* income of individual taxpayers. The tax rate schedules included in Chapter 2 are subject to two very important exceptions. They are the 50 percent maximum tax on earned income and an alternative tax rate which can be applied to certain long-term capital gains. The former exception will be discussed here; the latter one in the next chapter.

Abstracting from certain calculational details, the maximum tax on earned income says simply that the *marginal* tax rate to be applied to the earned taxable income of an individual taxpayer cannot exceed 50 percent. Application of this new provision obviously necessitates the separation of taxable income into two component parts which can be labeled "earned" and "unearned" income. The distinction intended by these terms is essentially the difference between (1) income derived from the rendering of personal service and (2) income derived from property. The former will not be taxed at more than 50 percent whereas the latter may be taxed at rates up to 70 percent. This aberration to the tax rate schedules plotted in Figure 3–1 can be depicted conceptually as shown in Figure 4–3, where the distance *ac* equals total taxable income; *ab* represents earned income; and *bc* represents unearned income. Distance *ax* represents the portion of earned taxable income (*ab*) that would be taxed at a marginal rate of less than 50 percent because of the normal progression in the regular rate schedule. The exact dollar amount of distance *ax* depends, of course, on the particular rate schedule in question. For single taxpayers utilizing Schedule X and for heads of households utilizing Schedule Z, the new maximum tax on earned income becomes operative whenever the taxpayer's earned taxable income exceeds $38,000. In other words, for these taxpayers the distance *ax* is $38,000. For married taxpayers filing jointly, it is $52,000; for married persons filing separately, it is $26,000.

The critical aspect of the business-organization-form alternative is related to the separation of taxable income into its earned and unearned components. The taxable income of many businesses is attributable jointly to the presence of a service and of capital. For example, the income derived from operating a grocery store, an automobile dealership, a gasoline station, a drug store, a farm, a truck line, a shrimp boat, or literally hundreds of other businesses is typically a combination of the taxable income attributable to the service rendered by the owner and the taxable income attributable to the capital that

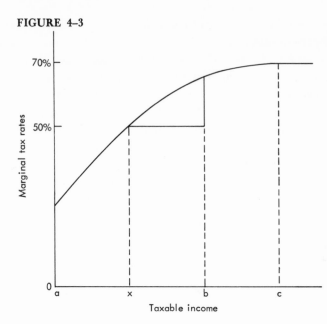

FIGURE 4-3

that owner has invested in his business. If the taxable income is sufficiently large, the new maximum tax on earned income will require that a taxpayer distinguish between these two component elements in the application of the appropriate tax rate. It has been arbitrarily determined that whenever income is derived from a business in which capital is a material income producing factor, not more than 30 percent of the taxable income so produced shall be deemed to be earned income.

Combining this arbitrary interpretation with the 50 percent marginal income determinations observed in the prior paragraph, we can conclude that a combined service-and-capital business that was not incorporated would have to produce a taxable income of more than $126,667 for a single person or a head of household before the owner could utilize the maximum tax on earned income (i.e., if 30% of X = $38,000, then X = $126,667). For married persons filing jointly, that amount would be $173,333 and for married persons filing separately it would be $86,667.

Presence of a corporate entity can magically transform unearned income into earned income for an owner-employee because salary earned as an employee is deemed to constitute earned income. To illustrate the tax-saving importance of this result, consider the effect that it would have on a taxpayer who owned a single business producing a $120,000 annual taxable income in which capital was a material income-producing factor. If the business were not incorporated and the owner were a married taxpayer who filed a joint return, the entire $120,000 taxable income would be subject to the regular rates since only $36,000 could be considered earned income. Thus, the owner's tax liability would be $57,580 annually. If the same business were incorporated and paid the owner-employee a $90,000 annual salary, and if the corporation were to retain and reinvest the remaining $30,000 in taxable income, the taxable income of the individual owner would be entirely earned income and his tax liability would be determined as follows:

Regular tax on first $52,000............	$18,060
Remaining $38,000 × 50%.............	19,000
Total individual tax on $90,000.........	$37,060

The corporate income tax on the $30,000 it retained would be $7,900 (i.e., 22% × $30,000 + 26% × $5,000). The total tax on the taxable income produced by this business would thereby have been reduced from $57,580 to $44,960, an annual tax saving of $12,260. Observe that in this illustration the tax saving can be attributed to minimization of the tax rate in two distinct ways: one, by utilization of the lower corporate rate on $30,000 of income which was retained in the corporate entity; the other, by converting the owner-employee's income to earned income and thereby utilizing the 50 percent maximum tax on earned income. A 40-year accumulation of this annual tax saving, earning a 5 percent after-tax rate of return, would yield a bonus of approximately $1.5 million!

Once again, an early word of caution may be appropriate. The success of the prior tax avoidance idea depends upon the ability of the owner-employee to sustain the fact that a $90,000 annual salary is "reasonable" in amount. Because the new maximum tax on earned income is so new—the 50 percent maximum rate became effective on January 1, 1972—we really have not yet had enough experience with the provision to predict safely what the final result will be. Two observations, however, may be pertinent to an intelligent guess. First, when judicial authorities are faced with such pragmatic problems as the interpretation of what constitutes a reasonable salary, they can only turn to the world and observe what other taxpayers in similar situations are being paid. Second, although a time lag is inevitable, all well-advised taxpayers eventually will realize the significance of this tax-saving opportunity, and this will cause them to increase their own salaries appreciably within the next few years. If this last prediction is correct, the court will be able to conclude only that such high salaries are normal and, therefore, reasonable.

The probable importance of the new maximum tax on earned income to owner-operated businesses can hardly be overestimated. To understand its economic significance, consider the fact that owner-operators in the past have tended consistently to accumulate income beyond their personal consumption needs within their corporations in order to take advantage of the lower corporate rates. As already explained, this was usually achieved through the use of multiple corporate entities so that the effective tax rate seldom exceeded 22 to 30 percent. The 1969 Tax Reform Act changed all that by concurrently eliminating the possibility of multiple surtax exemptions (as explained on pages 40–42) and by instituting the new maximum tax on earned income. The owners of middle-sized businesses soon will realize that leaving taxable income beyond approximately $25,000 in their corporations will subject that taxable income to an effective tax rate of 48 percent whereas immediate distribution of that same income will mean a tax of 50 percent, only 2 percent more, *if* the maximum tax can be made applicable. Given this minor penalty, these owner-operators are going to opt *en masse* for immediate distribution of more taxable income as owner-employee salaries in lieu of continued corporate retention because of the greater financial flexibility provided. No danger of a second tax will exist if the income can be immediately distributed by the corporation. In the past, the owner-operator always had to contrive some way of getting the taxable income out of the corporate entity if he needed it for personal reasons, or if he wanted to reinvest it in a new venture which was organized in a separate corporation. There never was a problem of getting it out of the old corporation if the owner was willing to declare a dividend and pay an individual tax of up to 70 percent. Typically, of course, he was not willing to pay such a high rate and tax advisors were kept busy finding ways to extract a little tax-free and a lot more in the form of a tax-favored long-term capital gain. All of those arrangements will become less important if the corporation can now begin to make immediate distribution of the income to its owners at essentially the same tax cost that would accompany the corporate-income retention alternative.

To summarize and restate, recent changes in the federal income tax law provide a basis for predicting massive changes in the way in which owner-operators of small- to medium-sized businesses will behave in a financial sense in the near future. In contrast to their previous tendencies to (1) create many corporations, (2) pay themselves relatively modest salaries, and (3) retain a maximum amount of income within their corporations, these same owner-operators will soon begin to (1) consolidate their multiple corporate activities, (2) increase their own salaries by substantial amounts, and (3) reduce accordingly the proportion of the taxable income retained in their corporations. Corporate boards of directors of closely held corporations may now find themselves short of cash; in the past, these same boards were often concerned with finding ways to invest excess cash in ways which would permit them to avoid imposition of the accumulated earnings tax.

The first line of defense offered by the IRS predictably will be an attack on the unreasonableness of the new look in owner-employee salaries. The more extreme cases will find their way into the courts. If enough owner-employees act in the same way at about the same time, proof of the normality of the high salaries paid to owner-employees will be available and cause the courts to conclude that such salaries are, after all, reasonable. In that event the Treasury Department will again turn to Congress for more remedial legislation. In the meantime, the reader should understand and remember the importance of the corporate form of business organization to achieving major tax savings in capital-intensive, owner-operated businesses.

Gaining a special tax deduction

For most purposes the individual taxpayer and the corporation are entitled to claim essentially the same deductions at least so far as business-related expenses are concerned. A major exception to that general rule exists as to the dividend-received deduction. As explained earlier, the corporation is granted a deduction equal to 85 percent of the dividends it receives from most other domestic corporations. An individual taxpayer gets no similar deduction, although he is allowed to

exclude from his gross income the first $100 of dividends that he re-
ceives each year. Each of these provisions—the 85 percent dividend-
received deduction and the $100 dividend exclusion—is intended to
minimize the double tax that is associated with the U.S. tax treatment
of corporate income and dividends.

Because of this important difference in the tax treatment of individuals and corporate entities, a major opportunity for tax avoidance
exists. Any wealthy individual earning a substantial *dividend* income
must consider the possibility of transferring some of his dividend-paying investment into a corporate entity. By doing this, he may significantly lower the effective tax rate on the dividends he receives. Ignoring complications that will be discussed later, suppose for a moment
that an individual receives $100,000 in dividends annually. Even after
making several favorable assumptions, this taxpayer would incur a
minimum tax liability of approximately $45,000 on the dividends he
receives. If this same individual were free to transfer his stock investments into his own corporation (created simply to receive them), the
annual tax liability on the same income stream could be reduced to
something like $3,300 were it not for some special restrictions. This
low tax liability would be the direct result of the corporate dividend-
received deduction which would operate as follows:

Dividends received by new corporation........	$100,000
Less 85% of $100,000 dividends received......	85,000
Corporate taxable income....................	$ 15,000
Times applicable corporate tax rate...........	✕ 22%
Equals gross tax liability....................	$ 3,300

Recognizing this tremendous opportunity that a corporation creates
for sheltering the dividend income of wealthy persons, Congress
enacted a Personal Holding Company Tax. The critical effect of this
tax is to take away the tax shelter provided for dividends received
by the corporation, but the special tax is applicable only in the more
obvious and extreme cases. It becomes effective only when the *passive*
income of a corporate entity is relatively more important than is income earned in more *active* business endeavors. That is, if a corporation is created to do little more than collect dividend checks, clip interest coupons, and/or cash rent checks, the Personal Holding Company
Tax will likely prevail. If, on the other hand, the dividend-rich taxpayer is careful to blend into a single corporate shell both some active

business venture and some passive business investments, he may be able to reduce the effective tax rate paid on his dividend income to something like 3.3 percent (i.e., 22 percent of 15 percent of the dividends received). This kind of tax planning obviously permits a maximization of reinvestment opportunities by gaining a tax deduction that would not be available in the absence of the corporate entity.

A second example which illustrates how a taxpayer might gain a benefit from obtaining a special deduction does not actually require the existence of a corporate entity, but its existence certainly may facilitate the end objective. This second illustration turns on the fact that every individual ordinarily is entitled to claim a $750 personal exemption deduction and a minimum $1,300 low-income allowance. Wealthy families were able to take advantage of the special deductions intended for low-income people by making certain that every member of the family received an income of no less than $2,050. Children and grandchildren were given sufficient property—often nonvoting, high-dividend preferred stocks in a closely held corporation—to insure their receiving the minimum amount of income. The tax result was partially restricted for years after 1971 because Congress passed a rule which disallows the $1,300 low-income allowance for any individual claimed as a dependent by another taxpayer, if his income is from passive sources. Thus, it now is necessary to insure that every child "earns" at least $1,300 of his income—probably as a salary paid by the family corporation—if the maximum tax result is to be achieved. Although the dollar amounts are relatively small, the tax savings can still be meaningful. In an extreme situation, this simple device can remove $2,000 of taxable income from the highest bracket and thereby save $1,400 in taxes each year since the new recipient would pay no tax on that same income. Incidentally, the parent will not lose the right to claim a second personal exemption for the child if he is under 19 or a full-time student and if a few other requirements are satisfied. This duplication of a single special deduction—that is, the claiming of a personal exemption by both the child and his parent—is a rare occurrence in taxation. Typically, only one taxpayer is entitled to claim any particular tax deduction.

Disposition of a business

The form in which a business was organized is particularly important when a taxpayer dissolves or otherwise disposes of that business.

On disposition of a sole proprietorship an owner is generally assumed to have disposed of the individual assets which comprise the business venture for tax purposes. The proceeds of the sale must be allocated among all of the assets based on their relative fair market values. As a consequence of this presumption, much of the profit realized on disposition may result in ordinary income since the sale of those same assets individually would have produced ordinary income. In contrast, the owner of a corporate entity usually has an option: either he can allow his corporation to sell individual assets or he can individually dispose of his business by selling the corporation's stock. In most instances he is able to claim the tax-advantageous capital gain treatment for any gain thus realized.

A corporation also provides a good vehicle for partial dispositions. It is relatively cumbersome to sell a partial interest in either a sole proprietorship or a partnership; a partial interest in a corporate entity may be more marketable. Disposition of a partial business interest through the sale of some part of a larger block of stock almost guarantees that any gain will be capital gain. The ease of making stock dispositions also makes the corporate form of business organization of major importance to estate planning for wealthy taxpayers.

Corporations were once widely utilized to convert what would otherwise have been ordinary income into capital gain in rather obvious situations. Perhaps the most celebrated use of the corporation for this purpose came to be known as the Hollywood corporation. Movie moguls, producers, and actors would jointly form a corporation to produce a motion picture. Each participant would contribute his talent and minimal capital in exchange for the corporation's stock. Then, after completion of the movie, but prior to its distribution, the corporation was collapsed and the stockholders were given the future royalty rights as a liquidating dividend. A liquidating dividend was taxed as a capital gain rather than as ordinary income. Thus, through the temporary use of the corporation, these Hollywood personalities were able to convert what was essentially their salary into a liquidating dividend and thereby change the applicable tax from an ordinary income tax into a capital gains tax. Congress, again at the urging of Treasury, closed this unintended tax loophole by creating a special set of tax rules which apply only to the disposition of stock in a *collapsible* corporation. Without going into details about the definition of a collapsible corporation here, it is sufficient to note that sale or other disposition of stock in such a corporation produces ordinary income rather than capital gain. Although the definitional provisions restrict the breadth of opportunity for converting ordinary income into capital gain through the use of a corporate entity, they do not eliminate this possibility entirely. Chapter 12, which considers selected tax traps, will note the few remaining possibilities.

Fluctuating income

Business ventures that are characterized by wide variations in annual income may find it advantageous to incorporate for several reasons. First, the steeply progressive feature of the individual income tax rates at relatively low levels of taxable income may result in a larger tax liability over a period of years than would application of the less progressive corporate rates. This tendency admittedly has been reduced by the introduction of income-averaging provisions which are available to individual taxpayers. Second, the adjustments that are required in converting a negative taxable income into a net operating loss carryback involve a greater chance for the loss of a tax deduction in the case of an individual taxpayer than they do in the case of a corporate taxpayer. Third, a corporation generally is presumed to be engaged in a trade or business; activities conducted directly by an individual carry no such presumption. Consequently, business ventures that could be considered to be a hobby (which are often characterized by widely fluctuating incomes) may be better able to withstand an IRS challenge if they are incorporated.

Although the preceding discussion is by no means exhaustive, it should give the reader some appreciation of the basic tax consequences which attach to the selection of any one of the various possible forms of business organization. What may not yet be apparent is that selecting the most advantageous organizational form is often dependent upon a diverse array of unknowns, including the amount of a taxpayer's future income or loss from all sources, the dispersion of that income or loss over several annual periods, the ultimate size of his family, the length of his life, and subsequent changes in the tax laws. Recognizing the degree of imprecision implicit in these variables, many knowledgeable taxpayers will concentrate their attention on one or two variables deemed to be of primary importance with the hope that other tax consequences can be reasonably accommodated as the business proceeds. Additionally, in other circumstances the nontax considerations may be sufficiently dominant to override what might otherwise be preferable from a tax standpoint. Any reader contemplating a new business venture should seek competent tax advice before selecting the business form within which he is going to conduct that venture. Special consideration must be given to business activities which involve more than one country.

SPECIAL CONSIDERATIONS FOR MULTINATIONAL BUSINESSES

The tax rules applicable to multinational business operations are inordinately complex. What appears here is only a capsule summary of a very few of the more critical tax aspects of doing business abroad. This brief discussion has been divided into unincorporated and corporate business activities. The more substantial tax-planning opportunities involve the utilization of a corporation.

Unincorporated businesses

The United States income tax is, as was previously explained, a global tax; it reaches the taxable income of all citizens and resident aliens regardless of where their income is earned. Also as previously explained, the U.S. income tax does not recognize unincorporated businesses as separate taxable entities but prefers, instead, to attribute any taxable income from an unincorporated business directly and immediately to the business' owners. As a consequence of these two rules, any U.S. citizen generally must pay a U.S. income tax each year on any income earned through business operations conducted outside the United States even though none of that income is immediately repatriated. Special rules are applicable, however, if a foreign government has blocked possible repatriation by currency restrictions.

Income earned in a foreign country by U.S. citizens is often taxed by the foreign government as well as by the U.S. government. To eliminate a double tax on the single income stream the U.S. usually allows the taxpayer to claim a tax credit against his U.S. gross tax liability for any foreign income tax paid. The net effect of this arrangement is to tax an unincorporated business venture operated by a U.S. citizen at the highest effective rate that is operative in the countries involved.

The *earned* income of a U.S. citizen who (*a*) is a bona fide resident of a foreign country or (*b*) remains abroad for not less than 510 days in 18 consecutive calendar months is eligible for a special exclusion. This exclusion applies to a maximum of $20,000 of earned income for the first 3 years that the taxpayer qualifies under either condition noted above; thereafter, the exclusion is $25,000 annually. If the taxpayer's income is derived from a business in which capital is a material income-producing factor, once again not more than 30 percent of such income can be treated as earned income and thus be excluded from gross income. The potential advantage of foreign incorporation by an owner-operator is again apparent.

Corporate businesses

U.S. corporations doing business abroad must reconsider the business-organization form question with specific reference to foreign operations. The corporation with a domestic (U.S.) charter can conduct its foreign operations as a branch of the domestic corporation, as a separate but domestic subsidiary of the U.S. parent, or as a foreign subsidiary corporation. In some instances it can also achieve its objectives through a licensing arrangement with a foreign corporation that is not a subsidiary. The tax consequences of each alternative are different and sometimes substantial.

Branch operations. Domestic corporations engaged in foreign business through branch operations are in essentially the same position as individual taxpayers conducting an unincorporated business abroad. That is, the domestic corporation must recognize and pay U.S. tax on all branch operations immediately regardless of the disposition of the taxable income earned by the branch. A tax credit may be claimed for any foreign income taxes paid by the branch.

Subsidiary corporations. A domestic corporation can, of course, create a subsidiary corporation to handle its foreign operations. This subsidiary can be either a second domestic corporation or one created under the laws of a foreign country. Subject to a few major exceptions which are discussed below, the domestic subsidiary doing business abroad will be treated, taxwise, like most other domestic corporations. The creation of a foreign subsidiary gives birth to a host of new problems and opportunities.

Recall the general rules which provide (*a*) that a stockholder is not generally taxed on the taxable income earned by his corporation until that corporation distributes its previously accumulated taxable income, and (*b*) that nonresident aliens are subject to the U.S. income tax only to the extent that they have income from U.S. sources. If applied literally, as it was until about 1962, these rules provide tremendous tax-planning opportunities for foreign subsidiary corporations. A U.S. taxpayer could create a foreign corporation (thus making it something like a nonresident alien) and withhold in that corporation all of its earnings until a most fortuitous moment without incurring a U.S. income tax. In addition, by a careful selection of the country in which the subsidiary is incorporated, the tax on the corporation's income could be minimized or even obliterated. No less than 25 countries, most of them tiny nations, clamored for years for these corporate shells by creating the most favorable possible corporate tax laws. These countries became known as "tax haven countries" and the corporate shells created in these countries became known as "base country corporations."

In their heyday, these foreign operations were further tax-blessed by price gerrymandering of the grandest proportions. To glimpse briefly the glorious tax opportunities of the recent past, consider the corporate superstructure shown in Figure 4–4. Although goods were

FIGURE 4–4

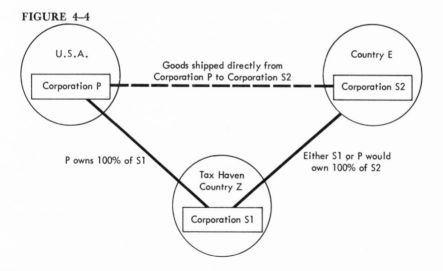

shipped directly from Corp. P to Corp. S2 for sale in Country E by Corp. S2, the legal title to these goods passed momentarily through island empire Z (a tax haven country) and Corp. S1. Corp. P would price its sales to Corp. S1 at something close to its cost, thereby reducing the reportable taxable income of P on foreign sales to a minimum or even to zero. Corp. S1 would resell the same goods to Corp. S2 at a price comparable to the ultimate sales price of the goods by Corp. S2 in Country E (which imposed a corporate income tax), thereby reducing Corp. S2's taxable income to zero. Corp. S1, in Country Z, needless to say, was a fantastic financial success! The owners of S1 were twice blessed by the coincidence that neither the U.S. nor Country Z would tax these profits until S1 paid P a dividend or P sold its S1 stock and reaped its bountiful capital gain.

So much for recent history. Specific statutory changes in the Code as well as more vigorous attempts by the IRS to force related taxpayers to deal with each other at something like arm's length prices have changed the foreign scene considerably. In the process the IRS has also created some of the most complex tax provisions ever known to mankind. The important result of the new rules is that (a) under prescribed conditions the U.S. stockholder of a foreign corporation *may be* required to report the taxable income earned by the foreign corporation immediately as this taxable income is earned and without regard for any actual repatriation of income from the foreign corporation to the U.S. stockholder; and (b) related to parties must be careful in all dealings with each other if they want to avoid a reallocation of their reported gross income and deductions by the IRS. The exact rules which chart these dangerous waters can be understood and interpreted only by an expert. International business ventures simply must have such an expert on board. A few special tax-saving opportunities related to foreign operations, which, by design, remain in our tax Code, should be examined briefly.

The DISC. In 1971 Congress, in response to a request from President Nixon, created a set of special tax provisions intended to reduce the perennial balance of payments problem. These new provisions create a special kind of corporation called the Domestic International Sales Corporation, or DISC. The stockholders in a corporation which qualifies and elects to be taxed as a DISC need report and immediately pay tax on only 50 percent of the DISC's taxable income unless a greater percentage is actually distributed by the DISC to the shareholder. If a distribution of more than 50 percent is made, that amount is immediately taxed to the shareholder. If a lesser amount is distributed, the untaxed 50 percent of the DISC's taxable income will remain untaxed by the U.S. until it distributes the income or the shareholder disposes of his interest in the DISC corporation. To qualify for DISC deferral privileges, a corporation must:

1. Have only one class of stock outstanding;
2. Have corporate capital of not less than $2,500;
3. Utilize 95 percent of its assets in direct export activities; and
4. Obtain 95 percent of its gross receipts from specified foreign operations.

To a limited extent, the DISC opportunity returns us to the tax-saving possibilities described above.

The WHTC. A domestic corporation that conducts all its business in the Western Hemisphere can qualify for special tax privileges as a Western Hemisphere Trade Corporation, or WHTC. The tax privilege in this instance takes the form of a special corporate deduction that is authorized in the computation of taxable income. The WHTC may claim a special deduction equal to nearly 30 percent (29.167 percent to be exact) of its adjusted taxable income. In order to gain this magical free 30 percent deduction a corporation must qualify as follows:

1. For the prior three years, or for its entire existence if that is less than three years, at least 95 percent of the corporation's gross income must have been from sources outside the U.S.; and
2. At least 90 percent of the gross income for this period must have been from the active conduct of a trade or business.

Remember, also, that all of the corporation's business must have been in the Western Hemisphere. The potential tax advantage of this special provision for a few corporations is obvious.

The special tax considerations for multinational business operations can be expanded to include such exotic topics as China Trade Act corporations, less-developed country rules, foreign personal holding companies, and many more special provisions. Because most readers could not take advantage of any tax-saving opportunities common to these provisions, they are dismissed without discussion. Hopefully this brief introduction to foreign operations may trigger an idea in some reader to justify even this limited discussion. Imagination often pays large dividends in tax matters, and this kind of creative imagination sometimes involves both the careful selection of a business form and a country of incorporation. Perhaps a classic example of vivid imagination came to light in the case of *U.S. Gypsum,* 23 AFTR 2d 1605. There the court found that a corporation which was created to own gypsum rock for the few seconds it took for the rock to fall from a related corporation's conveyor belt to the hold of a ship, which was owned by another related corporation, was not a valid WHTC because it was not actively involved in the conduct of a trade or business. The court report's diagram of the critical facts, which is reproduced in Figure 4–5, is most informative.

FIGURE 4–5

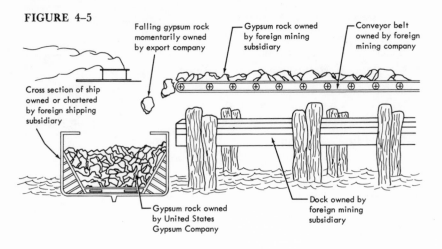

Falling gypsum rock momentarily owned by export company

Gypsum rock owned by foreign mining subsidiary

Conveyor belt owned by foreign mining company

Cross section of ship owned or chartered by foreign shipping subsidiary

Gypsum rock owned by United States Gypsum Company

Dock owned by foreign mining subsidiary

5

Capital gains and losses:
Basic rules

MOST TAXPAYERS realize that capital gains carry some form of special tax advantage in the United States. Very few taxpayers, however, can accurately explain either what those tax advantages are or exactly which gains represent capital gains. This chapter is intended to give the reader a clearer understanding of the complex rules applicable to the taxation of capital gains and losses and to illustrate the important tax differences that exist because of these complex rules. Even this rather lengthy chapter must be regarded as an incomplete discussion and the reader must proceed cautiously in applying these rules to real-world situations unless he obtains competent tax advice in the process.

Before we begin our examination of the many rules which must be understood in the area of capital gains and losses, we might recall that Treasury Department studies have consistently revealed that capital gains privileges constitute by far the single most important tax loopholes in our income tax laws. For persons earning over $50,000 to $100,000 per year, it is the capital gains privileges alone that explain why a substantial majority of these taxpayers in fact pay something like 30 to 35 percent of their income in income taxes rather than 60 to 70 percent as Figure 3–1 seems to imply. Treasury data prepared in 1969 revealed that of all the tax returns in the $100,000 to $500,000 income class, 11 percent actually paid an effective tax rate of something between 0 and 20 percent; 60 percent of the same group actually paid an effective rate of between 20 and 40 percent;

and only 29 percent paid an effective rate of more than 40 percent. If these figures were not so compelling, it would be easy to get discouraged while trying to untangle the web of rules that must be learned before a taxpayer can effectively utilize the tax-saving opportunities available in the capital gain provisions.

This chapter is divided into five major parts. The first is an explanation of the ultimate tax advantages that can accrue to certain forms of income commonly known as capital gains or, sometimes more precisely, as long-term capital gains. The second division is concerned with definitional problems necessitated by the separation of ordinary gain from capital gain for tax purposes. Part three interprets the most important corollary "basic rules" critical to the measurement of any capital gain or loss. The fourth part explains how short- and long-term transactions must be combined for tax purposes. The final division explains the special rules that apply when a taxpayer realizes more capital losses than capital gains in a particular year. Illustration of the many ways in which the capital gain rules can be advantageously utilized in specific situations is deferred to the next chapter.

UNDERSTANDING THE ADVANTAGES

Many persons believe that the ultimate tax advantage which accrues to income classifiable as a long-term capital gain is that such income is taxed at a flat rate of 25 percent. This belief is both incomplete and at least partially incorrect. A more accurate understanding of the ultimate tax advantages of a long-term capital gain needs to be separated into two sets of rules. Individual taxpayers and fiduciaries play by one set; corporate taxpayers by another.

Individual and fiduciary taxpayers

An individual taxpayer who has realized in any year a net long-term capital gain in excess of his net short-term capital loss has the option of (a) claiming a long-term capital gain deduction or (b) paying an alternative tax of 25 percent of such a gain. Since the Tax Reform Act of 1969, however, the second option is limited to $50,000 of qualifying gain per year. If a taxpayer has realized more than $50,000 in net long-term capital gains, he still has the option on the first $50,000; thereafter only the first of the two tax privileges can be claimed. This means, of course, that if a taxpayer realizes (say) a $200,000 qualifying capital gain, he can really claim both tax privileges: he can claim the alternative 25 percent rate on $50,000 of his gain and claim a long-term capital gain deduction based on the remaining $150,000.

The long-term capital gain deduction. The long-term capital gain deduction is by definition equal to 50 percent of the excess of net long-term capital gains over net short-term capital losses. Translated into English this means simply that a taxpayer can pretend that half of his gain does not really exist anytime that he can classify it as a capital gain rather than as ordinary gain. Although the technical computation proceeds on the basis of a special deduction that serves to reduce the tax base called taxable income, the real economic effect is equivalent to halving the applicable tax rates for certain capital gains. As a practical result our tax rates begin at 7 percent and increase to a maximum of only 35 percent any time that a taxpayer is entitled to claim the privilege of the long-term capital gain deduction. The obvious advantage of those rates in comparison with the apparent 14 to 70 percent rates printed in the Tax Rate Schedules (see again pages 51 through 54) needs no further comment.

The 25 percent alternative tax. The 25 percent alternative tax for qualified capital gains is conceptually similar to the 50 percent maximum tax on earned income introduced in Chapter 4. In effect, it suspends the normal progression of the apparent marginal tax rates implicit in Tax Rate Schedules X, Y, and Z any time that the income tax base can be realized in the form of a qualifying capital gain. As noted earlier, however, this alternative is limited in that it may be applied to a maximum of $50,000 of qualifying capital gains each year.

Which option to elect. Which of the two tax privileges available to qualifying capital gains should an individual taxpayer elect in any given fact situation? Common sense will lead the reader to the correct conclusion that an individual taxpayer generally will elect the 25 percent alternative tax rate when he has sufficient *taxable* income to put him in a marginal tax bracket of more than 50 percent using the normal rate schedules. This is true because any rational taxpayer would prefer paying 25 percent on the entire qualifying capital gain (to the extent permitted) rather than paying marginal rates in excess of 50 percent even when those rates are applied to only one-half of his real capital gain income.

In other words, a taxpayer ordinarily will elect the long-term capital gain deduction so long as the effect of claiming it is to reduce his effective marginal tax rate to less than 25%. This will be the result of claiming the deduction option until the taxpayer is in a marginal tax bracket of more than 50 percent, since the deduction option gives him the right to ignore exactly one-half of his qualifying capital gain income. Once he has passed that point in the marginal rate brackets, he will opt for the 25 percent alternative tax rate until that option is exhausted by the $50,000 maximum per year. Thereafter he will return to the effective rate created by the deduction option.

If a taxpayer's entire taxable income does not consist of qualifying capital gains, it becomes necessary to tier his income. Furthermore, to calculate the gross tax liability, it becomes necessary to rank-order the different tiers of income. The Code tells us in effect that in applying the alternative long-term capital gains tax we may consider ordinary (that is, noncapital) income as the first tier and qualifying capital gain as the second tier. This is fortunate for the taxpayer, of course, since it allows ordinary income to be taxed at the lowest possible marginal tax rates. If the tiers were reversed, the capital gain privileges would be less beneficial than they now are.

The correct and preferred application of the capital gain rules and options just explained to any given situation depends entirely upon the specific facts of that situation. Suffice it here to make these general observations:

1. A qualifying capital gain is always preferable to an equivalent amount of ordinary income.

2. An individual taxpayer generally will utilize the 25 percent alternative long-term capital gains tax rate if his *taxable* income is sufficiently large to place him in a marginal tax bracket of more than 50 percent. (Remember, in computing taxable income the taxpayer may ignore 50 percent of his qualifying capital gains.) For married taxpayers filing joint returns, this 25 percent rate option generally becomes preferable when taxable income exceeds $52,000; for single persons and heads of households, it is preferable after $38,000; and for married persons filing separately, it becomes advantageous after $26,000.

3. Whenever the taxable income is near the breaking points suggested in the preceding paragraph, the taxpayer should make both calculations because his income mix—that is, the ratio of his ordinary income to capital gain—may influence the selection of the preferable

option, because the taxpayer must treat the entire qualifying capital gain as a single amount. He cannot divide it between ordinary income and capital gains except in total and he cannot divide amounts between the two tax privileges except when forced to do so by the $50,000 annual limitation applicable to the 25 percent alternative rate.

4. Even if an individual taxpayer does not have sufficient taxable income to make claiming the 25 percent alternative rate desirable, he may elect to claim the capital gains deduction for qualified amounts of long-term capital gain.

A final complication. Solely for the benefit of the curious, we might observe that an individual taxpayer may find that he would like to claim the benefits of both the 50 percent maximum tax on earned income (discussed in Chapter 4) and the benefits applicable to long-term capital gains. When this happens, the taxpayer's taxable income must be separated into three tiers before his minimum tax liability can be determined. These tiers are: (1) earned taxable income; (2) taxable income which is neither "earned" nor "qualifying capital gain"; and (3) qualifying capital gains. The Code requires that the rate determinations be made in the sequence suggested in the preceding sentence which means, of course, that only rarely will a taxpayer's real income actually be subject to the highest possible marginal tax rates as they are stated in the Tax Rate Schedules. To further complicate matters, the determination of earned taxable income is dependent upon the amount of specified tax preferences claimed by the taxpayer, and one of these preferences is the long-term capital gains deduction. The translation of the actual rules into a specific example is so complex that it is best omitted from this book. The reader should simply be aware of the different tax shelters available to him and request an expert to make the necessary determinations whenever they appear pertinent. Fortunately the rules that harbor the tax advantage for a capital gain realized by a corporation are considerably simpler than are the rules applicable to individuals and fiduciaries, which we have just reviewed.

Corporate taxpayers

If a corporation realizes a net long-term capital gain in excess of a net short-term capital loss in any particular year, it has the option of taxing that excess at a flat alternative rate of 30 percent. The option is in lieu of taxing that same excess in the normal way for a corporation. Since the corporate tax rate schedule involves only a two-step progression, this means in most instances that a corporation with a taxable income of less than $25,000 will *not* elect the 30 percent alternative tax rate whereas the corporation with a taxable income of more than $25,000 will elect it. Again because of the income mix—that is, the ratio of ordinary income to qualifying capital gain—and because of the rule requiring that the entire qualifying capital gain be treated in the same way, corporations with taxable incomes slightly in excess of $25,000 should make both calculations to determine which alternative is more advantageous in their particular circumstances. It is important to observe that the corporation never has the option of claiming a long-term capital-gain deduction; that tax privilege is restricted to individual and fiduciary taxpayers.

The tax-saving potential of a qualifying capital gain is easily demonstrated. Assume that a taxpayer earns a $200,000 taxable income, and that all of his taxable income is ordinary income not eligible for any special privileges, while his neighbor also earns a $200,000 income, but all of that income can be classified as a long-term capital gain. Assuming that the first taxpayer is married and files a joint return, his tax liability amounts to $110,980 while his neighbor's tax liability (also married and filing a joint return) amounts to only $45,180. Observe that the first man's tax liability is nearly 250 percent of the tax liability of the second man! If the first taxpayer were a corporate entity, it would pay a tax of $89,900 while the neighboring corporation would pay only $60,000. As these comparisons amply demonstrate, the potential tax advantage of a capital gain is especially significant for individual taxpayers with substantial incomes. Because the potential for tax savings is so great, it is worthwhile reviewing the related and often complicated rules that determine exactly which gains may ascend into this tax haven and which gains are doomed to the tax purgatory known better as ordinary income.

DEFINING THE BOUNDARIES

Most persons believe that capital gains and losses are those gains and losses attributable to transactions involving either stocks and bonds or plant-and-equipment type assets. Once again, this common belief is both incomplete and at least partially incorrect. Fortunately, however, we do not have one set of definitions for one kind of taxpayer and another set for other taxpayers. For individual, fiduciary, and corporate taxpayers alike, a capital gain or loss is simply any gain or loss attributable to the sale or exchange of a capital asset. The real question, then, becomes one of defining a capital asset.

Surprising as it may seem, the Code defines capital assets by exception. That is, the Code states that *all assets are capital assets unless they are specifically excluded.* The list of excluded assets is initially both limited and surprising. It includes:

1. Inventory items ". . . or property held by the taxpayer primarily for sale to customers in the ordinary course of his trade or business";
2. Real or depreciable property used in a trade or business;
3. A copyright, literary, musical, or artistic composition, a letter or memorandum, ". . . or similar property" but only if such an asset is held either by the taxpayer who created it or by one who has assumed the tax basis of that creator—in the case of letters, memoranda, and similar property, the exception also applies to the person for whom it was prepared or produced;
4. Receivables acquired in a trade or business; and
5. Certain discount bonds issued on or after March 1, 1941.

Inventory assets

The first group of assets excluded from the capital asset category— that is, inventory items—is self-explanatory. If such an exclusion were not made, all routine profits of a merchandising operation would be capital gains by definition. The only practical problem with this first exclusion is the difficulty in applying it in situations where a taxpayer frequently, perhaps regularly, buys and sells certain assets, but which activity is not deemed to be his primary or even secondary source of income. A professional lawyer, for example, was surprised to discover that the IRS and the courts found that his dealing in real estate constituted a trade or business even though he did not have a broker's license and did not personally take an active part in the sales activity. The court found that the frequency and substantial nature of this activity was sufficient to sustain the IRS contention that such purchases and sales did constitute a trade or business and that, therefore, the profits were ordinary income from the sale of real estate held primarily for sale rather than capital gains from investments. Just why this same interpretation should not be applied to non-broker investors who are heavily engaged in stock market transactions is not at all clear. Suffice it to say that the frequency criterion has not been applied generally when the asset in question was a security although the literal wording of the Code makes no such distinction. The Service and the courts seem to have implicitly accepted a hands-off attitude in applying the capital gain definition to securities transactions for reasons known only to themselves. Only regular securities dealers realize ordinary income from trading transactions. With this notable exception, however, the reader should understand that there is absolutely nothing inherent in any particular kind of property that makes it capital or noncapital. That definitional result is based solely on the relationship between the taxpayer and the property: if an asset is held primarily for resale in the ordinary course of a trade or business it is not a capital asset for that particular taxpayer. And any one taxpayer can be engaged in multiple trades or businesses at the same time.

Real or depreciable property used in a trade or business

The second group of assets excluded from the capital asset category—that is, real or depreciable property used in a trade or business—is probably the most surprising entry in the list of noncapital assets. If it were applied without further modification it would mean that all profits and losses from the sale of plant-and-equipment type assets would be ordinary income or loss by definition. Stated in another way, it would mean that any profit on the sale of farm land by a farmer or rancher, on the sale of a factory by a manufacturing firm, or the sale of a cash register by a retail store would be categorized as ordinary income. There are several additional sets of rules which modify this conclusion in varying circumstances.

Before we concern ourselves with those modifications, we should observe that *this exclusion applies to either real or depreciable property but only if such property is used in a trade or business*. When the adjective "real" is used to modify the noun "property," it generally means land and anything permanently attached to land. Thus the term real property would include most buildings and building components, a lot of heavy equipment, and fences, tanks, tracks, and other assets permanently attached to the earth directly or indirectly. The adjective "depreciable" tries to distinguish a wasting asset from a nonwasting one. Any property, whether real property or nonrealty, that will waste away over time can be considered a depreciable property. In this context, however, the Code has reference to more than this physical wasting characteristic. The term as used here demands wasting plus a profit motive. Thus a taxpayer's personal residence would *not* constitute a depreciable property for purposes of this definition because there is no profit motive present in the taxpayer's ownership of that house. A single dwelling rented by a taxpayer to another person for a reasonable rent, however, constitutes a depreciable property for this purpose, since the Code permits that taxpayer to claim a depreciation deduction against the income he derives from the property. Observe that a property can be depreciable, then, without being part of a trade or business. When we classify an item for tax purposes from a profit motivation standpoint, we utilize a trichotomy which includes: (1) a full fledged trade or business class; (2) a profit-oriented, but less than trade or business, status; and (3) a wholly personal or not-for-profit category. This definitional distinction can be diagramed as below:

FIGURE 5–1

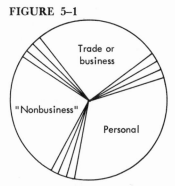

The term "nonbusiness" is often used in tax matters to describe something held for profit but not classifiable as a full-fledged trade or business. The definitional distinctions are sometimes very hazy even though the distinction may be critical to the capital asset definition. Returning to our earlier illustration, if a taxpayer rents a single dwelling unit to another party, and this rental activity is not deemed to constitute a trade or business, the rented unit remains a capital asset since the statutory exception applies only to real or depreciable properties *used in a trade or business.*

A book devoted to tax-planning ideas is not an appropriate place to review all the complex rules that modify the ultimate tax treatment of even the most straightforward trade-or-business type asset. Given our objective, it seems more appropriate to provide some summary statements that will usually be correct and then remind the reader that these statements should not be used in actual circumstances without first verifying their applicability in those specific settings. Table 5–1 summarizes, correctly in most circumstances, the present tax treatment of the gain and loss realized on the sale or exchange of a real

TABLE 5–1
Usual tax treatment of gain or loss realized on the sale or exchange of real or depreciable property used in a trade or business

Kind of property	If result is gain	If result is loss
Depreciable non-real property (e.g., car used by salesman, office desk and typewriter, hand tools, etc.).....................	Ordinary income	Sec. 1231 loss
Depreciable real property (e.g., retail store, warehouse, factory plant, etc.)		
if rapid depreciation was claimed.......	Partially or wholly ordinary income	Sec. 1231 loss
if straight-line depreciation was claimed...	Sec. 1231 gain	Sec. 1231 loss
Non-depreciable real property (land).......	Sec. 1231 gain	Sec. 1231 loss

or depreciable property used in a trade or business. The reference to Section 1231 gain or loss will be explained immediately.

Section 1231 is a very peculiar part of our income tax law. In effect, it provides that specified items shall be brought together and their ordinary or capital character held in suspense until the end of the year when their net result is known. If the net result of all Section 1231 transactions is a loss, each of the items is treated as if it involved a non-capital asset; if the net result of all Section 1231 transactions is a gain, each of the items is treated as if it involved a long-term capital asset. From a tax-planning standpoint, this is most favorable to the taxpayer. As noted earlier, capital gains are always preferred to equivalent amounts of ordinary income. Partially for these same reasons, and partially for reasons to be explained in the last portion of this chapter, ordinary losses are always preferred to equivalent amounts of capital losses.

Combining this terse explanation of Section 1231 with Table 5–1, we should note that a taxpayer may still be able to recognize capital gains from the sale or exchange of depreciable real property used in a trade or business. The likelihood of this result is increased if the gain is attributable to the sale or exchange of land, or if the taxpayer claimed only straight-line depreciation on depreciable real property before he sold or exchanged it. The opportunity to allocate a higher proportion of the sales price to land, and a smaller proportion to a building, may provide an opportunity to increase the amount of a capital gain even if rapid depreciation has been utilized. Because the buyer's best interest in any allocation of the sales price is typically adverse to that of the seller's, the IRS and the courts usually are willing to live with an allocation stipulated in a sales agreement. This continuing opportunity for a knowledgeable seller to convert potential ordinary income into a capital gain will be further illustrated in the next chapter. Suffice it to note here that the exclusion of property used in a trade or business from the capital asset definition has not always meant that transactions involving such assets necessarily will produce ordinary income or loss.

Copyrights

The third group of assets excluded from the capital asset category includes copyrights, literary, musical, or artistic compositions, letters, memoranda, and similar property. The rationale for the exclusion of most of these items turns on the belief that taxpayers should not be able to reap the rewards of their individual efforts in the form of a capital gain just because their efforts culminated in the production of a property. The potential inequity between a taxpayer who rendered a personal service without the production of a property—for example, a physician, an accountant, or a sales clerk—and a taxpayer whose service produced a property—for example, an author, a composer, or an artist—would be tremendous were it not for this exception. The obvious failure to include patents in the list of noncapital assets is notable. Congress apparently believes that it is preferable for our citizens to tinker and invent machines than to spend time in other creative ways. At least the substantial tax reward of a capital gain is retained solely for these activities.

The exclusion of letters and memoranda is closely related to recent revisions in the tax rules applicable to the contribution deduction. Without explaining these rules here, we might note that the important result is to deny a taxpayer a sizable tax deduction for any gift of property that would produce ordinary income if sold. As specifically applied to letters and memoranda, this means that all U.S. Presidents who hold office after Lyndon Baines Johnson will be denied a substantial tax deduction for the value of the many papers which these men typically donate to their Presidential libraries.

Note that this third category of exclusions usually applies only to the person who created the property or who received it without cost from such a person. If a taxpayer purchases a copyright or literary, musical, or artistic composition from the creator, the same asset in the hands of the purchaser may be a capital asset. Whether or not it will depends in large measure on the reason the purchaser had for acquiring the asset and the way he uses it after acquisition. If he purchased it with the intention of reselling it in the ordinary course of his business, or if it becomes a depreciable property used in a trade or business, the asset will remain a noncapital asset. If, on the other hand, the purchase was made as an investment or for personal enjoyment, it will become a capital asset in the hands of the purchaser.

All other exceptions

Accounts and notes receivable generally are not considered to be capital assets for the same reasons that inventory assets are excluded from the capital asset definition. If the receivables are derived from the ordinary conduct of a trade or business any gain or loss on the disposition of the receivables should be treated in the same way the income produced by those receivables would be treated. The exception of receivables from the capital asset definition effectively accomplishes this result.

The last exclusion—certain discount bonds—was instituted as a way of ending the conversion of ordinary interest income into capital gain. Prior to the exception of this item it was possible for a taxpayer to purchase a noninterest-bearing security at an appropriate discount and to later sell the same security at a "profit." The discount obviously was nothing more than an alternative to paying a stipulated rate of interest. The tax result, however, would be to create a capital gain rather than ordinary interest if this special exception were not included among the list of assets not to be treated as capital assets.

In summarizing this portion of Chapter 5 we should remember that the capital or noncapital status of any asset is determined by the relationship between the asset and the taxpayer. There is no inherent characteristic in a property that leads to a correct classification. For example, a car would be a noncapital asset to an automobile dealer because it is part of his inventory; the same car might be a noncapital asset to a contractor because he uses it entirely in his trade or business; to another taxpayer, who uses the car solely for personal enjoyment purposes, the same car would be a capital asset. Actually a single asset may be both a capital and a noncapital asset. If, for example, a physician used his car 80 percent of the time for business reasons and 20 percent of the time for personal reasons, that car would be both capital (20 percent) and noncapital (80 percent). The importance of this definition, and the complications it can create, will be demonstrated after we investigate further the rules associated with the measurement of a capital gain or loss.

MEASURING A CAPITAL GAIN OR LOSS

The amount of a capital gain or loss is simply the difference between the "amount realized" on the sale or exchange and the "basis" of the capital asset there surrendered. The amount realized is, in turn, the sum of (1) any cash received, (2) the fair market value of any noncash property received, and (3) the amount of any liability which the buyer takes from the seller. To illustrate, assume that in 1965 a taxpayer purchased, solely for investment purposes, a parcel of land for $50,000, paying $10,000 down and assuming a $40,000 mortgage for the balance. If the taxpayer decided in 1975 to sell the land for (1) $30,000 cash, (2) a boat worth $25,000, and (3) the new buyer's assuming the $20,000 mortgage which remained outstanding against the property, the selling taxpayer would realize a long-term capital gain of $25,000. The amount realized would be $75,000 (that is, $30,000 + $25,000 + $20,000) and the adjusted basis of the property surrendered would be $50,000 (the original cost of the land). The difference of $25,000 represents the measure of the taxpayer's capital gain.

In the real world, of course, it may not be easy to determine the fair market value of any noncash property received. A determination of that value is, nevertheless, necessary to the measurement of the gain or loss realized, and the IRS and the courts generally insist that taxpayers make such a determination immediately. In some situations the tax authorities will infer the value of the more-difficult-to-value property on the basis of an easier-to-value property, believing that a taxpayer would not engage in a sale or exchange of the two properties if those values were not equal. To return to our earlier illustration, if the value of the boat received in that exchange were difficult to determine but the value of the land surrendered were easier to determine, the IRS and the courts would not hesitate to infer the $25,000 fair market value for the boat if they could readily determine that the land was worth $75,000 at the date of the exchange.

The more difficult problem in measuring a capital gain or loss usually involves the determination of the basis of the capital asset surrendered. This difficulty is attributable to the fact that the basis rules differ, depending upon the way in which a taxpayer acquired the capital asset. One set of basis rules is applicable for purchased property, another set for property acquired by gift, another set for inherited property, and yet another for property acquired in a "nontaxable exchange." The first three of these four sets of rules will be considered here; the basis rules applicable to property acquired in a nontaxable exchange will be deferred to Chapter 9.

Basis of purchased property

The tax basis of purchased property is generally equal to its cost plus the cost of any subsequent capital improvements and less the amount of depreciation (or depletion or amortization) claimed for tax purposes. The term "cost" includes both the basic purchase price and all associated costs necessary to acquire the asset and make it operative. Thus, the cost of a security includes the broker's commission; the cost of equipment includes the freight and installation charges which may be incurred before the equipment can be put to its intended use; and the cost of land may include fees paid to realtors and lawyers. If a taxpayer purchases more than one asset for a single purchase price, he must allocate this cost between the several assets acquired. This allocation is based on relative fair market values.

After an asset is acquired, and before it is sold or exchanged, a taxpayer typically incurs numerous costs to "keep it going." Any costs that do not extend the original estimated life of the asset are usually treated as current expenses and (if authorized) deducted immediately for tax purposes. Costs that extend the original life, or that improve a property in some material way, are called "capital expenditures," which means simply that they are properly charged to the asset account rather than to an expense account at the time they are incurred. Because of the time preference value of money, a taxpayer typically wants to expense everything (and thereby reduce his tax liability) as soon as possible; the IRS agent seems to think that everything should be capitalized. The distinction between these two is sometimes very hazy and, in these instances, tax disputes are commonplace.

The amount of depreciation (or depletion or amortization) that a taxpayer can claim for any asset is a function of its cost, estimated life, salvage value, and depreciation method. These concepts are sufficiently complex to justify a separate discussion in Chapter 8. For our immediate purposes—the quantification of a capital gain or loss—we will avoid any problems associated with determining which costs must be capitalized and how much depreciation can be claimed, so that we may concentrate on the problems peculiar to the measurement of a capital gain or loss.

To summarize and illustrate the rules applicable to the determination of the tax basis of purchased property, consider the plight of a taxpayer who purchased land and a building in 1967 and who sold that same property in 1975 if, during the interim period, this taxpayer collected the following information:

Initial purchase price...................	$40,000
Legal fee associated with title search made at purchase date.........	1,000
Capital improvement to building made 3 years after purchase..........	8,000
Cost of routine repairs, taxes, etc., during ownership...................	12,000
Depreciation claimed on building during ownership...................	10,000

Before this taxpayer can determine the amount of his gain or loss on the sale made in 1975, he must determine the tax basis of the assets he sold. This begins with a separation of the initial purchase price of $40,000 between land and buildings. Assuming that the taxpayer can find good reason to do so, he might allocate $30,000 to the building and $10,000 to the land. A question then arises concerning the $1,000 legal fee: must this cost be capitalized, or could the taxpayer deduct that expenditure in 1967? If it must be capitalized, should the cost be divided between the land and the building or is it entirely allocable to the land? The answers to those questions are not apparent, but further investigation might substantiate the conclusion that the legal fee would have to be capitalized and that it might be allocated entirely to the land. Capital improvements would be added to the basis of the building; routine costs might be deducted as they were incurred. In summary, then, this taxpayer could determine the tax basis of his assets in 1975 as follows:

Building: $30,000 + $8,000 − $10,000 = $28,000
Land: $10,000 + $1,000 = $11,000

If the taxpayer sold the land and building for $60,000 and, at the time of the sale, $20,000 was properly allocated to the land and $40,000 to the building, he would have a gain of $9,000 on the land and $12,000 on the building. By reviewing the way in which the taxpayer utilized this building and by reference to the rules implicit in Table 5–1, he could finally determine the correct tax treatment of this $21,000 profit.

Basis of property acquired by gift

The tax basis of property acquired by gift is usually either (a) the donor's cost basis or (b) the fair market value of the property on the date acquired. The tax basis of property acquired by gift will be the donor's cost unless the fair market value of the property is lower than that cost on the date the gift is made. In the event that the fair market value is lower than the donor's cost on the date of the gift, the basis of the property cannot be determined until the donee finally disposes of the property. In this latter instance, if the donee eventually sells it for less than the depreciated value on the day he received it, his basis becomes the value on the day he received it; if the donee eventually sells for more than the donor's original cost, his basis becomes the donor's cost; if he sells for any value between the depreciated value on the day he received it and the donor's cost, he need not report either gain or loss.

These rules may seem unduly complex, and they probably are. However, they become easier to remember and to apply if the reader will but observe that the one thing the tax law will *not* tolerate is passing around a paper loss to a donee in a high tax bracket. In other words, if a man purchased a stock for $100,000 and that stock had depreciated in value to $60,000 the law would not permit the original owner to transfer this $40,000 paper loss to another taxpayer in a higher marginal tax bracket. If the man gave the stock away and the donee sold the stock immediately after receiving it, his basis would have become $60,000 and thus he would not realize any loss on the sale (that is, $60,000 amount realized less $60,000 basis). On the other hand, observe that the law will not penalize the donee if he waits and sells the shares at a date when their value has returned to something more than the donor's cost basis of $100,000. In that situation the donee's basis reverts to $100,000, and his gain is calculated from that value. If a donee sells for any price between $60,000 and $100,000 in this illustration, the tax rules essentially tell him to forget it—he has neither gain nor loss to report.

Observe again that the critical fact that initially determines the tax basis of property acquired by gift is the relationship between the donor's cost and the fair market value on the date a gift is made. If the fair market value on the date of the gift is equal to or greater than the donor's cost, the donee's basis will under all possible circumstances remain the donor's cost—subject only to a minor modification if the donor pays a gift tax on the transfer. As a practical matter, a taxpayer should seldom, if ever, make a gift of property which has decreased in value since he purchased it. To do so risks the possibility that an income tax loss may forever go unrecognized by anyone. Some of the important tax saving opportunities that remain because of the basis rules will be discussed in later chapters.

Basis of inherited property

The tax basis of inherited property is usually either (a) the fair market value of the property on the date of the decedent's death or (b) the fair market value six months after his death. The tax basis of inherited property will be the fair market value on the date of the decedent's death unless the estate is valued at $60,000 or more *and* the executor elects the alternate valuation date for estate tax purposes. In the latter circumstances, the tax basis of inherited property becomes the value of that property on the alternate valuation date— that is, six months after death—except for property distributed by the executor prior to that date. For property so distributed, the basis becomes the fair market value on the date of distribution. Since an executor will only very rarely distribute property prior to the valuation date, the basis is nearly always the fair market value on whatever date it is valued for estate tax purposes.

For income tax purposes, the rule just stated is of tremendous importance. Observe that no one ever pays an *income tax* on property that appreciates in value but that is not sold or otherwise disposed of prior to the owner's death. Any heir can sell inherited property shortly after he receives it and report little or no income tax since his tax basis will be approximately equal to the price he can demand for that property. If the deceased taxpayer had sold the same property just prior to his death, he would have had to recognize the entire gain and his executor would still have had to pay estate taxes on all assets owned by the decedent at the time of his death. Thus, the tendency to retain appreciated assets and allow them to pass through a decedent's estate is very large for persons of substantial means. This tendency has been commonly called the "locked-in effect" in obvious reference to the feeling of an older person that he cannot afford to dispose of an appreciated asset before his death because of the extra tax that would be imposed on such a disposition.

Application of the basis rules for property acquired by gift and for inherited property is important to family tax-planning ideas. The very large tax savings that are possible will be explained in Chapter 11 after we have reviewed the rules common to the Gift and Estate Taxes. For the moment, it is sufficient to observe that the income tax can be permanently avoided by the application of the basis rules for inherited property, but it cannot be avoided by application of the basis rules for property acquired by gift. Since a donee can never get a basis higher than a donor's cost (except for minor increases due to the gift tax), he will eventually recognize the income implicit in appreciated property that is made part of a gift unless the donee holds the property until his own death.

COMBINING SHORT- AND LONG-TERM CAPITAL GAINS AND LOSSES

The special tax privileges explained in the first part of this chapter apply only to the excess of net long-term capital gains over net short-term capital losses (if any). Application of this rule obviously necessitates the separation of capital gains and losses into two categories: namely, short and long term. This distinction for several years has been based on a six month holding requirement. Capital gains and losses derived from the sale or exchange of a capital asset held for more than six months are categorized as long-term gains and losses; those arising from sale or exchange of capital assets held for six months or less are characterized as short-term gains and losses. Observe again that the ultimate tax privileges are restricted to the excess of *net* long-term gains in excess of *net* short-term losses. This means that all long-term transactions must be combined separately and that all short-term transactions must be combined separately before the two net amounts can be considered. We can express this in formula fashion as follows:

$$(\text{LTCG} - \text{LTCL}) \text{ less } (\text{STCL} - \text{STCG})$$

where LTCG represents long-term capital gains, LTCL represents long-term capital losses, and so on.

Tax benefits are possible from capital gains if and only if the quantity in the first set of parentheses in this formula is both (*a*) positive *and* (*b*) greater than the quantity in the second set of parentheses. Be-cause this calculation is made on an annual basis a taxpayer obviously has a great deal of opportunity to influence the net result in any particular year by a careful selection of the date on which he elects to recognize certain gains and/or losses. By careful timing of capital gains and losses, a taxpayer can substantially change the tax liability attaching to these transactions. Some of the tax-saving opportunities will be explained in the next chapter. Before we consider these opportunities, however, we must become familiar with one additional set of rules. These rules deal with the tax treatment of net capital losses.

CORRECT TAX TREATMENT OF NET CAPITAL LOSSES

If a taxpayer realizes in the aggregate more capital losses than capital gains in any particular year, he is beset with another host of special tax rules. Once again these rules differ for individual and fiduciary taxpayers and for corporate taxpayers. We will review the rules applicable to individual and fiduciary taxpayers first and then consider the corporate rules.

Individual and fiduciary taxpayers

If an individual or fiduciary taxpayer realizes in the aggregate more capital losses than he does capital gains in any single year, he may offset a maximum of $1,000 of such losses against his ordinary income in that year. To make matters worse, if the losses were derived from long-term transactions, he can claim those losses only on a two-for-one basis, and he has no option but to claim them to the maximum extent allowed. If the taxpayer has both net short- and long-term capital losses he does, at least, have the right to utilize the net short-term losses on a one-for-one basis before he must begin to expend net long-term losses on the two-for-one basis. But what happens if the taxpayer's aggregate net capital losses exceed the $1,000 maximum?

In the case of individual and fiduciary taxpayers, any capital losses in excess of the maximum $1,000 that may be offset against ordinary income can only be carried *forward* and offset against taxable income of future years. Short-term losses are carried forward and treated as short-term losses in subsequent years, and long-term losses are carried forward and treated as long-term losses. There is no dollar limit on the amount of capital losses that can be offset against capital gains in either the current or future years. If, however, a capital loss is carried forward and the taxpayer does not realize sufficient capital gains in the next year to offset such a carryforward, he once again is limited in the next year to a maximum $1,000 offset against his ordinary income. All remaining losses are carried to later years until they finally have been utilized or the taxpayer dies.

Corporate taxpayers

If a corporation realizes in the aggregate more capital losses than it does capital gains in a single year, it cannot offset any of that capital loss against its ordinary income. However, the corporation can carry that loss *back* and offset it against any capital gain it reported in the third prior tax year. If the capital gains in that year are insufficient to absorb the current year's capital loss, the excess is carried to the second prior year and, if necessary, to the last taxable year. If the total capital loss in the current year exceeds the amount of capital gain reported by the corporation in the three prior years, any balance can be carried forward and offset against capital gains realized in the next five years. If the loss has not been utilized by the end of the fifth subsequent year, it expires without tax benefit.

Whenever a corporation carries a capital loss back or forward, that loss is magically transformed by law into a short-term loss regardless of how it may have been originally characterized. Under the proper circumstances, this transformation of long-term loss into short-term loss can be fortuitous for the corporate taxpayer, since the tax refund is based on whatever tax was paid on the income thus removed from the third prior year. If it happens that the corporation reported a net short-term capital gain in that year, it may have paid as much as 48 percent of that gain to the government in income taxes. In that event, a net long-term capital loss in the current year could actually provide a refund based on a 48 percent rate when it was reclassified as short-term loss and carried back to the earlier year.

A mathematically oriented reader may see the possible number of permutations and combinations implicit in these capital gain and loss rules and seriously question the sanity of anyone who would try to plan events to take maximum advantage of them. Other readers may simply be inclined to throw up their hands in disgust and say only that they know there are so many rules that they simply cannot remember and utilize them effectively. Although it is true that the number of complex rules is inordinately large in this area of the tax law, some reasonably obvious tax-planning situations can be described and appreciated by all readers. Because the tax-saving potential is so large in this area, it will pay the reader to persevere and follow the examples of the next chapter as best he can.

6

Capital gains and losses:
Some applications

IN CHAPTER 5 we became acquainted with the basic rules determining the tax treatment of capital gains and losses. In this chapter we will examine several separate situations that demonstrate the need for careful tax planning so as to maximize the benefits, or minimize the detriments, which attach to transactions involving capital assets. The chapter is not exhaustive, and some portions of the discussion are necessarily superficial. Understanding the chapter is complicated by the fact that the ideas do not flow logically to culmination in a single idea or two.

This chapter has been divided into two parts in an attempt to provide some structure to the otherwise scattered illustrations. The illustrations contained in the first section depend for their success or failure upon careful attention to definitional details. The taxpayer who is appropriately attuned to the capital asset definition is often in a position to amend his intended actions in some manner that will allow him to achieve his personal and economic objectives and, at the same time, modify the tax consequences in a favorable manner. The success or failure of the illustrations contained in the second section of this chapter depends largely upon careful attention to the timing of transactions. In almost all instances other than casualty events, a taxpayer has domination over the exact time at which a gain or loss will be realized. When dealing with capital assets, this time dimension becomes especially critical because of the tax distinction made between short- and long-term gains and losses.

DEFINITIONAL MANIPULATION

In the preceding chapter we learned that all assets are capital assets unless they have been specifically excepted from that classification by Code provision. The most surprising exception is that of real or depreciable property used in a trade or business. That same exception also provides an unusual opportunity for the owner-operator of a business to modify his use of a particular asset and thereby also modify its status as a capital or noncapital asset. In determining whether or not a particular gain or loss is a capital one, the tax authorities generally look at the relationship between the taxpayer and the asset on the date the sale or exchange is completed rather than on the date the asset was acquired or any intermediate date. By removing a depreciable asset from its original use in a trade or business and by utilizing it solely in a personal manner, a taxpayer *may be* able to change the classification of the asset from a noncapital to a capital status and thereby modify the tax result on disposition. The intended-use criterion may be subject to even greater manipulation when more than one taxable entity is involved. We will consider first the case where only a single taxable entity is involved.

Modification of use by a single taxable entity

Any taxpayer who operates a trade or business in the form of a sole proprietorship, a partnership, or a joint venture has multiple opportunities to modify his use of a particular property on a timely basis and thereby to modify its status as a capital asset. To illustrate the basic idea involved in this change of status, consider the tax consequences attaching to the disposition of an automobile by a taxpayer who had continually used that automobile 80 percent of the time in business and 20 percent of the time in personal use from the date of acquisition until the date of disposition. If we assume that the tax payer-owner originally paid $4,000 for the car, depreciated it a total of $2,800 for tax purposes, and finally sold the car for $1,000, we might be tempted to conclude that he had a $200 loss on the sale ($1,000 realized less $1,200 adjusted basis) and that $160 of this loss (80% × $200) was ordinary loss and $40 (20% × $200) was capital loss. Such a conclusion would be incorrect under the circumstances described, as the tax rules essentially view this transaction as involving two entirely separate assets, one capital and another noncapital. The correct calculation of gain and loss is as follows:

	Noncapital portion (80% business use)	Capital portion (20% personal use)	Total (100%)
Original cost	$3,200	$800	$4,000
Less depreciation	2,800	0*	2,800
Adjusted basis on sale	$ 400	$800	$1,200
Amount realized	$ 800	$200	$1,000
Less adjusted basis	400	800	1,200
Gain or (loss) realized	$ 400	($600)	($ 200)

* Personal-use assets are not depreciable for tax purposes because they are not income-producing.

To the dismay of the taxpayer, the correct determination of the tax consequences of this simple transaction would produce a $400 ordinary income and a nondeductible $600 capital loss! The tax treatment of the $400 "gain" is determined by the basic tax rules implicit in the preparation of Table 5–1 (page 88). Those rules provide that any gain on the sale of depreciable nonrealty used in a trade or business will likely be ordinary income. The correct tax treatment of the $600 loss is derived from the basic rules stated in Chapter 2. It was noted there that all income is taxable income unless the taxpayer can find some authority to exclude it; on the other hand, nothing is deductible unless the taxpayer can find some authority that makes it deductible. Search as he may, except in the case of casualty losses, the taxpayer will find no authority for the deduction of any loss incurred in the sale or exchange of purely personal assets. In other words, if a taxpayer sells his personal residence, car, or clothing at a profit he must pay tax on that profit as a capital gain. However, if the taxpayer sells his personal residence, car, or clothing at a loss, such a loss is properly classified as a capital loss, but, more importantly, it constitutes a capital loss for which no tax deduction can be claimed since no Code section authorizes the deduction of losses from the sale or exchange of purely personal assets. As explained on pages 29 and 30, losses arising from the sale of a specific property are deductible if attributable to properties used in a trade or business or to "non-business" properties (that is, profit-producing properties that do not constitute a trade or business) but not if attributable to purely personal properties. The only exception for purely personal properties applies to casualty and theft losses. In our illustration, no casualty was involved in the sale of the car for $1,000 and, therefore, the $600 loss attributable to the 20 percent of the car used for personal reasons would not be deductible.

Suppose that the taxpayer had converted the car from 20 percent personal use to 100 percent personal use for one week preceding the disposition at $1,000. Would this change in use for one week magically transform the classification of the transaction to one involving solely a personal property and thereby get rid of the $400 ordinary gain that otherwise would attach to the 80 percent of the car which had been used previously for business purposes? A literal reading of the Code might lead one to that conclusion. Anyone familiar with the tax game, however, would immediately predict that such a simple tax plan would have to fail, possibly on some rather nebulous judicial grounds. On numerous occasions, the courts have not hesitated to look through a "rigged" transaction to find either that a particular transaction had no "business purpose" or that "form should give way to substance" in tax matters. When the court makes this finding, it usually is trying to find good authority for ignoring the Code as it is literally written and to apply it as Congress probably intended that it be applied. The interesting part of such nebulous judicial doctrines is that they are not applied consistently and that taxpayers can help to improve their chances for nonapplication of such judicial rules by slightly modifying their own behavior.

Returning to our illustration of the car sold for $1,000 just one week after it had been converted to wholly personal use, we might note that the most "phony" aspect of that transaction involved the short time period that elapsed between the date of the alleged conversion from 20 to 100 percent personal use and the date of disposition. If the taxpayer had allowed one year rather than one week to elapse, several things would have happened. Most importantly, perhaps, the time lapse would have provided evidence that the conversion in use was "real," or "had substance," beyond its obvious tax-saving result. This difference quite likely would have been sufficient to convince any court that such judicial doctrines as substance-over-form or business-purpose were not applicable to this transaction and thus the taxpayer would have effectively avoided the need to recognize any taxable income on the disposition. This conclusion would also be buttressed by the fact that values would have changed sufficiently during the intervening time period to make any allocation of earlier and undetermined amounts difficult if not impossible—an interesting corollary of the realization criterion.

This illustration could easily be dismissed as unimportant because of the small dollar amounts involved. Such a peremptory dismissal would be unfortunate. The same principle can sometimes be applied in other circumstances where larger sums are involved. Consider, for example, the possibility of converting a well-depreciated rental home into a personal residence prior to sale. In this instance, the potential ordinary income to be realized on the disposition of the property at a profit would remain intact and the owner-turned-occupant may feel that he would have to remain in the home indefinitely if he were to achieve the apparent tax advantage just discussed. Because of some rather generous rules in the area of nontaxable exchanges, however, he probably could avoid recognition of this ordinary income permanently if he would be willing to live in the home for at least one year. The exact details of such a plan should be checked carefully by a competent tax advisor before being implemented.

The reverse possibility is equally pertinent. Consider, for example, the plight of the taxpayer who purchased a personal residence for $40,000 and who finds, a few years later, that his home has decreased in value so that he can sell it only if he is willing to realize a nondeductible loss on such a sale. Instead, this taxpayer might convert his former home to a rental property and then, some years later, proceed to sell it and thereby try to convert his nondeductible personal loss to a deductible loss on rent-producing property. In this instance, the tax rules have specifically attempted to preclude the deduction of this loss by providing that the tax basis on the date of conversion from a personal residence to a rental property must be the *lower* of (a) the owner's original cost or (b) the fair market value on the date of the conversion in use. The only fact that works to the taxpayer's benefit in this circumstance is the fact that fair market values are exceedingly difficult to determine, especially retroactively, and the taxpayer may be able to achieve his intended objective if he is sufficiently patient and allows a reasonable time to lapse before he realizes any loss, and if he is sufficiently adamant in maintaining his position on assumed fair market values at the earlier date. At least the taxpayer has given the real economic facts a maximum opportunity to become sufficiently confused so that a revenue agent might be convinced to yield on a debatable point that he recognizes as a distinct risk if the controversy proceeds to judicial settlement. Finally, even if the taxpayer cannot convince the revenue agent of the reasonableness of his contention, he has given a court or jury potential grounds on which to render a decision favorable to his position.

Modification of use involving more than one entity

Under some circumstances, a taxpayer may find it advisable to utilize more than a single taxable entity if he is to achieve a desired tax consequence. To illustrate this possibility, suppose that an individual taxpayer purchased a tract of land in 1955 for $150,000 and that he held this land solely for investment purposes for the next 15 years. Let us assume that, by 1970, the land had increased in value to $350,000 because of the growth of a nearby city and the favorable location of a new highway. Under these circumstances, the investor-taxpayer could sell the land and realize a long-term capital gain of $200,000. The same taxpayer might believe, however, that he could increase the value of the land by another $150,000 if he would but divide up the tract into smaller lots and expend an additional $50,000 for streets, curbs, gutters, sewers, and similar improvements. If this taxpayer proceeded with the development plans and eventually sold the smaller plots for a total of $500,000, he would discover that his $300,000 profit ($500,000 realized less basis of $150,000 plus $50,000) was entirely ordinary income. The IRS and the courts, with sufficient authority, would maintain that the lots were held primarily for sale to customers in the ordinary course of a trade or business venture, and the entire profit, therefore, would be classified as ordinary income.

If, instead of developing the land himself, the taxpayer had sold the land to a development corporation for $350,000 before making any improvements, he would have fixed his right to claim the $200,000 capital gain. If the taxpayer happened also to own 100 percent of the purchasing corporation, he might eventually reap the additional $100,000 profit even though that portion of the profit would have to be reported as ordinary income either by the corporation or by him (as salary). Certainly, the taxpayer would prefer to report $200,000 of long-term capital gain and $100,000 of ordinary income rather than $300,000 of ordinary income. Under these circumstances, it again is possible that the courts would look through the form of the transactions and, by ignoring the corporate entity, find that the entire income was ordinary income of the individual taxpayer. Even a brief reexamination of the facts suggests that the most vulnerable aspect of the proposed tax-saving plan is the fact that the original investor also owned 100 percent of the corporation which eventually developed the property. If this owner were willing to allow a non-related party to own, say, 25 percent of the stock in the development corporation, he would have gone a long way toward insuring his right to claim the capital gain status of the $200,000. In summary, through the creation of a viable second entity and the sale of property to that entity, the investor-taxpayer in this illustration might avoid an inadvertent conversion of a $200,000 long-term capital gain into ordinary income by making certain that the status of the property as an investment would not be lost prior to realization of the initial appreciation.

The reverse of this tax-saving idea was the basis for the collapsible corporation discussed in Chapter 4. Until the collapsible corporation provisions were enacted into law, it was possible for a taxpayer to develop land (or almost any other property) within a corporate entity and, after the increase in value had occurred but before the increase had been realized, collapse the corporation and convert the potential ordinary income attributable to the development work into a capital gain for the shareholders by virtue of the corporate liquidation provisions in the Code. Because this alternative is no longer generally available, it will not be further developed here. The possibility of converting a potential ordinary income into capital gain through the careful allocation of a selling price is much more likely to be possible today.

Favorable price allocation in property transactions

In Chapter 5 we noted the necessity of allocating a portion of the purchase (or sales) price to land whenever a taxpayer buys or sells a parcel of realty which includes both land and buildings. In the purchase transaction, this allocation is required to determine what portion of the initial cost is subject to depreciation (the portion allocated to the building) and which portion of the initial cost must remain intact and be recovered taxwise only upon disposition of the property (the portion allocated to the land). In the sales transaction, the same allocation is necessary to determine separately the amount of the gain or loss on the building and on the land. An examination of Table 5-1 further reveals that some portion or all of the profit on the sale of a building may be treated as ordinary income if rapid depreciation has been claimed on that building, whereas any profit on the sale of the land is likely to be treated as Section 1231 gain and therefore as long-term capital gain.

Because the interests of the buyer and the seller are generally adverse, the IRS is inclined to accept whatever allocation of the price is agreed upon by the parties to the contract. The opportunity to make a favorable allocation is especially great when the seller has depreciated the building on a straight-line basis and, therefore, has no tax reason for preferring one allocation to another. Sometimes it is also possible to obtain a favorable allocation when one of the parties to the transaction fails to understand the tax significance of the agreed allocation.

The cost allocation opportunity can also be combined with the change-in-use opportunity explained earlier in this chapter to achieve still greater tax savings. Suppose, for example, that you desired to acquire, at a cost of $400,000, several parcels of real estate including numerous old buildings with the idea that you would tear down the old buildings and erect a new office building on the same location. If you proceed openly and directly with your plans, the IRS would have every reason for allocating the entire $400,000 purchase price to the cost of land. If, on the other hand, you adequately disguised any possible intention to erect the new building behind an apparent intention to acquire and operate the several old rental properties, your tax consequences might be quite different. If you actually acquired the properties for $400,000, you might be able to find some authority—perhaps utilizing city property tax assessments—for allocating $250,000 of the $400,000 cost to the buildings and only $150,000 to the land. Then, after two or three years of rental experience, you could have a detailed study made of your rental activities which would show that you were ineffectively utilizing this land. Based on the independent study, you might have good authority for "changing your mind," tearing down the old buildings, and erecting the new office building. Under these revised facts, some portion of the $250,000 allocated to the buildings already would have been recovered taxwise through depreciation deductions which were offset against the ordinary rent income in the interim years. The remaining basis allocated to the buildings would become an ordinary tax loss deductible in the year the buildings were torn down. This quick recovery of much of the initial investment through tax deductions would be significantly more favorable than would the required capitalization of the entire $400,000 purchase price contemplated earlier.

Any attempt to quantify precisely the dollar value of the tax benefits of this alternative plan would require the selection of an appropriate discount rate, the stipulation of a useful life for the old and new buildings, the actual holding period for the old and new buildings, a marginal tax rate for the investment taxpayer both presently and in the future, and a probability of the tax plan succeeding without additional cost. All of these variables are sufficiently imprecise to support the conclusion that quantification of the benefit would not be sufficiently reliable to justify the effort required to make and understand it here. Nevertheless, the reader should appreciate the potential dollar significance of the tax-savings suggested.

Favorable price allocation in installment sales

Taxpayers often sell property under terms which require the buyer to pay for the property over a period of several years. Such sales, called installment sales, usually provide for interest on the unpaid balance. In effect, the seller has loaned the buyer a portion of the purchase price, and it is only reasonable to assume that the buyer will pay interest on the sum borrowed. From the standpoint of the seller, however, it will be preferable taxwise to provide a minimum of interest and a maximum in sales price any time that the asset sold is a capital asset that has been owned for more than six months. To illustrate, assume that a taxpayer sold a capital asset for $1,000,000 under a contract that required a $100,000 downpayment and $100,000 per year plus 8 percent interest on the unpaid balance. To simplify this illustration, let us assume that the seller had no remaining basis in the asset sold and, therefore, the entire sales price represents long-term capital gain. Under this extreme assumption, the seller's reported income for the next 10 years would be:

Year	Long-term capital gain	Ordinary income (8% interest)	Total received
1.	$ 100,000	$ 0	$ 100,000
2.	100,000	72,000	172,000
3.	100,000	64,000	164,000
4.	100,000	56,000	156,000
5.	100,000	48,000	148,000
6.	100,000	40,000	140,000
7.	100,000	32,000	132,000
8.	100,000	24,000	124,000
9.	100,000	16,000	116,000
10.	100,000	8,000	108,000
Total	$1,000,000	$360,000	$1,360,000

Even momentary reflection on these numbers will sustain the conclusion that the seller would prefer a sales contract providing for a $1,360,000 sales price and no interest to the one specified here. If this were possible, the seller could convert the $360,000 ordinary interest income into a long-term capital gain and thus reduce his tax liability on that income by at least 50 percent of what it otherwise would have been. The buyer, of course, would prefer the contract providing for a maximum rate of interest since interest payments generally can be deducted immediately for tax purposes. In this situation the seller often is in a dominant position and a buyer may accept almost any terms that the seller may dictate. In order to reduce the conversion of ordinary income into a capital gain, Congress has authorized the imputation of interest in situations in which the taxpayer either provides no interest or an unreasonably low interest on an installment sale. The present provision, however, states that interest will not be imputed if the sales agreement provides for at least 4 percent simple interest. During all recent years the market rate of interest has remained well in excess of 4 percent and, therefore, the opportunity to convert some ordinary interest income into capital gain remains a real possibility for the alert seller on an installment contract.

The corporate quagmire

As soon as a taxpayer places some portion of his assets into a corporate entity, he has created a whole host of new problems and opportunities that often involve the application of capital gain and loss rules. In the space available here, we can but scratch the surface of these opportunities. Two aspects of the corporation-corporate shareholder quagmire will be considered. First, we will consider the different tax consequences that might attach to the disposition of assets in corporate and noncorporate solution. Next, we will consider the different tax consequences that might attach to an asset distribution by a corporation to its shareholders.

Disposition of assets. If an individual taxpayer sells a bundle of assets outside a corporate entity, their capital or noncapital classification generally will be determined on an asset-by-asset basis. In other words, each asset sold will be examined in light of the capital asset definition and the gain or loss will be classified as ordinary or capital based on that definition. Suppose, for example, that a taxpayer owns

three assets (items A, B, and C) which have the following tax basis
and fair market values:

Item	Tax basis	Fair market value	Paper profit or (loss)
A.......	$100,000	$200,000	$100,000
B.......	150,000	100,000	(50,000)
C.......	200,000	450,000	250,000
Totals	$450,000	$750,000	$300,000

If the taxpayer were to sell these assets individually, and if items B
and C were *not* capital assets, the taxpayer would have to report a
$100,000 capital gain and a $200,000 ordinary income.

Suppose that this taxpayer instead transferred assets A, B, and C
into a new corporate entity in a nontaxable transaction. He then would
own stocks in his new corporation, rather than assets A, B, and C,
and these new stocks would assume a tax basis of $450,000. What
has changed is the number of options open to the taxpayer: he can
now indirectly sell the same assets by selling 100 percent ownership
in his new corporation's stock, or he can allow his corporation to
sell the old assets and thus have it recognize the paper gains and
losses implicit in these assets. If the individual owner sells stocks, he
will realize nothing but a capital gain and thereby effectively have
converted his potential ordinary income into a capital gain. Because
of the tax differential in this example, a knowledgeable buyer might
not be willing to pay $750,000 for the stock even though he might
agree that the assets individually were worth that amount. If the buyer
can acquire the assets only in corporate solution, he (the buyer)
will have the new and increased tax basis in the shares of stock and
not in the assets he purchased indirectly. Because of potential ignorance on the part of the buyer, or because of the possible application
of other tax rules which might be available to this buyer, a purchase
price of something approaching $750,000 is not entirely impossible.

In short, an individual taxpayer might be able to convert potential
ordinary income into a capital gain by transferring appreciated properties into a corporate entity and then selling the stock in the entity
which owns the assets. Once again, the time horizon may be critical
to the success of such a tax plan. A hasty transfer of assets followed
by an immediate sale of stock is certainly subject to question by the
IRS. A properly aged sale would raise fewer questions.

Extracting corporate income.   In prior chapters we learned that a corporation is not entitled to a deduction for dividends it pays and that individual stockholders, with minor exceptions, pay ordinary income tax on all dividends received. These rules have strongly influenced the ways in which closely held corporations distribute their accumulated profits.

To begin our study of this area we need to observe that the tax treatment of values received by corporate shareholders from their corporation varies depending on the classification of that distribution. The major classifications and the attendant tax results are as follows:

Classification of distribution	*Usual tax result to shareholder*
Salary, interest, rent, etc.	Ordinary income
Routine dividend	Ordinary income
Stock redemption	Ordinary income or capital gain
Partial liquidation	Capital gain
Complete liquidation	Capital gain
Repayment of debt	No tax (return of capital)

In earlier chapters we considered the first two of these six possibilities so we will consider here only the remaining four.

A stock redemption differs from a dividend in that a redemption requires the shareholder to surrender part or all of his shares of stock in the corporation in exchange for the assets distributed to him by the corporation. This critical difference can be illustrated as shown in Figure 6–1. If there is only one shareholder, or if each shareholder

FIGURE 6–1

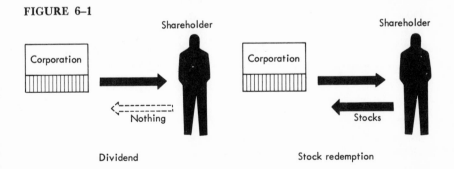

surrenders a pro rata share of his ownership, the act of surrendering shares is pointless in terms of real economic effects. The tax law has recognized this reality and, under these circumstances, provides that amounts received in a stock redemption generally will be treated as ordinary income. On the other hand, if one shareholder is completely removed from ownership through a stock redemption of only his shares, or if the redemption is not substantially proportionate among all owners, the Code provides that the amount received in such a stock redemption should be treated as a capital gain.

A partial liquidation is very much like a stock redemption except that; for tax purposes, we must look to the effect of the distribution on the corporation to determine the tax consequences for the shareholder. If the assets distributed by the corporation represent a "significant corporate contraction," the distribution may be characterized as a partial liquidation and the stockholders may be entitled to capital gain treatment. The corporate contraction concept implies some significant change, such as the liquidation of a branch operation, the decision not to replace a plant or division destroyed in a casualty combined with a distribution of the insurance proceeds, or some similar contraction of genuine business operations.

A complete liquidation requires, of course, the total termination of all business operations by the corporate entity and a distribution of the remaining corporate assets to the stockholders. Unless the corporation is a collapsible corporation, or the same stockholders hastily return the operating assets of the old corporation to a new corporation and continue the business pretty much as it was before the liquidation, the amounts received in complete liquidation will be taxed as a capital gain.

Even this superficial review of the differences between stock redemptions, partial liquidations, and complete liquidations should indicate the need for expert tax assistance any time a closely held corporation is considering the distribution of some portion or all of its assets. The way such a distribution is arranged may very easily make the difference between the shareholder having to report ordinary income instead of a long-term capital gain.

In limited instances, the shareholder may even be able to avoid capital gain treatment. If a taxpayer, at the time he originally organizes his corporation, takes sufficient care to designate some of his initial investment as a loan, and only the remainder of his investment as an equity investment, he has laid the necessary groundwork that will allow him later to extract some of the corporation's accumulated income tax-free. In the previous paragraphs we discovered that stock redemptions and partial liquidations produce either ordinary income or capital gain for the recipient shareholder. The repayment of debt, however, creates no taxable income because in that transaction the debtor is deemed to get back only his previously taxed capital. Realizing this critical difference in tax treatment, a taxpayer might be tempted to create a corporation with very minimal equity and maximum debt; for example, $10 in equity and $999,990 in debt would certainly be preferred to $1,000,000 in equity and no debt from the standpoint of the owner of a closely held corporation. Once again the tax authorities will use judicial doctrines to correct such obvious abuses in "thin corporation" cases. A more reasonable allocation of debt and equity, say $250,000 equity and $750,000 debt, would very likely withstand attack by the IRS if other indications of real debt are adequately maintained. And once again, the value of expert assistance cannot be overrated.

The preceding illustrations demonstrate sometimes subtle differences in behavior that may spell the difference between ordinary income and capital gain. In a limited number of situations, the same tax result stems from explicit statutory provisions that create special exceptions to the normal rules for specified transactions. Two such statutory exceptions will be considered here.

Statutory exceptions to "normal" rules

In select instances, the Code provides special rules that convert what would otherwise be ordinary income into a capital gain or what would otherwise be capital loss into an ordinary loss. Section 1231 is exemplary of the former kind of special rule; Section 1244 of the latter. Obviously it is to any taxpayer's benefit to take advantage of these special rules if he possibly can. Section 1244, which is of general applicability, will be discussed first.

Section 1244. Based on the normal rules reviewed in the previous chapter, we know that a taxpayer generally must report a capital loss when he sells or exchanges corporate stocks or securities for an amount less than his basis. We also know that capital losses are generally not as tax advantageous as are ordinary losses. Section 1244 is worth investigating precisely because it allows a taxpayer to treat a loss from the disposition of certain common stock as an ordinary loss rather than as a capital loss. The conditions specified before this result can obtain include:

1. The taxpayer claiming the loss must be an individual;
2. The loss must be attributable to stock issued to the taxpayer by the corporation—that is, it cannot be purchased from a prior owner, acquired by gift, etc.;
3. The stock must have been qualified as Section 1244 stock both initially and at the time the loss is sustained—this qualification includes specified dollar limitations (generally it is available only to corporations with equity capital of $500,000 or less) and an active trade or business requirement;
4. The stock must be common stock issued under a plan adopted by the corporation's board of directors after June 30, 1958; and
5. The amount deducted as ordinary loss under this provision cannot exceed $25,000 per taxpayer per year. (Thus, on a joint return, $50,000 per year is allowable.)

Any taxpayer who is the owner-operator of a closely held corporation should make certain that he qualifies a maximum amount of his stock under this special provision. In the initial planning stages, the owner-operator may be so optimistic that he simply cannot see the need for anticipating tax differences which become pertinent only if his new venture fails. Historical data supports the conclusion, however, that many more small businesses fail than succeed. For those businesses that do fail, the opportunity to obtain a tax refund based on a $50,000 ordinary net operating loss deduction is substantially more valuable than the potential use of a $50,000 net capital loss carryforward. This provision should also be of special interest to new corporations seeking venture capital. High marginal tax bracket investors are attracted by the possibility of investing in a new firm if they know that the government will share their risk of loss on a 70–30 basis but will share the potential profit on a 25–75 basis. Finally, except for knowledge of the provision and a little timely action, the cost associated with this tax-saving opportunity is essentially zero.

Section 1231. In Chapter 5 we learned that Section 1231 is the Code provision that makes it possible for a taxpayer to realize capital gain on the disposition of real or depreciable property used in a trade or business, even though such properties do not constitute a capital asset according to the pure statutory definition. Actually, Section 1231 is much broader than the previous discussion implied. It is also among the most complex provisions of the entire Code.

Under the circumstances, it seems most appropriate simply to observe that Section 1231 effectively converts into long-term capital gain what would otherwise be routine operating (ordinary) income from timber, coal, and domestic iron ore operations; from livestock held for draft, breeding, dairy, or sporting purposes (if held for more than 24 months); and from the disposition of certain unharvested crops. Just why these particular forms of business activity should be able to reap the substantial benefits of capital gains taxation while other business ventures must face the higher tax consequences of ordinary income is not at all obvious. The probable role of politics is apparent and possibly instructive—that is, for those with sufficient funds and connections, this is an alternative route to major tax savings. Because most readers will not be engaged in those particular forms of business endeavor, we will turn our attention to more common tax-saving opportunities which depend for their success on only the careful timing of a particular transaction by the taxpayer.

TIMING CONSIDERATIONS

Just as physicians advocate an annual physical examination for anyone over 30 years of age, tax advisors advocate an annual, year-end security examination for frequent investors. As any investor approaches the year's end, he typically has realized several capital gains and losses and has at his disposal a number of additional investments which could be manipulated if there were sufficiently compelling reasons for doing so. In numerous situations, the special rules applicable to the tax treatment of capital gains and losses provide such a compelling reason, and a careful consideration of the time horizon is often the controlling variable.

Year-end security review

Based on the rules explained in the previous chapter, we know that tax privileges extend to transactions in capital assets only when the taxpayer has realized a net long-term capital gain in excess of his net short-term capital loss. The year-end security review must begin, then, by quantifying the present position of the taxpayer. To illustrate this procedure, let us consider the tax position of a taxpayer who has engaged in six security transactions during the year with the following results:

Transaction no.	Long-term gain or (loss) realized	Short-term gain or (loss) realized
1.............	$ 60,000	
2.............	40,000	
3.............		($20,000)
4.............	(10,000)	
5.............		50,000
6.............	30,000	
Net position........	$120,000	$30,000

Going into the end of the year, this taxpayer has realized a net long-term capital gain of $120,000 and a net short-term capital gain of $30,000. If he does nothing further, the $120,000 will be eligible for the benefits known as the alternative long-term capital gains tax and/or the long-term capital gain deduction. The $30,000 net short-term capital gain, however, would not be eligible for special benefits and would be taxed exactly in the way any other $30,000 of ordinary income would be taxed. A taxpayer in this situation would almost certainly be in a high marginal tax bracket and, therefore, doing nothing further would mean that he would have to pay most of the $30,000 short-term gain to the government in the form of income taxes. Since he does not like that prospect, he begins to search for ways of negating that tax result.

The easiest way to change the tax consequences might well be suggested by a careful review of this taxpayer's remaining investments with implicit or "paper" gains and losses which he has not yet brought to fruition through a sales transaction. Such a review might, for example, reveal the following:

Stock	Original cost	Present fair market value	Potential LTCG or (LTCL)	Potential STCG or (STCL)
A.......	$100,000	$210,000	$110,000	
B.......	50,000	30,000		($20,000)
C.......	60,000	40,000		($10,000)
D.......	30,000	20,000	(10,000)	
E.......	70,000	100,000		30,000

Under the circumstances described earlier for this taxpayer, at a minimum it would be advisable to sell all of the B and C stocks so as to realize an additional $30,000 in short-term capital loss during the current year. By making such a sale, the taxpayer could remove the $30,000 in previously realized net short-term capital gains from the ordinary tax base at a minimum cost. Whether or not this taxpayer would choose to realize additional gains or losses would have to depend on further analysis of his economic expectations and the potential tax effect of those transactions.

Wash sales. In the previous illustration the taxpayer might be convinced that his investments in stocks B and C were still desirable from an economic standpoint. That is, he might believe that the present paper losses were only temporary and that further retention of these securities would eventually yield a profit. Under these circumstances, the taxpayer might be tempted to sell the stocks to obtain the offset of the loss against the $30,000 net short-term gain previously realized, but he might be further tempted to immediately repurchase the same shares to reestablish his economic position in stocks B and C. Such a sale-repurchase would become a "wash sale" which, for tax purposes, would negate the right of the taxpayer to recognize any of the loss he had thus realized. The wash sale rule provides that no capital *loss* shall be recognized for tax purposes if the taxpayer purchases substantially identical securities during a period 30 days before or 30 days after the sale in which he realized a loss. In other words, this taxpayer would have to be willing to go without an investment in B and C for at least 31 days if he wants to obtain the tax advantage just described. Note, however, that the wash sale rules do not apply to transactions involving gains and that they do permit an investment in other companies in the same industry and possibly even an investment in a different class of stock of the same corporation.

To illustrate the potential benefit of a wash sale resulting in a gain, consider the year-end security review of a taxpayer who has realized a net long-term capital gain of $20,000 and a net short-term capital loss of $60,000. If this taxpayer does nothing further his long-term gain of $20,000 will be offset by his short-term loss of $60,000 leaving him with a net $40,000 short-term capital loss. Only $1,000 of that loss could be offset against his ordinary income in the current year, the remaining $39,000 having to be carried forward to future years. The potential tax benefit of that loss is, thus, substantially deferred.

If this taxpayer had at least $39,000 in potential or "paper" short-term gains which he could realize, this would be an ideal time to do so. He could sell the shares with a short-term paper gain and immediately repurchase them if he desired to maintain his economic position. Such a transaction would cost him only the broker's fee in exchange for the right to immediately offset the previously realized short-term capital loss against a potential item of ordinary income; in addition, the taxpayer would have increased his tax basis in the shares he repurchased by the amount of the gain he had just realized. Thus, any subsequent sale at a later date could be made with less concern for tax consequences since much of the taxable gain had already been absorbed. There would be no way in which this taxpayer could benefit more taxwise since he has been able to utilize a short-term loss in offsetting what is potential ordinary income (i.e., the net short-term gain).

Generalizations. Obviously, there is an almost infinite possible array of circumstances which we could create for this kind of year-end security review. What action is preferred for any particular taxpayer will depend upon his present capital position, his anticipation of future economic events, and the marginal tax rates that will be applied to various gains and losses both now and in the future. In general, however, the taxpayer will prefer to:

1. maximize (LTCG − LTCL), and to
2. minimize (STCL − STCG).

Typically, this means that a taxpayer should allow capital gains to become long-term by holding them for more than six months. It also means that losses should be realized before they have been held for six months because such an early realization leaves open the possibility of offsetting those losses against short-term capital gains before they must be offset against long-term capital gains (which are the only form of tax-blessed capital gains). Finally, it usually means that short-term capital gains should be realized in any year in which the taxpayer has net short-term losses since the failure to realize the short-term gains at that time will mean that those losses may be utilized against known long-term gains which, obviously, are already tax-blessed whereas *potential* long-term gains (that is, those that are still short-term) have not yet guaranteed their tax strength. An exception to this last rule exists in any year in which a taxpayer can realize only net capital losses. In that event the taxpayer should make certain that he has at least $1,000 in net short-term capital loss to offset his ordinary income. If he has only long-term capital losses available, he will have to offset them against his ordinary income on a two-for-one basis. The long-term capital losses otherwise could be carried forward and applied against capital gains of future years on a one-for-one basis. Under the most favorable conditions, a long-term loss carried into a new year could be offset against a net short-term capital gain and thus effectively reduce potential ordinary income on a one-for-one basis even though that same loss otherwise could only be offset against ordinary income on the less favorable ratio.

Short sales. A taxpayer occasionally will discover that he already has so arranged his affairs that he is in the most desirable tax position, but his prediction of future economic events is such that he would very much like to "freeze" a particular economic gain or loss in the current year. If he proceeds to freeze this gain or loss in the usual manner, it will, however, upset the preferable tax position which he has already arranged. To illustrate, suppose that a taxpayer had already realized $80,000 in net long-term capital gains and that he had reduced his short-term position exactly to zero. The taxpayer may be very willing to pay the income tax on the $80,000 long-term capital gain, but he also has a $60,000 potential short-term gain which he thinks he must realize very soon if he does not want to lose it. Further, the taxpayer is aware that if he does realize this short-term gain he has no further available short-term losses which he could also realize to offset the gain he believes he must realize or lose.

Under the conditions just described, this taxpayer is a prime candidate for a "short sale against the box." A simple "short sale" involves the sale of something a person does not own. In the case of short sales of securities, the broker typically borrows the shares sold short for the seller, and, at some future date, the seller goes into the market and purchases the shares that he sold earlier and delivers these shares to the broker to "cover" his prior short position. If the value of the shares has decreased in the interim, the seller obviously has profited on the transaction, because he was able to sell for more than he paid. If the value of the shares increased between the two dates, the seller obviously lost, because he sold for less than he eventually paid.

The tax magic of the short sale is due entirely to noneconomic factors. The pertinent question involves the selection of a date that must control for tax *reporting* purposes. Two dates are potential candidates: it might be the date of the short sale (that is, the date on which the seller had the broker sell short), or it might be the date on which the short sale was covered (that is, the date on which the seller purchased and delivered to the broker the shares which had been borrowed in the interim period). In a pure short sale, the amount of the gain or loss cannot, of course, be determined until the cover date. Therefore, the tax rules provide that the cover date will control for purposes of determining the correct year of reporting gain or loss.

One final twist must be clarified before we can solve this taxpayer's problem. A short sale against the box is like a pure short sale except that, in this instance, the seller already owns what he purports to sell short. However, he allows the broker to go out and borrow the stock temporarily, and only after the new year has dawned does the seller deliver his shares to the broker to cover the short sale. By application of the short sale rules, this taxpayer has just been able to defer the recognition of his $60,000 short-term gain into the next taxable year by withholding delivery of his shares against the earlier short sale. Through this simple device, the taxpayer has maintained his desirable tax position and put the additional short-term gain into a new tax year which gives him an entire year during which he can again offset this gain in the most appropriate manner.

Observe that short sales *cannot* be used to convert short-term gains into long-term gains. For purposes of determining whether a capital gain or loss should be classified as short- or long-term, the pertinent time lapse is that between the date of purchase and the date of the short sale, *not* the date of covering the short sale. If six months or less have elapsed between the purchase date and the date of the short sale, the gain or loss will forever remain a short-term gain or loss even though delivery of the shares is postponed beyond six months. In summary, a short sale is useful only in shifting the year of reporting, not in transforming short-term transactions into long-term ones.

Learning to count six months

Remember that a capital gain achieves no special tax benefits until it can be classified as a long-term capital gain, and that requires that the capital asset be held for *more than* six months prior to disposition. A quick review of some of the technical rules used to implement the holding period requirement may pay handsome dividends. Generally, the holding period begins to run on the day a taxpayer acquires title and stops running on the date title passes from him; the taxpayer may include one but not both of these two days in counting to 6 months. In other words, a stock purchased on October 10, 1973, will "go long term" on April 11, 1974, which is exactly six months and one day later. The tax authorities will not divide time periods into less than one day. In other words, even if a taxpayer could prove that he made a stock purchase at 10 A.M. on October 10, 1973, and that he sold the same stock at 2 P.M. on April 10, 1974, that transaction would continue to be classified as a short-term one.

Special problems may also be encountered with month-end sales and purchases. Purchases made on the last day of any month must be held until the first day of the seventh subsequent month before they are considered long-term. Thus, purchases made on February 28 (in nonleap years) must be held until September 1 before they are classified long-term. Any sale of a February 28 purchase on August 29, 30, or 31 would remain short-term.

Care must also be exercised to make certain that any gain or loss can be reported in the most desirable year. We have already considered why it may be desirable for a taxpayer to utilize a short sale to defer the tax recognition of a particular transaction. Under other circumstances, year-end sales can present similar problems or opportunities. Generally, an accrual basis taxpayer must report all gains and losses in the year in which a transaction is completed; for securities transactions, this would be the year of sale. Cash basis taxpayers would normally expect to report gains and losses in the year they received their cash settlement. The normal rules apply for securities transactions with one major exception: cash basis taxpayers must report losses in the year a sale is executed even though cash settlement is deferred until the next year. Obviously, to a limited extent, a cash basis taxpayer can alter the year of reporting by making special arrangements with his broker to modify the usual time lapse which occurs between the sale and settlement date common to securities transactions.

Use of installment sales

A taxpayer typically has some control over the time and manner in which he will receive the proceeds from the sale of a capital asset. Usually, he can either insist on immediate payment, even if this necessitates borrowing by the purchaser from another source, or allow the buyer to make payments over several years. As explained earlier, the latter option is known as an installment sale. If a sale qualifies for installment treatment, it means that a taxpayer can defer recognition of any gain until the years in which he receives the proceeds of the sale. For tax purposes, an installment sale may be especially useful when the asset sold is a capital asset for one of two reasons.

The alternative tax rate. Some taxpayers are typically in a high marginal tax bracket even though they do not realize large amounts of capital gains in most years. A physician, for example, might easily be in this circumstance. Under these circumstances, the most advantageous aspect of the long-term capital gain is its eligibility for the 25 percent alternative rate. We noted in the last chapter, however, that the alternative rate can be applied only to a maximum of $50,000 of qualified capital gains in each year. Thus, a taxpayer might utilize an installment sale to spread out a single but large capital gain in a most advantageous manner.

To illustrate, assume that a surgeon ordinarily earned a $200,000 taxable income and that in one particular year he also realized a $250,000 long-term capital gain. If he recognized the entire long-term capital gain in a single year, he would in effect pay 25 percent on $50,000 and 35 percent (one-half the maximum marginal ordinary rate) on the remaining $200,000. By utilizing an installment sale and spreading the long-term capital gain over a five-year period, he could reduce the effective rate on the total $250,000 to 25 percent and thereby save $20,000 in income taxes.

Declining ordinary rates. Another circumstance in which a taxpayer will find it advantageous to utilize the installment sale is when he is anticipating a decline in his ordinary income and, therefore, a decline in the marginal rate of his ordinary income tax in future years. This situation is often typical for a person facing imminent retirement. Even if such a taxpayer could not utilize the 25 percent alternative rate available for long-term capital gains, he would do well to defer recognition of any long-term capital gain through the use of an installment sale since the deferral would mean that he could wait and pay tax on the gain at one-half his future and lower ordinary tax rate. Thus, if the taxpayer were in a 50 percent marginal ordinary tax bracket before retirement, and if he anticipated being in a 30 percent marginal bracket after retirement on December 31, an installment sale could be utilized to decrease the effective tax rate on a long-term capital gain realized in his last working year from 25 percent (50% of 50%) to 15 percent (50% of 30%).

Obviously, the opposite prescription is equally valid for the person anticipating a substantial increase in his income. For example, an M.B.A. student living on the G.I. bill would be ill advised to utilize an installment sale in the year preceding his graduation. Under these circumstances the taxpayer student should protect his right to report any income in his low-income year and thus insure the application of the lowest possible marginal tax rate whether the income be ordinary or long-term capital gain.

By application of a series of tax rules commonly known as the "nontaxable exchange provisions," it may be possible for a taxpayer to defer recognition of a taxable gain for an even longer period of time. In the most favorable circumstances, a taxpayer may be able to defer recognition indefinitely. For individual taxpayers, an indefinite deferral may amount to a permanent avoidance of the *income* tax if an appreciated property is finally passed to another person by inheritance. The possibility of longer-term deferrals will be considered in Chapter 9.

In summary, every taxpayer should be aware of the many ways in which he can influence the tax liability attaching to common transactions. He should be aware that his inadvertent action may convert what once was capital gain into ordinary income. He should also be aware that his deliberate action can be helpful in converting what would otherwise be ordinary income into capital gain. And he should be aware that nondeductible capital losses can occasionally be turned into deductible ones and that capital losses might be turned into ordinary losses under still other circumstances. The possible array of variations in tax consequences is almost endless. Hopefully, this chapter has helped to sensitize the reader to those situations over which he personally may have some control.

7

Compensation considerations

EMPLOYEE COMPENSATION TRANSACTIONS have been more significantly affected by tax considerations than virtually any other common business occurrence. A majority of the tax-saving techniques available in this area demand that the employer be a corporate entity either because the technique depends in part for its success upon the existence of corporate stock, or because the law makes the particular privilege available only to employees. Self-employed persons—the proprietors of sole proprietorships, and the partners of partnerships— are not considered to be employees of their own firms and, therefore, any tax shelter given to employee benefits is unavailable to them.

Largely because of the distinction between employees and self-employed persons and the dollar significance of the differences between the tax treatment of pensions for employees and those for self-employed persons, the professions—such as medicine, law, accountancy, dentistry, and engineering—recently brought great pressure to bear upon the state governments to pass legislation authorizing the right of professionals to incorporate in professional service corporations. By 1970, 49 states had responded affirmatively to this pressure. Although the Treasury Department for some time fought the recognition of the new professional corporations, the courts were generally unsympathetic to the IRS view, and the battle now taking shape seems destined for a Congressional solution. In retrospect, this is not surprising since most of the major restrictions in the area of tax-oriented compensation considerations have required legislative action to curtail their success.

The degree to which tax laws have influenced compensation packages in large corporate enterprise is hard to overestimate. The most thorough study of compensation experience in large organizations was undertaken a few years ago by the National Bureau of Economic Research. Wilbur Lewellen, author of the NBER studies, reported many interesting statistics in several reports. Summarizing extensive data for the period 1955–63, Lewellen found that the average before-tax cash payments to the five most highly paid corporate executives in each of the 50 large manufacturing companies studied was in the neighborhood of $135,000 per year. These cash payments, however, amounted to only 50 percent of the real remuneration of these top executives; the remaining amount went largely into tax-shielded benefits. If the employer corporations had attempted to provide the executives with a cash salary that would have been sufficiently large to allow them to purchase, from their after-tax salaries, an equivalent collection of benefits without a tax shield, their before-tax salaries would have had to increase to something like $734,000 per executive per year!

The many tax shields available in the compensation area can be classified in several different ways. One of the most meaningful ways to classify them seems to be in terms of their differential tax effect on the employer corporation and on the employee. The importance of the alternatives comes into particularly clear focus when we think about the small to medium-sized, owner-managed business venture. In terms of priority ranked preferences, few owner-managers would disagree with the following preferences:

Preference ranking	Tax effect to employer corporation	Tax effect to employee recipient
1.	Immediately deductible	Never taxable
2.	Immediately deductible	Tax deferred and, if possible, realized in a preferential form
3.	Immediately deductible	Immediately taxed
4.	Deferred deduction	Deferred tax
5.	Never deductible	Taxed immediately or at a later date

As a matter of fact, each of these is a viable possibility, and the specific techniques commonly used in compensation arrangements have been classified under each of these five headings in the remaining pages of this chapter.

TECHNIQUES PROVIDING AN IMMEDIATE CORPORATE DEDUCTION AND A BENEFIT THAT IS NEVER TAXED TO THE EMPLOYEE

In Chapter 2 we observed that, generally speaking, an individual is taxed on any economic benefits he receives for services rendered, no matter how indirect his benefit may be. In that same chapter, however, we also observed that the Code does provide a limited number of exceptions to the preceding rule in the form of specific statutory exclusions. We further noted there that a taxpayer is entitled to deduct all ordinary and necessary business expenses incurred in a trade or business, including any reasonable compensation paid to an employee. By carefully combining the exclusion provisions with the deduction authorizations, it is possible in a limited number of circumstances to provide an employee with a real economic benefit which is never taxed at the same time that the employer corporation is entitled to an immediate deduction.

Group-term life insurance

Code Section 79(a) provides that an employee need not report as gross income the value of group-term life insurance premiums paid by his employer for his benefit so long as the insurance coverage provided him under this group policy does not exceed $50,000. Observe that, before this special exclusion can apply, the insurance in question must be *group, term, life* insurance. Proposed regulations issued by the Treasury Department suggest that a group plan must include at least ten full-time employees if it is to be recognized as a separate group. For very small organizations, the group might cover less than ten employees, but, in that event, the plan cannot discriminate in favor of corporate owners if it is to be recognized as a legitimate plan. If the coverage exceeds $50,000, the employee is taxed only on the cost of the premium for the excess; this cost is based on tables provided in the pertinent regulations. Suffice it to note that the tax cost of coverage in excess of $50,000 is minimal. The economic advantage attaching to tax-free life insurance, in comparison to insurance purchased from after-tax salary dollars, is obvious.

In the case of life insurance, a double exclusion is actually possible. Note that the employee need not report the premiums paid by his employer for this insurance and that, further, if the employee dies and his beneficiaries collect insurance under the policy, they need not report as gross income the amount they received by reason of the insured person's death. Furthermore, an employer can provide up to $2,000 in additional group-term life insurance for the employee's spouse and each of his children under the same tax-sheltered conditions.

Health and accident plans

Code Section 106 provides for a very similar tax treatment of health and accident insurance plans purchased by an employer for the employee. In the case of health and accident insurance, however, it is necessary to distinguish between the tax treatment of the premium payments and the amounts actually received under such coverage. It is the cost of the premiums that can be excluded by the employee under Section 106. Other sections of the Code determine the tax consequence of compensation (a) for injuries and medical expenses and (b) for wage continuation payments received under health and accident plans. Generally, the employee can exclude the former amounts whereas the latter are excludable only to a maximum of $100 per week and then only after certain waiting periods have been satisfied. The details of the many rules are best left for other books.

It again is pertinent to note that, relative to health and accident insurance, an employer corporation can provide a very real economic benefit to an employee without tax cost. If the employee were to purchase his own equivalent insurance coverage from after-tax salary, it would cost him more for the same coverage; the exact amount of the increased cost depends upon the employee's marginal tax bracket. Alternatively, of course, the employee might be forced to purchase a less desirable coverage for the same dollar cost. Incidentally, this tax-saving opportunity can include the increasing cost of an annual physical examination for any employee.

Meals and lodging

Code Section 119 permits an employee to exclude from his gross income the value of meals and lodging furnished on the employer's premises for the convenience of the employer. The potential benefit of this section seems to have gone largely unrecognized in the past, and it should be carefully examined by many more taxpayers. Apparently Code Section 119 is the statutory authority which explains the presence of beautiful executive dining rooms, high in the metropolitan skies, as well as the authority which allows our presidents to live in regal splendor (at least for the period of their presidency), and corporate presidents and university chancellors their right to live in million-dollar homes without tax consequence. The critical nexus in succeeding taxwise lies in the ability to establish a valid corporate employer's reason for having an employee eat while at work or having him live in a particular home. In regard to company homes, the success of beer magnates Adolph and Joseph Coors is encouraging. (See *Adolph Coors Co.,* T. C. Memo, 1968-256.) The undeveloped but potential use of this section by ranchers with livestock seems to be substantial since they should find it easy to explain why their constant presence would be required by their own employer corporation. Other taxpayers in other businesses may find equally good business reasons. The economic impact of this alternative can be substantial since it effectively provides the taxpayer, through his own corporation, the right to deduct depreciation on his home, the cost of utilities and insurance, and many other costs not otherwise deductible. Observe that, under the proper circumstances, even the cost of the food eaten by the employee becomes deductible by the employer corporation.

Death benefits

Code Section 101 allows a taxpayer the right to receive up to $5,000 in tax-free death benefits paid by a deceased employee's corporate employer. The employer can also deduct the amounts paid under such a death benefit plan. Although the dollar significance of this opportunity is obviously rather limited, any taxpayer who takes the trouble of incorporating his business to obtain other employee tax benefits should also take the necessary action to insure his right to this small additional benefit as well.

Some tax shelters are available not because of specific statutory exclusion provisions, but because of the way in which other Code provisions are applied and interpreted. The net effect of these interpretations may be to provide an employee with the equivalent of a tax-free (or tax-cheap) economic benefit.

Travel and entertainment

The detailed rules which regulate the correct tax treatment of travel and entertainment expenses are so lengthy that they cannot be examined here. However, it would be equally inappropriate to gloss over the obvious benefits available in this area. Country club memberships, theater tickets, admissions to athletic events, box seats in domed stadiums and outdoor tracks, elegant dining, superior alcohol, and other perquisites too numerous to mention can all be deducted as a reasonable entertainment expense under the proper circumstances. Travel which combines business with pleasure is equally rewarding from a tax standpoint.

The critical tax result is that under prescribed conditions all of these costs can be deducted as proper business expenses while those who enjoy the fruits of the expenditure either (a) need not report taxable income or (b) report equivalent amounts of income and deductions. Although there is no specific statutory authority for an exclusion, the end result apparently derives from the notion that individuals required to travel and to entertain business associates in this manner really are at work, and it is virtually impossible to design a tax law or tax administration which can measure the indirect benefits which one derives from working in pleasant surroundings. On the other hand, for those who have been there, it is equally impossible to measure the implicit costs associated with the many long evenings spent in boring company and away from home, no matter how luxurious the surroundings. On balance, any implicit deductions might be greater than any implicit income an academic theoretician could identify.

In a practical sense, what these rules should say to the entrepreneurial class is that they ought to give adequate consideration to the tax aspects of alternative ways of doing business combined with pleasure. When the conditions are favorable, it is not terribly difficult to convert a great deal of personal pleasure expenditures into tax deductions. Relative to domestic travel, for example, once the taxpayer can establish that the primary purpose of a trip is business, the cost of the transportation and most related expenses during business days become tax deductible. Relative to foreign travel, slightly different rules are applied. These interesting little rules sometimes make the entire scene look like part of a comic opera. If any business is done during a day, the entire day becomes a business day. If business is done anytime on Friday and Monday, the weekend can be wholly devoted to pleasure with no loss in tax consequences. On and on the rules go. In this area more than many others, an ounce of prevention is worth a pound of cure, so see your tax advisor and go well prepared. The way can be both rewarding and enjoyable for those who know the rules. For the poorly advised, the same road is pocked with pitfalls.

Automobiles (and airplanes?)

The company car has become as much a part of the American scene as the Florida convention in winter. For the fortunate employee, under the correct circumstances, the company car is the one which produces no taxable income but the entire cost of which is deductible by the employer corporation. The model may vary from the Ford Pinto to the chauffeur-driven, black Cadillac limousines parked two deep around Wall Street and Rockefeller Center at 3 P.M. The tax results are the same. Use the car for purely personal purposes and you suddenly have realized gross income. Use it solely for business purposes and you escape tax free. Use it for both personal and business purposes and anticipate an argument with an IRS agent. Business purpose? Personal use? Definitions are a dime a dozen.

Why stop with automobiles? For the jet set a Lear is vastly more effective. After all, if the company plane is scheduled to fly to Acapulco to pick up a business client, there can be little basis for imputing income to the corporate executive (or member of his family) who happens to have the day off and flies along just for the fun of it. Or, if Air Force One happens to be flying the President to Hawaii, why shouldn't the astronauts' wives and families accompany the President tax free? And a Senator or Congressman on the military jet bound for a fact-finding mission in Cambodia just may find enough time to do Christmas shopping in Hong Kong.

The opportunities for tax saving obviously are as real as the social inequities created by what has to be class legislation. Unfortunately, there are no easy answers. Business travel and business entertainment are as legitimate a business expense as are expenditures for heat, light, water, and rent. The unique social problem created by travel and entertainment, however, is the fact that it is next to impossible to distinguish on any reasonable basis between the legitimate and the disguised. What is unfortunate is that only so few have the opportunity to abuse the tax law. No social order or system of government can change that conclusion. It is simply unfortunate that the taxpayer who inevitably gets tagged is the poor salesman whose wife has been invited to the Las Vegas convention at company expense. That salesman knows that he very likely will have to report as taxable income at least the marginal cost of the company's sending his wife while other, more fortunate taxpayers, ride high, wide, and handsome.

Employee discounts

If an employee is given the opportunity of purchasing the employer's ordinary inventory at a small discount, and if this discount is extended to all employees, the employee generally need not report the bargain price element as gross income. On the other hand, if the price discount becomes too great, or if it is not generally made available to all employees, the IRS will be quick to find that the employee must report as taxable income the difference between the fair market value and the lower price that he actually paid to acquire the employer's property. The opportunity to escape any substantial amount of tax liability in this manner initially seems to be small and hardly worth investigating.

Conceptually, however, it really presents an entirely new idea and for that reason it may be important. Observe that what really happens in the courtesy discount situation is that the corporate employer achieves its potential tax advantage *not* by gaining a deduction, but by reporting less gross income itself. In other words, the corporate employer cannot deduct the value of the "bargain price" element so long as the employee need not report any income. The net effect to the corporation, however, is the same as the creation of a deduction because the sales to employees simply reduce the employer's gross revenue from sales and thereby reduce taxable income by the amount of the net price reduction. The employee's benefit depends upon his right to exclude the economic benefit received from income. In the case of courtesy discounts this results from an administrative pronouncement, not from a Code provision. Probably the reason for the generosity of the IRS is attributable to the administrative difficulty of applying any other standard. Imagine, for example, the practical problem that the IRS would create for itself if it tried to tax the small employee discounts given to literally millions of employees.

In a few industries the same administrative difficulties probably keep the IRS from trying to apply a stricter standard to what have become much more than small or minor employee discounts. In the airline industry, for example, one of the really significant tax-free economic benefits available to employees is the coveted pass which may allow the employee to circle the world on a grand vacation at little cost. This real economic benefit may be quite significant to young, travel-oriented employees, and it may even induce them to accept a lower than normal rate of pay. The extra benefit stems from the fact that there is almost no way that the IRS could ever tax this economic advantage since measuring the real value of the pass to any particular employee is next to impossible. Observe, again, that the employer airline gets no additional deduction in this instance; it simply deducts all of the usual operating expenses incurred in running an airline, and the fact that a particular passenger happens to be flying on a free pass makes little difference in terms of the expense incurred. Economically, what does happen, however, is that the airlines' gross revenues do not increase for this passenger and, therefore, it effectively has been able to give the employee a tax-free benefit without increasing its own revenue which, in one sense, is tantamount to a deduction.

Interest-free loans

A short leap of the imagination will quickly lead the reader to other opportunities based on the same fundamental idea as company discounts and airline passes. For example, why shouldn't an employer corporation make an interest-free loan to a very special corporate officer (or to a special star athlete)? Certainly, the corporate employer will not get a deduction for anything in this instance because it has incurred no real out-of-pocket expense. Very importantly, however, the corporate employer has avoided earning any taxable income on the $50,000 or $100,000 loaned to the employee, and it has thereby reduced its taxable income by an equivalent amount. At the present time there is some authority for the recipient employee to receive an interest-free loan tax-free. A quick look at any compound interest table, at market rates of interest, will demonstrate just how important this opportunity could be to the lucky employee. The eventual imputation of interest by the IRS in this situation seems inevitable if enough taxpayers begin to take advantage of it. In the meantime, the desired tax result may be possible as long as the parties take all necessary precautions which will allow them to prove that the loan is a bona fide debt which the employee will repay.

Before we proceed to the second ranked form of compensation, a word of caution seems to be in order. Obviously, the IRS and the courts are not ignorant of what is taking place in the area of disguised compensation. They examine the records of closely held corporations with particular care just because the opportunity for owner-managers to divert corporate funds for purely personal purposes is substantial. In the large publicly owned corporation, even the very top executives may eventually have to answer to a higher authority at the next stockholders' meeting. The most obvious abuses in this area frequently lead to the courtroom and an eventual judicial settlement. The owner-manager must be particularly careful to establish sound business purposes for whatever he does, and he must take extra caution in maintaining the proper records to give any transaction the bona fide look. This is not a job for an amateur.

TECHNIQUES PROVIDING AN IMMEDIATE CORPORATE DEDUCTION AND A TAX-DEFERRED BENEFIT TO THE EMPLOYEE

A second class of compensation techniques can be characterized by the ability to produce an immediate deduction to the corporate employer and only a deferred (and sometimes preferential form of) gross income to the employee. In terms of the absolute dollar amount of tax-sheltered compensation, there can be little doubt that this class of tax-saving techniques dominates in the aggregate. The most common forms of this second-ranked class are the qualified pension and profit-sharing plans. In the same class of benefits, but of much less common occurrence, is the qualified stock bonus plan. Every *qualified* pension, profit-sharing, and stock bonus plan shares several common characteristics. On the other hand, two fully qualified plans may differ significantly from one another. In the discussion that follows we will first examine the common characteristics; then look at some of the more important differences between qualified plans; and finally consider briefly a few of the related considerations that should be given careful thought before undertaking the implementation of any of these plans.

Common characteristics of all qualified pension, profit-sharing, and stock bonus plans

All qualified pension, profit-sharing, and stock bonus plans attain their preferred tax position because of certain unique tax provisions that are applicable to them. They all must meet common requirements before they can be considered to be qualified plans. And they all trigger tax consequences for the employee under similar circumstances. Before we begin to consider the many requirements applicable to qualified plans, let us look briefly at the available benefits.

The tax shelters available. The tax benefits available in most qualified pension, profit-sharing, and stock bonus plans can be separated into six distinct considerations. They are:

1. Subject to varying maximum limits, the corporate employer will get an immediate tax deduction for its contribution to the employee trust fund created to administer these assets.
2. The employee trust fund will be treated as a tax-exempt entity which allows it to accumulate earnings and grow at a substantially faster rate than otherwise would be possible.
3. The employee will not be taxed on either his employer's current contributions or on the growth from prior contributions until he either withdraws the funds or they are otherwise made available to him.
4. An employee may designate, in the vent of his death, that his interest in an employee trust fund is to be paid to someone other than the executor of his estate, and he can thereby remove from the value of his estate (for estate tax purposes) any interest in the trust fund that is attributable to the employer's contributions.
5. If the employee withdraws his entire rights from a pension trust in a lump sum settlement in a single year, he can treat all of the previous growth in the fund as well as the employer's contributions made before December 31, 1969, as a long-term capital gain. Non-lump-sum withdrawals—for example, an ordinary retirement annuity or "pension"—as well as withdrawals of any employer contributions made after December 31, 1969, will be treated as ordinary income but the latter, if made in a lump-sum payment, will be subject to special income averaging rules.
6. The employee may be able to contribute additional funds to the pension trust out of his own pocket, and thus these funds, too, may be put to work for him in a tax-free environment. In rare circumstances, the additional contributions made by an employee may be taken from his own salary by the employer on a before-tax basis. In other words, the employee may be able to contribute a larger number of dollars to the fund if they can be treated

as a salary *reduction* rather than as a salary *deduction*. In other cases, the employees' personal contribution must come from after-tax dollars, but, to the extent that this is true, the employee will be able to recover those amounts free of any further tax on separation from service or retirement.

This list of tax shelters available through a qualified pension plan is truly impressive and the dollar significance of this opportunity to any employee can hardly be overrated. The magnitude of the tax savings is, of course, directly related to the marginal tax bracket of the employee. For upper-income-bracket individuals, it would require a tremendous increase in cash salaries to purchase an equivalent retirement annuity in a taxable commercial enterprise. The compounding effect of tax-free contributions and tax-free growth is almost phenomenal over the working life of an individual. To grasp better the significance of the difference, consider the result of two taxpayers who each are in the 50 percent marginal tax bracket, who each divert $5,000 per year to a retirement plan, and who each earn an annual 8 percent return on their retirement investment for a period of 25 years. The only difference between the two taxpayers is that Taxpayer A prepares for his retirement in a non-tax-sheltered way whereas Taxpayer B prepares for his retirement through a qualified pension program. At the end of the 25 years, Taxpayer B's retirement fund will amount to approximately $365,000, while Taxpayer A's fund will have grown to only $104,000. Obviously, these two amounts are not appropriate as a final comparison since Taxpayer B still has to pay an income tax on all of his retirement income, while most of Taxpayer A's retirement income will be free of further income tax (that is, all but the additional earnings produced by the remaining assets during the retirement years). Nevertheless, the dollar difference in terms of their retirement pensions will be substantial. The larger size of B's fund will permit much larger payments to be made, and the larger fund will continue to earn larger sums during B's retirement. In addition, B probably will now be in a lower marginal tax bracket, so even an ordinary income tax might not be onerous. And if B elects a lump-sum settlement, his after-tax proceeds would still be in the neighborhood of $210,000, which is more than twice the value of A's accumulation. Perhaps in no small measure it is because these benefits are so impressive that requirements for qualification are so demanding.

Qualification of a plan. A pension, profit-sharing, or stock bonus plan will not qualify for the tax shelters listed above unless its satisfies the numerous Code requirements of Sec. 401(a). Among the conditions required for qualification are the following:

1. That the plan be created for the exclusive benefit of the employees and/or their beneficiaries;
2. That the sole purpose of the plan be either to give the employees a share of the employer's profits or to provide them with a retirement income;
3. That the plan be a permanent plan, be made in writing, and be communicated to the employees;
4. That the plan *not* discriminate in favor of corporate officers, stockholder-employees, supervisory or highly paid employees; and
5. That the plan provides for a vesting of benefits if and when it ceases to exist.

Each of these requirements is stipulated with considerable detail in the Code and the related regulations. For anything other than the smallest corporate enterprise—that is, for all but the "one-man" corporation—the most important requirement is perhaps the one which precludes discrimination among employees. Most owner-operators would be delighted to provide themselves with a tax-sheltered pension or profit-sharing plan, but they are more reluctant to do so when that also requires that all other employees share the pot. Actually, the Code does provide for something less than total coverage of all employees and it does permit a limited degree of discrimination. For example, part-time and seasonal employees as well as 20 to 30 percent of otherwise eligible employees may be excluded from coverage under a particular plan, and that plan may still qualify for tax purposes. In addition, because contributions to the plan may be made a percentage of the employee's salary, the real benefits obtained are not equal for every employee by any means.

Taxpayers owning more than one corporation could, of course, be selective in determining which corporation would institute the most generous qualified pension or profit-sharing plan. The corporation with the highest ratio of owner-employees to total employees is the obvious candidate. The opportunity to discriminate through the careful selection of one from several related corporate entities presents numerous problems that cannot be regarded lightly. In some instances multiple businesses under common control must be treated as a single business. Profit-sharing plans may also be affected by discriminatory pricing policies on interrelated corporate transactions. In other words, the price of intercorporate transfers between related entities could be rearranged to the maximum benefit of the one corporation having the generous profit-sharing plan for the (mostly) owner group. Once again, however, the IRS and the courts do not hesitate to recalculate corporate profits of related businesses where tax avoidance motives are grossly apparent.

Assuming that a pension or profit-sharing plan meets all Code requirements for qualification, the accumulated assets of the employee trust fund must sooner or later be distributed to the employees. When this happens the employee must recognize taxable income. As noted earlier, that income may be either ordinary income or a capital gain.

Taxation of employee benefits. The employee covered by a qualified pension or profit-sharing plan need not report as taxable income any benefits under that plan until they are paid or otherwise "made available" to him. Usually, benefits are not distributed by employee trust funds until an employee terminates his employment, retires, or dies. Very often a qualified plan will allow the employee to select from several options when deciding how to take his accumulated benefits. He may, for example, be given a choice between (1) a lump-sum settlement; (2) a lifetime annuity for his own life; or (3) a smaller lifetime annuity for so long as either he or his spouse shall live. Another common option is a "refund" feature, which guarantees the employee or his heirs the right to receive a minimum payment regardless of how long the employee may live. The option selected by the employee significantly determines the tax consequence of any distribution. Once again, the specific rules which determine the exact tax results are too numerous and too complex to justify their inclusion in a book aimed at tax recognition rather than tax solution. Suffice it to repeat here the important conclusion that, at least for the next several years, lump-sum settlements generally produce mostly capital gain whereas annuity payments spread over more than one year generally produce ordinary income. Taxpayers who are fortunate enough to retire with large continuing incomes will, therefore, usually opt for lump-sum settlements while taxpayers retiring on small incomes may well prefer the annuity option even though that requires their recognition of ordinary income.

If all details are properly arranged in advance, an employee sometimes may be able to obtain an earlier benefit from his economic interest in a qualified plan without termination of his employment and without triggering the usual tax consequences for all accumulated benefits. For example, qualified profit-sharing plans have provided that employees could make a partial withdrawal of any vested rights under the plan if they could show need (such as the purchase of a new home, medical costs, or college expenses), and they could gain the approval of either the fund trustee or an administrative committee created to make such decisions. As long as the employee does not have an absolute right to make such early withdrawals, but only has the right to request withdrawal in appropriate and specified circumstances, the usual tax deferral privilege may be maintained.

Some important differences in qualified plans

Although all qualified pension, profit-sharing, and stock bonus plans have many things in common, they also differ in many important ways. Some of the important differences have more to do with everyday economics than they do with taxation. Some of the differences are of primary importance to the employer corporation; others are of greater importance to the employee. Perhaps the most important differences relate to funding and to the tax deduction limitation.

Pension plans. A pension plan has as its primary purpose the provision of a retirement fund for covered employees. Once instituted, a pension plan generally becomes a fixed obligation of the employer corporation. This means, of course, that the employer must make the contractual contribution without regard for the presence or absence of corporate profits. Because of the substantial cash requirement implicit in a pension plan covering any sizable group of employees, new and more risky ventures are typically reluctant to institute such a plan. Employees, especially middle-aged and older employees, on the other hand, strongly prefer the relative security of a fixed contractual arrangement. Because pension plans are intended to provide for retirement income, they seldom make provision for any acceleration of benefits, even in cases of demonstrated need.

Vesting rights continue to present the most controversial aspect of qualified pension plans. Labor, supported by a growing list of business-related organizations, argues for the full vesting of employees' rights within some reasonable time period; say, for example, after five or ten years of service. This would mean that an employee who had served an employer the specified period would be guaranteed his rights under the pension program whether or not he continued his employment with the same firm until his eventual retirement. Obviously, an employee who left the employ of a corporation after a few years would expect to receive a smaller retirement pension than would an employee with many years of service. By accumulation of two or three small pensions with different employers, however, the more transitory employee might look forward to a reasonable retirement income even if it were not paid wholly from a single fund. Congressional action in the area of vesting rights is imminent, but the precise vesting formula is sufficiently undetermined at the date of this writing to justify omission of speculation as to detail. Until Congress acts, however, vesting of all employee rights is not a requirement of qualified pension plans.

The maximum tax deduction which an employer corporation may claim in any tax year for its contribution to a qualified pension plan depends in part upon the funding method it elects. The actuarially determined cost of the plan determines the maximum deduction under any method. Pension costs are based upon assumptions about the future including estimated employee earnings, mortality, turnover, retirement, and vesting rights, among other factors. Because qualified pension plans can include credit for prior service (that is, for services rendered to the employer prior to the institution of the pension plan) as well as for future service, the current year's tax deduction may well exceed the cost, which relates only to current employee services rendered to the employer. In any case, however, the IRS will allow a deduction of not less than 5 percent of the current taxable compensation paid. Under some funding plans, an employer can deduct up to an additional 10 percent of the cost related to prior services in a single tax year.

Profit-sharing plans. Rights under a profit-sharing plan depend, as the name implies, upon the presence of employer profits. If the corporate employer earns no income in a particular year, it has no obligation to make a contribution to a qualified profit-sharing plan that year. Firms with highly volatile income find this feature especially appealing. Young, new employees, who look forward to several prosperous years, may also find profit sharing a desirable alternative while older employees, with fewer years remaining prior to retirement, generally prefer some other plan.

The maximum deduction for amounts contributed by the employer to a profit-sharing plan is generally equal to 15 percent of the compensation paid to participating employees. If an employer contributes less than the maximum deduction in one year, it obtains a carryover credit which allows contribution deductions in subsequent years to exceed the normal maximum by the amount of any carryforward. In no instance, however, can the deduction in a single year exceed 30 percent of current employee compensation. This carryover credit is unique to profit-sharing plans; underfunding of pension plans in any year simply goes into the formula calculation for subsequent years. Amounts contributed in excess of the current year's maximum deduction generally can be carried over and deducted in succeeding years to whatever extent the succeeding year's contributions are less than the maximum deduction.

Stock bonus plans. The tax rules for qualified stock bonus plans generally parallel those applicable to profit-sharing plans. The major difference between the two is the fact that stock bonus plans are payable in the stock of the employer corporation rather than in cash. This means, of course, that the employees' rights under the plan depend not only upon the presence of profits but also on the value of the employer's stock. New corporations may be especially attracted to stock bonus plans because they minimize cash requirements and many new corporations are critically short on cash. Young employees may find that the additional risk associated with the future value of their employer's stock is well worth the possible increase in benefits. Older employees and majority stockholders may find stock bonus plans less acceptable because of the extra risk and the dilution of equity, respectively.

As noted earlier, it is easy to underestimate the significance of the tax shelter available through qualified pension, profit-sharing, and stock bonus plans. Implementing the plans, and selecting the most desirable options within those plans, is a much more difficult task. Some of the more important considerations will be reviewed very briefly.

Related considerations

Any taxpayer considering the possibility of implementing a qualified pension, profit-sharing, or stock bonus plan should consult with a team of experts to assist him in making a wise decision. The team normally will consist of representatives of the employer and the employees as well as an accountant, attorney, and actuary (or life underwriter).

The taxpayer should carefully estimate the cost of implementing any plan as well as the benefits he expects to obtain from it. The costs and benefits are doubly difficult to predict not only because they are based on many estimates of the future, but also because they may significantly influence that future through changes in employee morale and, thus, the corporate performance generally. A good plan is one which helps develop and retain a strong and permanent complement of employees who are anxious to do their part to make the corporation more profitable.

Decisions related to the vesting provisions are especially difficult. Full vesting at too early a stage may unnecessarily encourage employee turnover. The absence of any vesting may undercut employee morale and encourage the most capable employees to seek greater security elsewhere. On the other hand, amounts contributed on behalf of departed employees who did not stay long enough to acquire a vested interest serve to decrease the employer's cost for those who remain. If Congress enacts a mandatory vesting requirement in the near future, as it appears it will, this aspect of qualified plans may require less attention than it has in the past.

Qualified pension plans may provide the retired employee with either a "fixed" or a "variable" annuity. A fixed annuity is one which stipulates in advance the exact number of dollars which the employee may claim at some future date under any given option. A variable annuity is one which provides benefits of varying amount, depending upon the relative success or failure of the trustee's investments during the years he controls the employee trust fund assets. Many authors describing fixed annuities suggest that they are less risky than variable annuities because the dollar benefits paid to the employee are not subject to the vagaries of the securities markets. Unfortunately, that statement is at least as misleading as it is accurate. Although it is true that the employee may know how many dollars he will receive under a fixed annuity, he has no knowledge about what that number of dollars may or may not buy for him at some future date. The more rapid the inflation prior to his retirement, the greater the risk in a fixed annuity and the less the risk in a variable annuity. Few if any employees contemplating retirement in the period from 1940 to 1960 would have accurately estimated the absolute dollar cost of a minimal retirement living in 1974. Given the importance of the unknowns, it is often very difficult to select wisely as between fixed and variable annuities.

Contributions made by an employer to an employee trust fund obviously do not lie idle pending the employee's retirement. These assets might be directly invested by the fund trustee; they might be turned over to a mutual fund or to some other professional for investment; they might be put into government bonds; or they might be lodged directly with an insurance company which could provide an annuity contract for each covered employee. The eventual financial success of the employee trust fund is directly determined by the investment decision. In some circumstances employee trust funds have even loaned cash back to the contributing employer corporation and retained their tax-exempt and qualified status. The risk of losing the tax-exempt status of a trust fund because of self-dealing or other prohibited transactions is so great that the few taxpayers who would travel this road should be advised to do so only with the greatest of caution and the very best counsel. After all, it is only reasonable that the tax law not allow the closely held corporation an immediate tax deduction for money contributed (at least partially) for the benefit of its owners and then allow that same corporation the right to use that same money in the meantime!

Life, health, and accident insurance are sometimes made a part of the qualified pension, profit-sharing, or stock bonus package. Generally, the presence of one or more of these benefits makes some part of the employee's rights immediately taxable to him. Other plans combine pension and profit-sharing plans into a single "combined" plan. Such a plan may maximize the number of dollars that can be tax-sheltered. Still other plans facilitate the transfer of employees between related employers by providing a single qualified plan for a group of related employers. Affiliated corporate groups can create plans which allow profitable members to make contributions for the benefit of an unprofitable member corporation's employees. Deciding whether or not to include these or many other benefits within the context of a qualified plan complicates the decision. Even with the multiple complexities, however, few tax-saving plans create more impressive benefits than do qualified pension, profit-sharing, and stock bonus plans.

The next class of compensation arrangements to be discussed is the class which includes the most common form of employee compensation, that is, the routine wage or salary. The tax planner should always remember that the aggregate compensation paid to an employee must be *reasonable in amount* before it can be deducted by the employer corporation. This reasonableness test encompasses all forms of compensation considered together.

TECHNIQUES PROVIDING
AN IMMEDIATE CORPORATE DEDUCTION AND
IMMEDIATE TAX TO THE EMPLOYEE

In addition to cash wages and salaries, this third class of techniques includes almost all nonqualified compensation arrangements. For example, if a corporate employee is given the right to make a bargain purchase of a corporate asset, the amount of that bargain generally will be included as part of his compensation. If a corporation purchases an entertainment facility—say a boat, or a hunting lodge—and makes it available only to corporate executive stockholders, the value of their use of such a facility could very easily be treated as additional compensation. If an employee's wife and family are provided at company expense with a "free trip" in connection with a convention or other business trip, the employee can anticipate having to report the amount expended by his employer for the wife and the family as additional gross income. In summary, assuming that the aggregate value of all of the items paid by the employer primarily for the employee's benefit is a *reasonable* compensation, it will be immediately deductible by the employer and immediately taxed to the employee unless it can be fitted into one of the special exceptions discussed earlier in this chapter.

Cash salary

The regular cash wage or salary is still the most common form of employee compensation. It may be surprising that it qualifies only as a third-ranked class of compensation techniques, that is, as one which produces an immediate deduction for the employer and an immediate gross income for the employee. The reason for its overwhelming popularity is, naturally, the need and desire of every employee to obtain cash and the personal flexibility in spending that goes with it. Even if an expert were able to create a tax-sheltered world in which every employee was adequately provided with a company home, company food, company car, company entertainment, company medical plan, and company pension, the need and desire for additional cash salary would remain. In fact, in such an extreme world, the implicit or psychic cost associated with any further tax shelter would almost certainly be greater than the benefit of the additional tax saving under even the most onerous income tax that the mind of man could devise.

Nonqualified stock options

Stock options have had a long and checkered history in the tax annals of the United States. Because of the many and very restrictive conditions put upon qualified forms of the stock option over the past 20 years, the preferred form of stock option today is quite likely to be the *nonqualified* one. To understand the reasons which explain this apparent puzzle we had better review the basic economics involved in a stock option.

A stock option is, of course, nothing more than a right to purchase a corporation's stock for a given time period at a given price. Even if the price is set equal to the market price on the date the option is granted, the option itself will have real economic value if the period of the option is of any reasonable length. To illustrate, if someone were to offer you the guaranteed right to purchase General Motors common stock at today's market price, wouldn't you be willing to pay something for that option if it ran for, say, a period of five years? Wouldn't you be willing to pay even more if it ran for, say, 10 or 20 years? Under these conditions the opportunity to make a substantial profit with a minimum investment is very real. The option holder would simply hold his rights unexercised as long as the value of the stock remained constant or decreased. If the market price decreased and remained depressed for the term of the option, it would finally expire and prove to be worthless. On the other hand, if the value of the stock increased, the option would become as valuable as the spread between the later market price and the option price multiplied by the number of shares authorized in the option.

At one time the tax laws were worded so that an employee was required to report as ordinary income only the initial spread between an option price and the fair market value of the stock at the date the option was granted. Any subsequent increase was capital gain. Today, the employee stands to report much more of his gain as ordinary income. The rules which control the tax consequence of a nonqualified stock option differ depending upon whether or not the fair market value of the *option* is readily ascertainable when granted. If it is, the employee must immediately report that value, less anything he might have to pay to acquire the option, as ordinary income; the same amount is immediately deductible by the employer corporation. In this situation any further increment in value will be reportable as a capital gain. If the fair market value of the option is not readily ascertainable when granted, the employee will not realize any taxable income until he exercises his option and acquires the property. At that time, the employee reports the entire fair market value of the property received, again less any payment that he must make to acquire the property, as ordinary income, and the corporate employer receives a corresponding deduction at that same time. The appropriate rules, although difficult to state in words, can be illustrated simply, as shown in Figure 7–1.

FIGURE 7–1

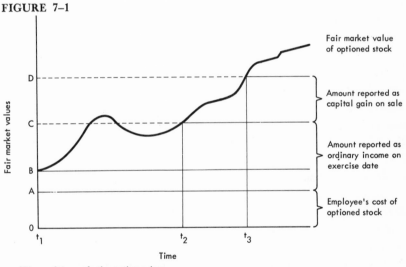

Where: OA equals the option price;
   OB equals the fair market value of the stock on the date the nonqualified stock option was granted;
   OC equals the fair market value of the stock on the date the nonqualified stock option was exercised;
   OD equals the fair market value of the stock on the date the stock was sold;
   t_1 represents the date the option was granted;
   t_2 represents the date the option was exercised; and
   t_3 represents the date the stock was sold.

The distance OA represents the amount of capital that the employee must contribute to the corporation to acquire the stock when he exercises his option. Distance AB represents the spread between the option price and the fair market value of the stock on the date the option was granted; as long as the option is a nonqualified one, there is no limit on the amount of this spread. If distance AB is known on date t_1, it is immediately taxed to the employee and deducted by the employer. Distance BC represents any additional increment in the value of the stock which takes place between the option date and the date the employee exercises his option and acquires the property. On this date (t_2), the employee acquires additional gross income equal in amount to distance BC and the corporation acquires an equivalent deduction. (If the distance AB was not known on date t_1, then distance AC would be taxed on date t_2.) Thus, the only element of capital gain remaining in this form of the nonqualified employee stock option is the distance CD, the increment in value after the exercise date and before the sale date. If the time lapse between t_2 and t_3 is more than six months, the distance CD will be long-term capital gain and will carry with it the usual advantages associated with such gains.

Given the fact that most of the increment in the value is presently taxed as ordinary income, the reader may wonder why the nonqualified stock option has any potential compensation value remaining. The answer has to lie in nontax considerations. First, note that the option price (OA) can be set low enough to allow even a nonpropertied junior executive a "piece of the action" with a minimum investment. Second, note that the value of the option eventually depends upon the value of the stock. If the stock becomes very valuable, so does the option. Initially, all stock options were defended on exactly these grounds: the proponents argued that the value of any corporate executive was entirely dependent upon what he could do with the company. If he could make the company highly profitable, and thus make the stock increase substantially in value for the shareholders, the executive was a very valuable person and should be compensated accordingly. Stock options made a direct relationship between stock prices and compensation arrangements possible. For the third and final advantage remaining, note that a stock option may provide a real economic benefit to an employee with no cash cost to the corporation. In fact, if the option is exercised, the corporation actually receives an additional cash contribution to its own capital. This cash-free cost assumes that the corporation can issue either (1) previously authorized but unissued shares, or (2) treasury stock already owned by the employer. The real economic cost is shifted to the stockholders by dilution of their equity interests. In large corporations, where no one person owns anything but a small fraction of the total, this dilution of equity is minimized if the executive can increase the shareholders' dollar value in this corporation's stock, notwithstanding the small dilution of each shareholder's relative interest. In summary, under the appropriate circumstances, a nonqualified stock option may still be a wholly viable form of compensation even though it presents relatively little by way of tax-saving opportunities.

The number of possible variations on the basic stock option theme is amazing. Some options involve additional restrictions on the property acquired by the employee which may affect the date and the measurement of his taxable income. Other plans involve phantom stock rather than actual shares. The phantom plans are useful whenever the stockholders desire to avoid any dilution of their ownership interests but still desire to give an employee a compensation based on stock values. Under the phantom plan the employee acquires an "equivalent unit," based on stock prices and on his stock plan agreement, which units every pay "dividend equivalents" which are accumulated and held on the employee's behalf. On separation from service, the employee claims his vested rights and withdraws his accumulated benefits over an agreed time period. Details of these and other plans could be described at length. The fundamental ideas would not change significantly, however, and, thus, it seems preferable to move to other techniques utilized in compensation arrangements.

TECHNIQUES PROVIDING A DEFERRED CORPORATE DEDUCTION AND A DEFERRED TAX TO THE EMPLOYEE

In relatively rare instances an employee may be provided with an unfunded equivalent of a pension plan. These arrangements are commonly known as deferred compensation plans which essentially involve an employer's promise to make continued payments to a particular employee following his retirement from service. The payments supposedly represent additional compensation for services already rendered by the employee. If the plan is a nonqualified one, no corporate assets are actually set aside to cover the contractual agreement, and the employee's rights are forfeitable, the employee will not report any gross income until he actually receives payments under the deferred compensation agreement, and the corporate employer will not claim a tax deduction until that same year. If the plan is funded and the employee's rights become vested, the tax consequences may be accelerated for both parties. Typically, the tax benefit of such a deferred compensation plan must derive from the deferral of income to a date at which the executive is in a lower marginal tax bracket. Economically speaking, these arrangements place the retired employee in the position of a general creditor of his former employer. If all goes well with the corporation financially, his contract is valuable and his comfortable retirement assured. If the company gets into financial difficulty, however, the nonqualified deferred compensation arrangement may be essentially worthless to a former employee. Perhaps for this reason as much as any other, deferred compensation arrangements are often limited to smaller businesses and to a key executive or two.

TECHNIQUES PROVIDING NO CORPORATE DEDUCTION BUT A TAX TO THE EMPLOYEE

A reader might well question whether or not any technique which provides no deduction to a corporate employer can really constitute an employee compensation device. It can be argued that, definitionally, such an item cannot exist. Although that conclusion may be justified on definitional grounds, as a practical matter it might pay to examine briefly two situations in which an apparent compensation is associated with a nondeductible result to an employer corporation.

Disguised dividends

If a court sustains an IRS contention that payments made to an employee are unreasonable in amount, the court is also likely to find that such payments are in effect a disguised dividend if the recipient also is a corporate stockholder. If a payment is found to constitute a dividend, we know that the corporation will not be entitled to any deduction even though the recipient shareholder will be required to report the entire amount received as ordinary income. The likelihood of this disastrous tax conclusion is significantly increased in the closely held corporation in which the corporate executives are also the major stockholders and dividend payments are kept to a minimum. Taxpayers in this situation may be able to provide some protection against the initial conclusion if they have an advance contractual agreement with their corporate employer which provides that they must return to the corporation any amount finally determined to constitute unreasonable compensation. If successful, such an agreement will remove the initial problem of ordinary income with no deduction, but it may create further problems in the area of the accumulated earnings tax. Again, the need for expert assistance in such a sensitive area is obvious.

The reader should also understand that, in making the reasonableness determination, the IRS will look to the entire compensation package, not just to cash salaries. To the extent that fringe benefits increase the aggregate compensation, they also increase the likelihood of the reasonableness issue. The successful defense against an unreasonable compensation charge may turn upon such facts as the special skill and ability of the employee; the scope of his services; the dividend history of the employer; the relative ownership interests of the employees whose salaries are being questioned; the adequacy of compensation in prior years; and general comparisons with other taxpayers in the same industry. Each case stands on its own, and generalization of results is hazardous.

Qualified stock option plans

The qualified stock option does not provide a corporate employer with a tax reduction at any time, even though it may create taxable income for the recipient employee. If a qualified stock option plan is successful taxwise, it means that the employee will report only a capital gain on the disposition of the optioned shares. Before a stock option plan can be a qualified one, and before the employee can report only capital gain on the disposition of optioned stock, the following conditions must be satisfied:

1. On the date the option is granted, the option price must be set equal to or greater than the fair market value of the stock.
2. The employee must exercise his option within five years from the date it is granted to him.
3. The employee cannot sell the stock for at least three years after he acquires it.
4. The employee cannot be a major stockholder in the employer corporation. (The definition of major stockholder varies with the size of the corporation's equity capital, but anyone with more than 10 percent interest would be so classified and sometimes as little as 5 percent will suffice.)
5. The stock option must be approved by the shareholders.

Because these conditions are so restrictive, the tax advantage which remains in the qualified stock option is limited. Such options may still be used, however, for valid nontax reasons. Perhaps the most important use of them today is to involve more of the rank-and-file employees in corporate ownership with potential attendant results in improved employee morale. If one or more of the above conditions are not satisfied, it does not necessarily mean that the entire gain on the sale of optioned stock will be treated as ordinary income. Usually, however, some portion of that gain must be reported as ordinary income under those circumstances. The exact details of the many possibilities are once more best left to other books with different objectives. Before leaving the topic of compensation, however, we ought to examine briefly the plight of the self-employed person.

SPECIAL TAX CONSIDERATIONS FOR
SELF-EMPLOYED TAXPAYERS

Many of the tax sheltered compensation techniques simply are not available to the self-employed taxpayer. Those not available to such a person include group-term life insurance, health and accident insurance, meals and lodging opportunities, and any arrangements dependent upon stock for their success. The one notable exception to the above list is the pension plan. Since 1963, a self-employed individual can claim a deduction on his own tax return for amounts contributed to his own retirement plan. As usual, a number of restrictive conditions and related factors must be considered before anyone can determine whether or not this tax shelter is desirable for a particular taxpayer.

Before a self-employed individual can claim a tax deduction for amounts contributed to his own retirement plan, that plan must be a qualified plan. These plans are commonly known as "Keogh" plans or as "H.R. 10" plans because Congressman Keogh introduced House bill number 10 which first authorized this particular deduction. The most demanding condition for qualification is that the plan must also include pension coverage for all full-time employees who have worked for the self-employed person for three years or longer. Thus, the tax value of the additional deduction for the self-employed owner may be more than lost to the extra cost of covering other employees. The most restrictive condition of a qualified Keogh plan is that the self-employed individual can never deduct more than $2,500 per year for the contribution made on his own behalf. In addition, before such a plan will be qualified the taxpayer must have sufficient income from an unincorporated personal service business; income from passive investments will not qualify for this deduction.

If a self-employed taxpayer person succeeds in creating a qualified pension plan, the tax shelter available to him is much like that available to the corporate employee in a qualified pension plan. In other words, the important tax results stem from the facts that (a) the contributions to the plan (to the $2,500 maximum) come from before-tax income and (b) the accumulated amounts can grow tax-free in a retirement fund. Most self-employed persons utilize an extant mutual fund, a bank trust fund, or an insurance plan to administer the assets during the years of accumulation. The self-employed individual with an annual earned income of more than $25,000 and a small number of permanent employees is the most likely prospect for a Keogh plan. Corporate employees who conduct a limited independent trade or business outside their corporate employment may also benefit from such a plan. Under the right conditions the tax shelter provided can be quite substantial. The chance to accumulate tax-free dollars of income in a tax-free growth fund should never be overlooked.

In summary, compensation arrangements more than almost any other common business transaction provide a host of opportunities for major tax savings. The entrepreneur and the corporate business manager would do well to review their own compensation arrangements in light of the broad outlines described in this chapter. Sometimes the need to create a new corporate entity will be obvious, but this is rarely a difficult task today. If suggested improvements appear to be possible, the reader should discuss his particular situation in detail with a competent tax advisor.

8

Tax factors in the acquisition, use, and disposition of fixed assets

THE TERM *fixed asset* is used to refer to any asset which will benefit more than a single accounting period. Thus, this term usually encompasses such mobile assets as cars, trucks, and airplanes as well as more "fixed" buildings, land, and utility poles; it also covers both tangible and intangible properties. For tax purposes income generally is measured in intervals of one year. Because fixed assets benefit more than one year, they present some unique problems in income measurement. One basic problem involves the proper method of allocating the total cost of a fixed asset over its estimated useful life.

The tax rules governing the acquisition, use, and disposition of fixed assets have become increasingly volatile in recent years because Congress has been convinced that changes in these rules have a greater than normal impact on the way our economy performs. In years in which economic stimulation is deemed necessary, we find that Congress tends to increase the amount of the depreciation deduction that may be claimed and, in some years, to allow a tax credit based upon the cost of certain fixed assets purchased during the year. In years when an economic repressant is deemed necessary, we have come to expect the opposite changes; that is, the amount of the depreciation deduction is typically reduced and the investment tax credit is suspended or rescinded. Because these changes have been so frequent, and because the rules are so diverse, we will concentrate our attention in this chapter on the general planning opportunities associated with investments in fixed assets.

Before we look at more specific details, we might pause to observe the range of alternative treatments available for fixed assets in general.

At the one extreme, it is possible for the law to authorize as an immediate deduction the entire cost of a fixed asset notwithstanding the fact that the expenditure will benefit one or more future accounting periods. The result of this alternative, of course, is to understate income in the year of purchase and to overstate it in subsequent years. In a limited number of circumstances, the Code actually authorizes such an immediate deduction. At the other extreme, it is possible for the law to deny a taxpayer the right to claim any deduction for the cost of a fixed asset until disposition. Generally, this is the tax treatment prescribed for all nonwasting assets, such as investments in stocks and land, which are deemed to be indestructible. The third and intermediate alternative is the possibility that requires the taxpayer to capitalize the cost of a fixed asset initially, but then allows him to recover this cost over the intended life of the fixed asset utilizing some predetermined cost allocation technique. This last alternative is the most widely used one and the cost allocation technique authorized is commonly known as a depreciation method. The several depreciation methods authorized, and some restrictions on their application, will be discussed later in this chapter.

Chapter 8 has been divided into five major sections. The first section explains the very fundamental relationships between tax rules, present value concepts, and profit opportunities. The second, third, and fourth sections deal with tax factors related to the acquisition, use, and disposition of fixed assets, respectively. The fifth and final section provides an illustration demonstrating the potential importance of tax rules on fixed-asset investment decisions. Although this organizational arrangement has certain pedagogical advantages, the reader should understand that he may have to examine several sections of this chapter if he wants the "whole story" on one specific form of investment. For example, if he really wants to understand the tax factors associated with ownership of an apartment house or an oil well, he must sequentially evaluate the tax factors pertinent to the acquisition, use, and disposition of that particular form of fixed asset.

FUNDAMENTAL RELATIONSHIPS BETWEEN TAX LAWS, THE PRESENT VALUE CONCEPT, AND SIMPLE ECONOMICS

The reader should observe that acquisition of a fixed asset may provide a tax deduction without an immediate cash disbursement.

Suppose, for example, that a taxpayer acquired in one day two identical fixed assets to be used for the same purpose but that he paid $10,000 cash for asset #1 and signed a $10,000 promissory note payable, due in five years, for asset #2. In each case the taxpayer's basis in the asset is $10,000 and he would be entitled to exactly the same tax deductions and credits on each asset. This ability to acquire a tax deduction, and possibly an investment tax credit with a minimal cash disbursement, is one of the basic reasons that high marginal bracket taxpayers have for their continuing interest in certain fixed assets.

To illustrate the critical interaction between tax rules and fundamental economics, let us begin with a grossly oversimplified illustration. If on January 1, 19x1, Taxpayer A acquires a $200,000 fixed asset with a four-year life by signing a $200,000, 10 percent simple-interest note, which will be payable on January 1, 19x5, and if we know with 100 percent certainty that this fixed asset will provide its owner with new assets that can be sold on January 1, 19x5, for exactly $280,000, and that the initial fixed asset will vanish into dust on exactly that same date, the reader might conclude that the taxpayer should not proceed with the investment. If we assume that there is no income tax, the result can be detailed as follows:

Year	Item	Cash inflow	Cash outflow
19x1	No cash transactions . . . . $ ...		$ ...
19x5	Sale of new assets.	280,000	
19x5	Payment of note		200,000
19x5	Payment of interest.		80,000

Obviously, this investor would have to utilize his entire proceeds to pay off the note and have no profit for his time and trouble.

If we want to illustrate the critical interface between tax rules and simple economics, we will have to begin to modify our stated assumptions. This time let us assume that Taxpayer A lives in a country that imposes a flat-rate 50 percent tax on all income; that authorizes the amortization of fixed asset costs equally over the life of an asset; that authorizes the deduction of interest expense; and that collects the income tax on January 1 of each year for income earned in the previous year. These extreme assumptions might still lead a reader to conclude that Taxpayer A should not proceed with this investment since the inevitable result will be cash-receipt equivalents equal in value to cash disbursements. The revised calculations would be as follows:

Year	Item	Cash inflow or equivalent	Cash outflow
19x1	Tax saving due to new $50,000 depreciation deduction allowed taxpayer.	$ 25,000	
19x2	Same as 19x1	25,000	
19x3	Same as 19x1	25,000	
19x4	Same as 19x1	25,000	
19x5	Payment of note—face amount		$200,000
19x5	Payment of note (the deduction for interest provides new tax saving)	40,000	80,000
19x5	Sale of new assets.	$280,000	
19x5	Income tax on sale of new assets		140,000
	Total over life of investment	$420,000	$420,000

Interestingly, the effect of introducing a 50 percent income tax into our earlier illustration is simply to increase the cash-receipt equivalents and cash disbursements by 50 percent; that is, from $280,000 to $420,000. The desirability of the investment does not seem to be changed by this fact alone.

The next step in understanding the interface between tax and simple economics involves appreciation of the present value concept. Stated in its most elementary terms, this concept suggests that money has a time-preference value. A dollar today is worth more than a dollar that you cannot have until one year from now, and that dollar is worth more than a dollar that you can not have until five years from now. The exact difference in the present value between these dollars depends upon the investor's discount rate. Stated crudely, the discount rate is the rate of income that an investor can earn on capital during an interim period. If we assume that a taxpayer has a discount rate of five percent, a dollar that he cannot have for one year is presently worth about $.95238095. In other words, if the taxpayer puts that latter amount to work for him at five percent (after-tax), it will be worth exactly $1.00 to him one year later. The dollar that he could not have for five years, discounted at five percent, would be worth approximately $.78352617 right now.

Returning to our previous calculations, we can now determine the discounted present value of the investment opportunity, based upon an assumed five percent (after-tax) rate of return, as shown.

Year	Item	Present value of inflows	Present value of outflows
19x1	'$25,000 tax saving discounted for 1 period ($25,000 × .95238095)	$ 23,810	
19x2	Same tax saving discounted 2 periods	22,676	
19x3	Same tax saving discounted 3 periods	21,596	
19x4	Same tax saving discounted 4 periods	20,568	
19x5	$280,000 sales discounted 5 periods	219,387	
19x5	$200,000 note discounted 5 periods		$156,705
19x5	$80,000 interest discounted 5 periods . . . . .·. . . .	31,341	62,682
19x5	$140,000 tax liability discounted 5 periods		109,694
	Total present value of investment	$339,378	$329,081

In other words, the effect of the tax law is to give this investor dollar-receipt equivalents (in the form of tax savings), which he can invest at five percent (after-taxes). Assuming that he actually makes these investments at this rate of return, this investment opportunity will actually provide him with a $10,297 profit *solely because of the combined effect of tax laws and the time-preference value of money.*

If we were to make a systematic study of this example to discover the magic of the $10,000 profit and what it has to say about pragmatic investments in fixed assets, we would not have to tarry long to observe that the sooner the tax deduction (and thus the cash-inflow equivalent) can be realized, and the longer the taxable income can be deferred, the greater the opportunity to profit. The tax magic of many fixed assets can be explained this simply: they provide immediate tax deductions with deferred income recognition possibilities. Obviously, it is even possible to create illustrations in which the nondiscounted cash outflows actually exceed the cash-inflow equivalents but which still yield an actual profit on a discounted basis. In the daily financial press, such losses are termed *tax losses* to distinguish them from real economic losses. The longer the time period between the tax deduction and the income realization, and the higher the discount rate, the greater the opportunity to reap a tax loss and an economic gain.

When we further relax the extreme simplifying assumptions made in our initial illustration, we can begin to understand why many high-tax-bracket investors continue to look to fixed asset investments for tax relief. For example, if a taxpayer is in a high marginal bracket at the time he is entitled to claim a deduction—say, for example, during his prime working years as a corporate executive, a successful athlete, or a surgeon—while he may be in a substantially lower marginal tax bracket at the time he must realize the income—say, for example, after retirement—the opportunity for profit is increased.

Another possibility involves the right to claim a tax deduction against ordinary income and to reap the deferred income as a capital gain. The differential in the marginal tax rates applicable to the early deduction and the deferred income really becomes significant in very short time periods when this difference in classification can be arranged. Prior to the Tax Reform Act of 1969, investments in cattle breeding operations and in citrus groves provided exactly this kind of investment. The rules have been restricted in these areas, however, and these particular forms of investment have lost some of their tax appeal. Similar opportunities remain viable in the mineral industries and, to a more limited extent, in apartment projects, shopping centers, and cattle operations.

To demonstrate the double parlay available when capital gains become involved, let us consider another very simple illustration. This time let us assume that a taxpayer invests $50,000 in an asset which the tax law authorizes as an immediate deduction and which produces a $55,000 investment two years later. Let us again assume that the taxpayer borrows the entire $50,000 on an 8 percent prepaid interest note, due when the asset is sold; that he is in a 60 percent marginal tax bracket relative to ordinary income; and that the entire gain of $55,000 can be reported as a long-term capital gain and be taxed at 30 percent (just one-half his ordinary rate) two years later. Initial calculations, without giving effect to either tax rules or to discounted present values, would look like this:

Year	Item	Cash inflow	Cash outflow
19x1	Prepayment of interest...............		$ 8,000
19x2	Sale of investment	$55,000	
19x2	Payment of note principal		50,000
	Total over life of investment	$55,000	$58,000

In summary, without considering either present values or income tax effects, it seems that the taxpayer will lose $3,000 on this investment.

If we add the tax effect, we observe that the picture changes as follows:

Year	Item	Cash inflow or equivalent	Cash outflow
19x1	Prepayment of interest.		$ 8,000
19x1	Deduction of interest expense saves taxes of $8,000 × .60	$ 4,800	
19x1	Immediate deduction of basic investment saves taxes of ($50,000 × .60).	30,000	
19x2	Payment of note principal		50,000
19x2	Receipt from sale of investment.	55,000	
19x2	Capital gain tax on sale.		16,500
		$89,800	$74,500

In effect, the tax rules have changed a $3,000 tax loss into a $15,300 real economic profit without giving consideration to the time preference value of money in this illustration.

If we add time-preference calculations, and presume that the taxpayer can make his investment during the final days of one tax year and defer the income recognition until the first days of the second subsequent tax year (thus holding the investment for just a few days in excess of two years), we can squeeze out a little larger profit even with a low discount rate. A five percent after-tax return has been assumed in the following calculations:

Year	Item	Present value of inflows	Present value of outflows
19x1	Prepayment of interest which is immediately deductible	$ 4,800	$ 8,000
19x1	Immediate deduction of investment	30,000	
19x2	Present value of note payment (deferred 2 periods)		45,351
19x2	Present value of proceeds on sale (deferred 2 periods)	49,887	
19x3	Present value of capital gain tax (deferred 3 periods)		14,253
	Total present value of investment	$84,687	$67,604

Finally, then, tax rules plus present values have changed an apparent $3,000 tax loss into a $17,083 real economic profit, assuming the accuracy of all values and a correct interpretation of tax laws.

These illustrations should have demonstrated that the real economic success of an investment in any fixed asset is critically affected by several variables, including: (1) the timing of the tax deduction; (2)

the timing of the income recognized; (3) the marginal tax rate applicable to the tax deduction; (4) the marginal tax rate applicable to the income recognized; and (5) the discount rate assumed by the taxpayer. Generally speaking, real economic profits will be increased if (*a*) the time between the tax deduction and the income recognition is lengthened, and (*b*) the deductions are claimed in high marginal tax bracket years and the income is recognized in either low marginal tax bracket forms or years. These differences substantially influence investors' decisions relative to the acquisition, use, and disposition of various fixed assets.

TAX FACTORS PERTINENT TO THE ACQUISITION OF FIXED ASSETS

When a taxpayer first considers the prospect of acquiring a fixed asset, he should give adequate consideration to the form in which he makes that acquisition since each form may produce significantly different tax and financial results. The most obvious and common way of acquiring a fixed asset is, naturally, by direct purchase. Even in this simple case, however, we have observed how the tax result may vary significantly if the taxpayer pays for the asset with his own cash or if he borrows the funds required to make the purchase. As an alternative to the direct purchase of an asset, a taxpayer sometimes has the opportunity to acquire a controlling interest in the stock of a corporation which owns the assets that he wants to acquire. In this way the taxpayer has acquired the effective use of the asset desired even though his ownership of the asset is indirect, through the corporate entity. This alternative may create tax problems or opportunities for the unsuspecting investor. As an alternative to either a direct or an indirect purchase, the taxpayer can also consider the possibility of leasing an asset. In this way he acquires use of an asset without acquiring legal title to the asset, and he probably will be entitled to a deduction for the lease rents paid. Finally, in some circumstances, a taxpayer may be able to construct or develop his own asset. This method of acquisition presents several new and interesting tax consequences for many.

Direct purchases

The most common form of acquiring a fixed asset is the outright purchase of the finished product from an unrelated party. Tax factors in this sort of acquisition are reduced to such fundamental problems as determining the correct amount to capitalize in the fixed asset account (for example, the cost of freight charges and installation expenses are properly added to the asset account in addition to the initial purchase price); estimating a useful life and eventual salvage value for the asset acquired; and selecting an appropriate depreciation method. Also, the taxpayer must determine if the asset is one which qualifies for an investment credit. Each of these tax factors will be discussed in remaining portions of this chapter.

Indirect acquisitions through stock ownership

If Taxpayer A desires to acquire a certain collection of assets which are owned by Corporation XYZ, he has essentially two alternatives. He can try to negotiate for the direct purchase of these assets with the executives of the XYZ Corporation, or he can negotiate for the purchase of a controlling interest in the stock of XYZ with its stockholders. Significant tax differences attach to each alternative from the standpoint of both the buyer and the seller. The most important differences for the seller were considered in Chapter 6.

To understand the important differences between direct and indirect acquisitions of assets from the standpoint of a buyer, consider the two alternatives which appear in Figure 8–1. In this illustration Taxpayer B owns 100 percent of the stock of XYZ Corporation and XYZ owns assets 1, 2, & 3. Let us assume that all parties agree that the fair market values of assets 1, 2, & 3 are $10,000, $20,000, and $30,000 respectively. If the only assets owned by XYZ are assets 1, 2, and 3, one might conclude that the stock of XYZ ought to be worth $60,000 since the ownership of this stock would give the stockholder the indirect ownership of the assets. If we assume, however, that XYZ has depreciated these assets so that the remaining tax basis in them is $1,000, $2,000, and $3,000 respectively, a special problem in valuation is presented. If A acquires the assets *directly* for $60,000, A's tax basis in these assets will be $10,000, $20,000 and $30,000 respectively. This means, of course, that A can proceed to depreciate the assets and thereby reduce his future taxable income by that same amount.

If A had made an *indirect* acquisition for $60,000, his tax basis would be *in the stock of XYZ, not in assets 1, 2, and 3.* The assets would still have their low tax basis ($1,000, $2,000, and $3,000),

FIGURE 8–1

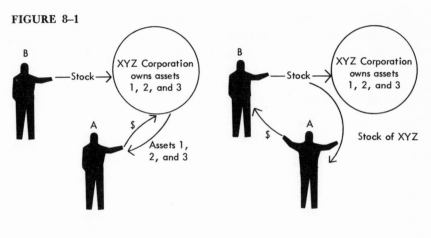

Direct acquisition   Indirect acquisition

and the taxable income of XYZ would be substantial in the future because it would have only very limited amounts of depreciation to deduct in future years. Under some questionable judicial authority, Taxpayer A *might* be able to liquidate the XYZ Corporation shortly after he acquired control over it and thereby transfer his higher ($60,000) basis from this stock to the assets.

This opportunity is guaranteed, under prescribed conditions, for corporate taxpayers acquiring a second (subsidiary) corporation in Code Section 334(b)(2). However, if any acquiring taxpayer does liquidate XYZ, it (XYZ) will have to recognize as taxable income the "paper gain" on assets 1, 2, and 3 in the year of liquidation. This would mean, of course, that XYZ would have to pay a corporate income tax on a $57,000 taxable income in its final year and the owner of XYZ would not find this solution of much help.

To summarize, if A understands the tax factors associated with an indirect acquisition of assets 1, 2, and 3, he would not under the circumstances described here be willing to pay $60,000 for 100 percent of the stock of XYZ even though he might be willing to pay that same amount for the assets acquired directly. The appropriate price reduction for an indirect acquisition would depend upon the kind of income—that is, capital gain or ordinary income—that would have to be recognized on the liquidation of XYZ and the marginal tax bracket of Taxpayer A. Observe also that under the reverse conditions—that is, when the fair market value of assets in less than their tax basis—an indirect acquisition may provide an economic benefit to the purchaser so that he may be willing to pay more than the apparent fair market value of the assets to acquire the tax advantage that would go along with an indirect acquisition.

Leasing fixed assets

A lease quite obviously provides a taxpayer with an opportunity to acquire the use of a fixed asset without acquiring other risks or benefits of ownership. In many instances the utilization of a lease in preference to other methods of acquisition is predicated upon financial considerations alone. A new company with limited capital, for example, may find the lease to be the only effective way to acquire certain assets. A leasing arrangement usually will prove to be more expensive than direct ownership because it must include a profit for the lessor. Thus, under many circumstances, the lease is less attractive to an established firm with large amounts of capital and adequate credit. However, even under these conditions, the tax consequence of a lease may make it more profitable than ownership.

Perhaps the easiest situation in which to demonstrate the potential tax value of a lease arrangement is in connection with land. If a taxpayer purchases land (for cash or on credit), he will not be entitled to any tax deduction for that investment until he disposes of the land since land is deemed to be a nonwasting asset. This means, of course, that a taxpayer may make a substantial real economic investment with no immediate tax benefit. We observed earlier that the chance to obtain a real economic profit usually increases if we can accelerate the timing of a tax deduction. Thus, a taxpayer may be inclined to lease land rather than to purchase it for tax reasons. The cost of a few hundred feet of ocean frontage in Miami Beach, Southern California, or New England might be prohibitive for anything but the largest hotel corporation. A lease arrangement, with attendant tax deductions for (land) rents paid, may change this financial requirement substantially.

The temptation for all taxpayers to disguise certain purchases through alleged lease arrangements has resulted in a close scrutiny of certain rent deductions by the IRS. If, for example, a document was written as a lease of land by providing for a series of 30 annual payments of $100,000 and giving the lessee the option, at the end of 30 years, to pay an additional $50,000 to acquire title to the land, the IRS would have no trouble in getting a court to agree that this contract was in reality a purchase agreement and in taxing it accordingly. On the other hand, if the same lease were written without the final option to purchase, or if that option were stated in realistic financial terms, the acquiring taxpayer would be entitled to immediate tax deductions for each lease payment made. The need for expert legal assistance in drafting lease arrangements, and thus in obtaining maximum tax deductions, must be obvious.

Constructing or otherwise creating fixed assets

A taxpayer sometimes will construct or otherwise create his own fixed asset simply because the particular asset which he desires is not already extant and he knows no one capable of making it for him. In other cases, a taxpayer will construct or create such an asset only because he believes that he can do it more cheaply himself. In many more situations, however, the primary reason for a taxpayer joining in a project to construct or otherwise create a fixed asset must be found in the peculiar tax treatment that will be accorded such a project. The most notable tax rules pertain to (1) the construction of an apartment house or other commercial building; (2) locating and developing a natural resource; and (3) land development and certain agricultural growth opportunities.

Constructing buildings. Many taxpayers prefer to join in the construction of a building, rather than buying an extant building, because of a few tax rules. First, during the often lengthy period of construction a building project typically incurs substantial losses. Major costs contributing to these losses are expenditures for interest and property taxes. If a taxpayer makes the proper elections, he will be entitled to deduct immediately both the interest and the taxes paid during construction. This treatment is contrary to the normal rule that requires a taxpayer to capitalize as part of the cost of a fixed asset all costs necessary to acquire the asset and to make it operative. The opportunity to deduct a cost immediately, especially when coupled with the demand for a minimal cash investment, is important for the reasons explained earlier in this chapter. In addition, as we will discover in the next section of this chapter, the most rapid depreciation methods authorized generally are restricted (a) to residential housing projects and (b) to initial owners. Once again, because taxpayers desire to accelerate tax deductions, there is good reason to prefer an investment in a new apartment project to many other investments.

Locating and developing oil and gas wells. The tax law provides that all *intangible* drilling and development costs associated with locating and developing an oil or gas well can be deducted immediately. These costs usually represent in the neighborhood of 80 percent of the cost of a producing well. The obvious benefit of the right to deduct 80 percent of an investment in a fixed asset explains one reason why these investments are far more attractive than many others to certain taxpayers.

It should be equally obvious that the right to an immediate tax deduction is *not* tantamount to the promise of an economic profit. The chance of drilling a dry hole is something like 8.5 to 1. And a dry hole is still essentially worthless to everyone. The tax law authorizes the deduction of any remaining costs associated with an attempt to locate and develop an oil or gas well when the drilling venture proves to be worthless. The right to immediately deduct the entire cost of a worthless venture, as well as a majority of the costs of a successful oil venture, serves to make oil and gas drilling ventures an attractive form of investment for high marginal bracket taxpayers. If things go badly for them, the government stands ready to share up to 70 percent of their losses (through tax savings to the investors). On the other hand, if things go well, the government still stands ready to share 70 percent of the initial cost but to demand, for reasons which will be explained later, as little as 25 to 35 percent of the final profits in income taxes.

In conclusion, in the oil and gas business, the risks are high. The wealthy taxpayer, however, might very well find the high risk to be preferable to other low risk forms of investment because of the liberal tax treatment of (1) the initial investment, (2) the income produced from a successful investment, and (3) the proceeds received on the disposition of an investment in mineral rights.

Land development and agricultural growth. In a series of special provisions the Code has tried to encourage investments in agriculture. The exact limitations of the several separate rules are again too detailed to justify our investigation of them. However, we should note in passing that under prescribed conditions the tax rules do authorize the immediate deduction of (*a*) soil and water conservation expenditures including ". . . levelling, grading and terracing, contour furrowing, . . . drainage ditches, earthen dams, watercourses, outlets, . . . and the planting of windbreaks"; (*b*) expenditures for fertilizer and ". . . other materials to enrich, neutralize, or condition land used in farming"; and (c) certain land clearing costs. Until the Tax Reform Act of 1969, the right to an immediate deduction usually was coupled with the right to claim a capital gain on the deferred disposition of the improved land. The double parlay of the immediate deduction of the expenditure against ordinary income, coupled with the deferred recognition of a long-term capital gain, served to increase the attractiveness of investments in agricultural land. The Reform Act reduced the popularity of these investments, however, by providing that some portion or all of the gain may have to be reported as ordinary income if the improved land is sold in less than ten years after the tax deduction is claimed. Taxpayers willing to wait the ten-year period retain many of the former benefits which, under the proper circumstances, can be very valuable.

A similar incentive to invest in livestock and citrus groves also existed prior to the 1969 Act. A large portion of such investments was immediately deductible as an expense of farming, while gains from the sale of those investments generally were turned into long-term capital gains by operation of Section 1231. Changes in the Reform Act tend to reduce substantially the possibility of a long-term capital gain from investments in either livestock or citrus groves and, therefore, their attractiveness recently has decreased. The chance to benefit from the present value differential of an immediate deduction and a deferred ordinary income remains viable. However, because of the relatively high economic risk associated with agricultural investments, the limited benefit of the present value differential is not usually sufficient to induce large investments in these assets. If a taxpayer can foresee a sudden and major downward shift in his ordinary marginal tax bracket, however, an investment in cattle could still provide substantial tax savings.

The investment credit

An investment tax credit was first introduced into the federal income tax in 1962; it was revised in 1964; suspended in 1966; reinstated in 1967; repealed in 1969; and reenacted in 1971. Given this checkered ten-year history, one is tempted to ignore the investment credit and to proceed with more stable aspects of our tax system. That temptation should be overcome solely because of the potential dollar significance of the investment tax credit in certain fixed asset acquisitions.

At the present time, the Code authorizes a taxpayer to claim as a tax credit an amount equal to seven percent of his investment in qualified property. In other words, if a taxpayer purchases qualified property at a cost of $10,000, the government will authorize him to reduce his actual income tax liability by $700 just because he made that investment. The real economic result of the investment credit is, quite obviously, tantamount to a seven percent reduction in the cost of a fully qualified asset. The only reason the government is willing to pick up such a large tab—in terms of lost revenues, this credit was estimated to have cost the government $3.6 billion in 1972 and to be even more in later years—is that investment spending is deemed to be a key variable in the way our economy performs. The threat of a recession in 1971 was responsible for the present credit. When the difference between a projected profit or loss on a fixed asset investment is small, an immediate seven percent tipping of the scales in favor of investment just may be sufficient to accomplish the intended objective.

Before a taxpayer can claim an investment tax credit he must make certain that his investment is made in a qualified property. In general qualified investments are of three types:

1. Tangible, nonreal property for which a depreciation deduction is authorized.
2. Tangible, real property *other than buildings and building components—*
    a. If used in manufacturing, producing, extracting, or furnishing a good or a utility service; or
    b. If the property constitutes a research or storage facility.
3. An elevator or an escalator.

Observe that the first category covers, among many other things, most factory and office equipment; automobiles, trucks, and airplanes; hotel and motel furnishings (similar furnishings in a nontransient apartment are usually made ineligible by other provisions of the Code); and even livestock used for draft, breeding, or dairy purposes. The second category includes blast furnaces, pipelines, tanks, and similar facilities but it specifically *excludes* all buildings and building components.

After a taxpayer determines that he has made a qualified investment, he must examine many additional rules to determine the exact amount of his investment tax credit. The second step in this determination usually involves the separation of qualified investments into one of four categories based upon the estimated useful life of the asset purchased. Only assets which are estimated to last seven years or longer are eligible for the full seven percent credit. The four possible categories are as follows:

Category	Estimated useful life	Fraction of cost deemed to constitute a qualified investment
1	Less than 3 years	0
2	3 to 5 years	$\frac{1}{3}$
3	5 to 7 years	$\frac{2}{3}$
4	7 years or longer	all

To illustrate this second step, assume that a taxpayer purchased qualifying property in each estimated life category at a cost of $6,000. His qualified investment tax credit would be computed as follows:

Category	Total investment	Qualified investment
1	$6,000	$ 0
2	6,000	2,000
3	6,000	4,000
4	6,000	6,000
Total qualified investment		$12,000 × 7 percent = $840.

Thus the taxpayer in this illustration could actually claim an investment tax credit of $840.

Even this cursory examination of the rules applicable to the investment tax credit suggests some planning opportunities. The following ideas are illustrative:

1. When in doubt, extend the estimated useful life to the next appropriate life estimate category. For example, if you think that an asset may last either four or five years, estimate five years and gain the additional tax credit. If a taxpayer initially underestimates the life of a fixed asset, he is never given the opportunity to go back and claim the larger credit on the longer life actually used.

2. Time purchases of qualified assets wisely. A tax credit can only be claimed when the tax return is filed. Given the present value of money, it makes eminent sense to purchase qualifying assets late in one tax year rather than early in the next year.

3. Select and install assets carefully. A built-in television set may constitute a building component in a motel and, thus, be ineligible for an investment credit. A mobile set would constitute a furnishing and qualify.

Other opportunities for tax planning are hidden in more esoteric rules that generally apply only to large taxpayers. There are, for example, annual limits on the amount of *used* property that can qualify for the investment credit ($50,000); there are other limits on the maximum credit that can be claimed in any single year; and there are still other rules disqualifying property used to furnish lodgings rented to nontransients. Every rule creates new pitfalls and new opportunities in slightly different situations. Large taxpayers, especially, must get advice before they act if they want to maximize their investment tax credit each year. In some years, certain dates become all important.

TAX FACTORS PERTINENT TO THE USE
OF FIXED ASSETS

After a taxpayer acquires a fixed asset, he typically encounters another series of tax considerations. The first major question that commonly arises involves the selection of a cost allocation method. If the fixed asset is a tangible fixed asset other than a natural resource, we refer to this cost allocation as "depreciation"; if it is a natural resource, as "depletion"; if an intangible asset, as "amortization." Because of the interaction of the tax rules and the present value concept, which was explained earlier in this chapter, a taxpayer typically wants to claim a maximum depreciation, depletion, or amortization deduction as quickly as possible for tax purposes. For financial accounting purposes, he may prefer just the opposite prescription: that is, for financial accounting he may prefer to defer these deductions as long as possible so that he may report a favorable financial income in the interim period. The need to report a maximum nontax income is increased in large, publicly owned corporations and in closely held corporations seeking external credit. Interestingly, a taxpayer is generally free to use one depreciation, depletion, or amortization method for tax purposes and a wholly different method for accounting purposes. The income reported to the government for income taxation is quite obviously, then, often a different and smaller figure than is the income reported to stockholders, which may be still different from the income reported to banks and other credit agencies. In this book we are interested only in the best tax alternatives.

Depreciation methods

Code Section 167(a) authorizes a deduction for depreciation in broad terms, as follows: "There shall be allowed as a depreciation deduction a reasonable allowance for the exhaustion, wear and tear (including a reasonable allowance for obsolescence)— (1) of property used in the trade or business, or (2) of property held for the production of income." The next subsection of the Code proceeds to authorize certain specific depreciation methods as "reasonable" methods under varying circumstances. The authorized methods include what are commonly known as a straight-line method and certain rapid methods. The rapid depreciation methods include all methods which provide a relatively larger depreciation deduction in the earlier years and a relatively smaller deduction in the later years of an asset's life. The most common rapid methods are the sum-of-the-years-digits method (SYD) and the declining balance methods.

Straight-line method. A straight-line depreciation method is one which allocates the total depreciable cost equally over the estimated life of an asset. Thus, if an asset has a tax basis of $10,000 and an estimated life of 10 years, straight-line depreciation would amount to $1,000 per year: that is, tax basis divided by estimated life equals straight-line depreciation. For tax purposes, it generally is acceptable to ignore estimated salvage values unless they are expected to exceed 10 percent of the cost of the fixed asset. Theoretically estimated lives are a question of fact to be determined in each specific instance by the taxpayer. In order to administer the depreciation provisions more uniformly and to reduce unnecessary conflicts, the IRS, in 1962, published tables which suggest specific lives as being reasonable estimates for thousands of specific properties. These IRS estimated lives are known as guideline lives. The guideline lives first divide all fixed assets into broad groups of properties and then subdivide them into industry classes. Finally, the government tables specify an estimated life for each category. Thus, for example, Group One includes all assets used by business in general; Group Two includes assets used in Nonmanufacturing Activities, Excluding Transportation, Communications, and Public Utilities, and so forth. Group One is next broken down into office furniture, fixtures, machines, and equipment (each of which is assigned an estimated life of 10 years); transportation equipment, land improvements, buildings, and so forth. The latter categories are further broken down into other subclasses. Under transportation equipment, for example, the subclasses include automobiles (with an estimated life of 3 years) and vessels and other water transportation equipment (with an estimated life of 18 years).

Early in 1971, the Nixon Administration further modified the existing guideline lives by authorizing a taxpayer, under specified conditions, to increase or decrease the previous life estimates by as much as 20 percent. This last modification, eventually approved by Congress, is properly referred to as the ADR (Asset Depreciation Range) system. Thus, ADR authorizes a taxpayer to utilize an estimated life as short as 8 years, or as long as 12 years, for any asset with an original guideline life of 10 years. Everyone anticipates that the vast majority of the taxpayers will opt for the shorter life, thus increasing their profit potential still more. The ADR reduction in estimated lives was, of course, another attempt to stimulate the economy through further increases in investment spending.

Sum-of-the-years-digits method. One of the popular rapid methods of depreciation authorized in the Code is the sum-of-the-years-digits (SYD) method. To determine a depreciation deduction for a particular year using this method, a taxpayer must know (1) the adjusted basis of the asset, (2) the number of years of estimated remaining life of the asset as of the first of the year, and (3) the *sum* of the total years estimated originally. To illustrate this method, let us determine the SYD depreciation for an asset which had an adjusted basis of $10,000 (initially) and an estimated life of 5 years (initially). Before we can determine the depreciation for any year we must find the sum of $5 + 4 + 3 + 2 + 1$, which is 15. Knowing that sum we can find the depreciation for any year as follows:

Year 1: $\frac{5}{15} \times \$10,000$, or $3,333;
Year 2: $\frac{4}{15} \times \$10,000$, or $2,667;
Year 3: $\frac{3}{15} \times \$10,000$, etc.

Obviously the SYD method yields a larger depreciation deduction in the early years of the asset's life than does the straight-line method.

Declining balance method. Another popular form of rapid depreciation is known as a declining balance method. In this method a fixed percent is multiplied by a declining adjusted basis of the asset to determine any year's depreciation deduction. The constant percent to be used depends upon (1) the estimated life of the asset and (2) the particular variant of the declining balance method being used. The Code authorizes a 200 percent declining balance method (also called "double declining balance" or DDB); a 150 percent declining balance method; and a 125 percent declining balance method. To determine the constant percent, the taxpayer must first determine the straight-line *rate* of depreciation for the asset. The straight-line rate is the percent obtained by dividing the asset's original estimated life into the number 1. Thus the straight-line rate for an asset with an estimated life of 20 years is 5 percent ($\frac{1}{20}$); for a 10 year life, 10 percent ($\frac{1}{10}$); and for a 5-year life, 20 percent ($\frac{1}{5}$). Once the straight-line rate has been determined, the taxpayer can readily convert to the desired declining balance constant by multiplying the stipulated percent by the straight-line rate. In other words, the constant fraction for a 200 percent declining balance method when applied to an asset with a 5-year life is 40 percent—200 percent of 20 percent. The constant fraction for a 150 percent declining balance method, applied to an asset with a 5-year life, is 30 percent—150 percent of 20 percent.

A comparison of results. A comparison of the depreciation deduction as determined under (1) the straight-line method, (2) the sum-of-the-years-digits method, and (3) the 200 percent declining balance method is made in Table 8–1. This is based upon an assumed asset costing $10,000, having an estimated life of ten years, and having no salvage value. A brief review of Table 8–1 would reveal that the 200 percent declining balance method yields the largest depreciation deduction in the first year but the least over a 10-year period. The sum-of-the-years-digits method provides the second largest deduction in the first year and, like the straight-line method, allocates the total cost over the estimated useful life of the asset. The straight-line method provides the smallest deduction in the first year. If the 150 percent declining balance method and the 125 percent declining balance method were added to this table, they would, of course, lie between the straight-line method and the SYD method in terms of the size of the first year's deduction.

Generally speaking, a taxpayer is free to switch from any rapid depreciation method to the straight-line method at any time. He cannot, however, switch in the opposite direction without the consent of the IRS. A taxpayer usually will switch to the straight-line method if the change will provide him with a larger deduction than would

TABLE 8–1
A comparison of the depreciation deduction determined under three common depreciation methods

Year	Straight-line method		Sum-of-the-years-digits method		200% declining balance method	
	Deduction for year	Adjusted basis on January 1	Deduction for year	Adjusted basis on January 1	Deduction for year	Adjusted basis on January 1
1 . . .	$ 1,000	$10,000	$ 1,818	$10,000	$2,000	$10,000
2 . . .	1,000	9,000	1,636	8,182	1,600	8,000
3 . . .	1,000	8,000	1,454	6,546	1,280	6,400
4 . . .	1,000	7,000	1,273	5,092	1,024	5,120
5 . . .	1,000	6,000	1,091	3,820	819	4,096
6 . . .	1,000	5,000	909	2,730	655	3,277
7 . . .	1,000	4,000	727	1,821	524	2,622
8 . . .	1,000	3,000	545	1,094	420	2,098
9 . . .	1,000	2,000	364	549	326	1,678
10 . . .	1,000	1,000	183	186	270	1,352
Total . .	$10,000		$10,000		$8,918	

continuation under the old method. In Table 8–1, for example, a taxpayer initially electing the 200 percent declining balance method would be likely to switch to the straight-line method in the seventh year because that would increase his authorized depreciation deduction from the scheduled $524 to $655; that is, the $2,622 remaining basis is divided by four years' remaining life. By making this change on a timely basis, the taxpayer would also insure his right to deduct the full $10,000 cost rather than the $8,918 shown in Table 8–1.

Depreciation method restrictions

A taxpayer is not free to apply any depreciation method that he wishes to any investment in a fixed asset. The current rules provide that, under most circumstances, for assets acquired after July 24, 1969, a taxpayer cannot claim a depreciation deduction that would be larger in amount than one determined according to the method indicated in Table 8–2. If the reader understands the present value notions introduced earlier in this chapter, it will be easy for him to review the restrictions stated in Table 8–2 and, thus, identify yet another reason for the conclusion that investments in certain assets may be preferred to investments in other assets by high marginal bracket taxpayers. For example, the reader should now understand more clearly why many taxpayers continue to look at investments in furnished residential rental units as a preferred form of investment. Very

173

TABLE 8–2
Depreciation method limitations applicable to fixed assets acquired after July 24, 1969

Type of property	Maximum depreciation method authorized
Depreciable tangible property other than buildings	
If the property is new	200% declining balance
If the property is used	150% declining balance
Depreciable buildings	
If residential rental property	
Acquired new.	200% declining balance or SYD
Acquired used with an estimated remaining life of 20 years or more	125% declining balance
Acquired used with an estimated remaining life of less than 20 years	Straight line
If other than residential property	
Acquired new.	150% declining balance
Acquired used	Straight line
All intangible property.	Straight line

few other opportunities provide for such a large depreciation deduction so quickly.

Other special rules related to depreciation

Even though this book makes no pretense at being comprehensive, a brief look at two related and special rules seems to be appropriate. One of these rules authorizes an extra first-year depreciation deduction which may be of particular interest to small taxpayers. The other rules, commonly known as the rapid amortization provisions, are of greater interest to the large investors.

First-year depreciation deduction. In addition to the regularly authorized depreciation deduction discussed above, every taxpayer can claim an additional first-year depreciation deduction if he purchases qualifying property. Any investment in tangible personal property (that is, nonrealty) acquired after 1957, with an estimated life of six years or longer, is eligible for this special 20 percent deduction. The maximum deduction authorized under this special provision is $2,000 per taxpayer per year. In other words, a taxpayer can claim the first-year deduction only on the first $10,000 (cost) of qualifying property purchased in any year—20 percent of $10,000 yields the $2,000 maximum. On the joint return of a married taxpayer, this can be increased to $4,000 because both the husband and the wife are deemed to be taxpayers on the joint return. If the taxpayer claims the special first-year deduction, the adjusted basis utilized in determining the depreciation deduction under the regular provisions must be adjusted downward accordingly. In other words, if a married taxpayer filing a joint return purchased qualifying property at a cost of $20,000 and he utilized the 200 percent declining balance method of depreciation on a ten-year life, his calculations would be made as follows:

```
First year
    Special deduction (20% × $20,000) . . . . . .  $4,000
    Regular DDB deduction on remaining basis
        (20% × $16,000). . . . . . . . . . . . . . .    3,200
            Total depreciation deduction authorized
                in first year. . . . . . . . . . . . . . . .  $7,200
Second year
    Regular DDB deduction (20% × $12,800) . .  $2,560
```

The important effect of this special deduction provision is to allow the taxpayer a quicker-than-normal recovery of his investment which tends to increase the profitability of making an investment.

Rapid amortization provisions. In a limited number of cases, the tax rules authorize the deduction of an investment in a particular fixed asset over a 60-month period without reference to any of the usual rules. The restricting conditions on each of these investments vary substantially; however, the special rules presently are all scheduled to expire on December 31, 1974. Expenditures which generally qualify for this special 5-year amortization include investments in: (1) low-income-housing rehabilitation projects; (2) certified pollution control devices; (3) railroad rolling stock; and (4) coal mine safety devices. Because these four provisions are of restricted application they will not be investigated further here. The important effect of the rapid recovery of an investment through a special tax deduction is intended to increase investments in these assets by making them more profitable for the few investors who take advantage of the special provisions. Hopefully, the increased investments would also help to cure certain social ills.

Depletion methods

As minerals are extracted from the ground and sold, a taxpayer owning an economic interest in the mineral rights is entitled to recover his investment through a depletion deduction. Except for the fact that an extracted mineral cannot be restored by human action, a depletion deduction effectively provides for a replacement of basic capital in the same manner that the depreciation deduction does. In an operational sense, however, depletion and depreciation are radically different because the Code authorizes a method of depletion, called "statutory depletion," which may continue to provide a tax deduction even though the adjusted basis of the investment has been wholly recovered in prior periods. The alternative method, called "cost depletion," does *not* provide that same opportunity.

Cost depletion. Cost depletion effectively guarantees the right of a taxpayer to recover his original investment in a mineral property, assuming production. To illustrate this cost recovery technique, we will consider the tax factors associated with a $500,000 investment in a mineral venture. If, as usual, the intangible drilling and development costs approximate 80 percent of the investment, this taxpayer will have recovered $400,000 of his initial $500,000 investment as an immediate tax deduction in the first year. He has a $100,000 investment remaining which he is entitled to recover from the production proceeds without further tax. This recovery is accomplished through the depletion deduction. If the engineers estimate that the mineral deposit contains 500,000 barrels of oil (or cubic feet of gas), the taxpayer can deduct 20 cents for each barrel of oil extracted and sold. The $100,000 unrecovered tax basis is divided by the 500,000 estimated barrels of oil to determine a cost depletion allowance of 20 cents per barrel. When the well is exhausted, the taxpayer will have recovered taxwise his entire investment: $400,000 as an immediate deduction for intangible drilling and development costs and $100,000 as cost depletion over the productive life of the well. If the initial estimates of the mineral deposit prove to be erroneous, an appropriate adjustment must be made to the cost depletion allowance. Under all circumstances, however, the effect of *cost* depletion is to guarantee the taxpayer's right to recover only his total investment, and not a dollar more.

Percentage depletion. The tax magic of the percentage depletion deduction is that it is *not* restricted to the unrecovered cost of an investment in a mineral deposit in terms of the total dollar amounts that can be deducted. Percentage depletion may go on and on and provide a lucky taxpayer with a tax deduction that is many multiples of his unrecovered investment if the well continues to produce. This tax distinction of percentage depletion is of major economic significance to potential investors.

Technically, the percentage depletion deduction is determined by multiplying (1) a statutory rate times (2) the gross income from the mineral property. The statutory rate varies from one mineral to the next. The Code currently authorizes a rate of 22 percent for oil and gas wells and for sulphur and uranium deposits; a rate of 15 percent for gold, silver, oil shale, and copper; a rate of 5 percent for gravel, sand, and other minerals; and many other statutory rates for many other minerals. Because we are interested only in the principle of percentage depletion, we will utilize a 22 percent rate in the remaining illustrations. The "gross income from the property" is usually an estimated value or a posted price of a mineral in its crude state, before transportation and refining have increased its value. Thus, if an oil well produced $50,000 in gross income in a particular year, the taxpayer with the rights to that production would be entitled to claim a percentage depletion deduction of $11,000 (22 percent of $50,000). Incidentally, a taxpayer can always claim cost depletion if it is larger than percentage depletion.

Percentage depletion is limited, however, in that it cannot exceed 50 percent of the *net* income from the property in any particular year. This rule effectively sets a ceiling on statutory depletion which will come into play in high-cost operations. If, for example, the $50,000 gross income produced for the taxpayer in the previous illustration required a $40,000 expense to obtain it, percentage depletion would be reduced from the apparent $11,000 determined earlier to $5,000, that is, to 50 percent of ($50,000–$40,000).

Because of the net income limitation, a complex series of rules is brought into consideration in some circumstances. Note that both percentage depletion and the net income limitation are based upon the gross or net income *from the property*. Exactly what are the definitional bounds of "the property"? Is each well a "separate property"? Are all wells on a single lease "a property"? Must all wells on one lease be combined or can they be treated separately? If contiguous leases are obtained at the same time, can wells on different leases be combined? Must they be combined? Is the date of the lease significant? The answers to these and many other related questions are much too complex to state here. The reader should simply observe that, when allowed, certain combinations may prove to be very valuable, taxwise. The two illustrations below amply demonstrate this conclusion, which, like so many other tax opportunities, turns on definitional considerations.

TABLE 8–3
These two wells should be combined and treated as one property if possible

Well no.	Gross income	Net income	Percentage depletion	
			If separate	If combined
1	$100,000	$10,000	$ 5,000	
				$27,000
2	100,000	80,000	22,000	
1 + 2	$200,000	$90,000		$44,000

TABLE 8–4
These two wells should not be combined and treated as one property if possible

Well no.	Gross income	Net income (loss)	Percentage depletion	
			If separate	If combined
1	$100,000	($20,000)	$ 0	
				$15,000
2	100,000	30,000	15,000	
	$200,000	$10,000		$5,000

In summary, the tax advantages associated with the *use* of an investment in mineral properties (that is, during the production period) stem from the fact that the taxpayer may claim percentage depletion in excess of the unrecovered tax basis. Before this opportunity is meaningful, however, the taxpayer must have (1) invested in a producing well that (2) can be operated commercially at a reasonable cost so that the net income limitation does not come into play. The final tax factors pertinent to such an investment involve disposition considerations. Before we turn to disposition factors, we must examine briefly one remaining tax problem associated with the use of fixed assets.

Expenditures during use—repair or improvement?

After a taxpayer begins to use a fixed asset, he typically will incur a number of expenses presenting additional tax difficulties. Expenditures in the nature of routine repairs are quite properly deducted immediately; expenditures in the nature of capital improvements are to be added to an asset account and recovered through subsequent cost allocation provisions. At the extreme, the difference between such expenses is easy to illustrate. For example, the gasoline used in an automobile is, quite obviously, a deductible expense. A major overhaul of an automobile is an equally obvious capital expenditure. The problem, of course, lies with all of those intermediate expenditures such as new tires, paint jobs, and minor overhauls. Are they immediately deductible, or must they be capitalized and recovered through depreciation? The classification problem with buildings is greater than with automobiles because of the major differences in estimated lives, potential changes in use, dollar amounts involved, and related values. Yet the need to distinguish between an expense and a capital expenditure is common to the use of all fixed assets.

In this problem area, as in the area of depreciation, the taxpayer may want to make one election for tax purposes and another for financial accounting purposes. The usual answer, naturally, is to expense as much as you can for tax purposes but to capitalize much of it for accounting purposes. To a limited extent, the different treatment is possible, although the right of the taxpayer to differentiate here is not as clear cut as it is in the case of depreciation.

The reader should simply be aware that one of the tax benefits which will attach to his election to report depreciation deductions under the new ADR (asset depreciation range) system is the right to use new percentage repair allowances. Stated very crudely, what the new rules do is provide the taxpayer with a dollar range—determined by administratively stated percentages and the taxpayer's total dollar investment in certain fixed assets—within which the IRS agent cannot challenge the taxpayer's treatment of repair-type expenditures. In other words, as long as the expenditure was not for a specifically excluded addition, an IRS agent cannot challenge a taxpayer's decision to expense a certain item, rather than to capitalize it, as long as that expenditure does not exceed the prescribed dollar limitations.

TAX FACTORS PERTINENT TO THE DISPOSITION OF FIXED ASSETS

The tax factors associated with the disposition of a fixed asset can be classified into three basic areas. The first and most important factor is classification of the gain or loss realized on disposition as a capital or an ordinary gain or loss. The second factor involves the potential recapture of an earlier investment tax credit. The third factor relates to each of the first two in that it considers alternative ways of disposing of a fixed asset in order that the taxpayer might influence the character of the gain or loss or the need to recapture the investment credit. Fortunately we have considered each of these problems elsewhere in this book and only a brief review is necessary here.

Capital gain or ordinary income?

Chapter 5 includes a discussion of the definitional problems associated with capital gains and losses. Table 5–1 adequately summarizes the most probable tax treatment of the gains and losses typically realized on the sale or exchange of a fixed asset used in a trade or business. As demonstrated in the first section of this chapter, that distinction has a major impact on the profitability of many fixed asset investments. What the taxpayer usually seeks, of course, is a long-term capital gain on disposition. The likelihood of a capital gain is common to the following assets:

1. All "pure" capital assets per the statutory definition;
2. Any depreciable *real* properties used in a trade or business *if:*
    a. The gain can be attributed to the land;
    b. The gain can be attributed to a building or building component *and* that building was depreciated on a straight-line method;
    c. The gain can be attributed to residential rental property *and* the property was owned for more than 16 years and 8 months. (Note: If the residential rental property was held for more than 10 years and less than 16 years and 8 months some portion of the gain will be ordinary income and some portion will be capital gain.)
3. Any gain associated with a mineral right *if* the disposition is complete and the transaction is worded properly.

Most other dispositions of fixed assets will produce ordinary income rather than capital gain.

Investment credit recapture

If a taxpayer originally estimates that a fixed asset will be used for a longer time period than it is actually used, he may have to recover part or all of the investment credit claimed in an earlier year. On page 167 we noted the critical importance of the estimated life of an asset to the amount of the investment tax credit that could be claimed. If a taxpayer estimates a longer life and disposes of the asset in a shorter time, he must recalculate the correct investment credit based upon the actual holding period and repay the government any difference between the original amount claimed and the revised amount.

To illustrate, let us assume that a taxpayer purchased qualified assets costing $6,000 and that he estimated the life of these assets at seven years. Based on his initial estimate the taxpayer would claim an investment tax credit of $420. If, after five years of use, the taxpayer disposed of that same asset, he would know that the proper amount of the investment credit should have been $280. In the year in which the taxpayer makes this disposition, he must add $140 to his tax liability to recapture the investment credit erroneously claimed in the earlier year. Incidentally, the taxpayer need not pay interest or penalty on this additional tax liability; thus, he has effectively had an interest-free loan from the government in the interim.

In a few instances, a taxpayer might be able to delay a disposition for a very brief period and thereby avoid the need to recapture any investment credit. The need for detailed records is obvious. Finally, the reader should observe that the term disposition covers many events in addition to the obvious sale or exchange.

Form of disposition

Just as a taxpayer can change the tax consequences associated with the acquisition of a fixed asset by changing the form of the acquisition, so he can also change the tax consequences associated with a disposition. In Chapter 6 we noted how a taxpayer might convert a potential ordinary income into capital gain by (a) transferring assets into a corporation and then selling the corporate stock or (b) converting a property from business to personal use on a timely basis. Unintended dispositions, through casualty or theft, initially create the usual tax problems associated with all other dispositions. However, special rules often apply to alleviate the tax burdens which might attach to an unintended disposition if the taxpayer makes certain elections on a timely basis. Some of these options will be considered in the next chapter. Finally, the reader should observe that it may be desirable to modify his intended disposition plans at least temporarily to achieve certain desirable tax consequences. For example, instead of selling a fixed asset, a taxpayer may be able to lease it to another and thereby modify his holding period or change the year of reporting so that his tax benefits can be maximized. The number of alternatives is almost unlimited and a good imagination combined with some knowledge of the tax rules (directly or through an advisor) can occasionally pay handsome dividends.

AN ILLUSTRATIVE COMPARISON OF TAX EFFECTS ON INVESTMENT DECISIONS

The multiple interrelationships between tax rules and economic benefits make understanding even a relatively simple illustration difficult. Nevertheless, if a reader is to understand the potential impact of the several tax rules studied in this chapter, it seems necessary to attempt a meaningful comparison. To do this, let us assume that a taxpayer invests $100,000 cash in an unincorporated venture and that this venture produces nothing the first year, but that, for the next five years, it generates a new cash flow of $20,000 and that it incurs additional cash expenses of $10,000. This leaves the venture with $10,000 excess cash which is returned to the investor in each of the next five years. Finally, let us assume that at the end of the six-year period the investor sells his rights in the venture for $80,000. *If we exclude all tax considerations* the initial projections might look something like this:

Year	Item	Cash in	Cash out
1	Initial investment		$100,000
2	Excess cash generated by new investment . . .	$ 10,000	
3	Same as year 2.	10,000	
4	Same as year 2.	10,000	
5	Same as year 2.	10,000	
6	Same as year 2.	10,000	
6	Sale of investment	80,000	
	Totals	$130,000	$100,000
	Net before-tax profit	$30,000	

If a person were totally unaware of the interface between tax rules and the profit concept, he might conclude simply that the investor in this situation could simply multiply the before-tax profit by his marginal tax rate to determine the tax effect and then, by simple subtraction, determine the net after-tax profit. In other words, if this were an investor in the 60 percent marginal tax bracket, the reader might conclude that the income tax on the $30,000 profit would total $18,000 and that the after-tax profit would be $12,000. Whether or not the taxpayer should proceed with the investment would then depend upon whether or not he would be satisfied with that minimal after-tax return on an investment of $100,000 for six years. An application of the actual tax rules and the present-value calculations would provide a more accurate analysis and would permit the investor to make a better decision.

The appendix tables to this chapter contain three projections based on the facts mentioned in the two previous paragraphs. The only additional fact assumed is that the taxpayer pays a marginal tax rate of 30 percent on all long-term capital gains. In Table A–1 the investment is made in used industrial equipment; in Table A–2 it is made in a new apartment house; in Table A–3 it is made in a successful oil well. A comparison of the net results on a non-discounted basis, but giving full consideration to all tax rules, is as follows:

	Equipment	Apartment	Oil well
Non-discounted after-tax profit......	$14,333	$12,000	$37,200

It is interesting to observe that the results for the apartment project coincide with the more simplistic solution suggested earlier so long as one ignores discounted present values. The modification in the solution for equipment is largely attributable to the investment tax credit. The major difference in the oil well investment in this illustration is attributable to the capital gain treatment on the sale—percentage depletion has only minimal effect on these results because the total depletion recovered exceeds the tax basis by only $6,400 in five years.

If we finally assume that this investor would demand no less than a five percent after-tax rate of return on his capital before he would make an investment, the comparisons on a discounted basis become much more meaningful. The discounted present value comparisons are as follows:

	Equipment	Apartment	Oil well
Discounted present value of after-tax profit or (loss).....	($4,808)	($5,638)	$20,624

These comparisons suggest that the investor should *not* proceed with plans to invest in either the equipment or the apartment house based on the prospectus of profits and giving full consideration to all tax laws *if* the investor really demands a five percent after-tax return on his investments. The oil well investment quite obviously will more than satisfy this investor's demands if the profit prospectus proves to be accurate.

In summary, this comparison should have demonstrated to the reader that tax rules must be given careful consideration in making investment decisions. The three illustrative cases used in this comparison are not grossly unrealistic. One cannot generalize from this single comparison, however, because the results will vary substantially depending upon how we slant the illustration in terms of absolute gains and losses as well as how we distribute the proceeds from an investment between interim income and final disposition gain. The time factor can also modify the results significantly. In this comparison, for example, the benefit of the rapid depreciation implicit in the apartment project was not sufficient to override the benefit of the investment credit in the machine. The results are also biased by the fact that the illustration demands an immediate cash outlay of $100,000; many investment projects, including most apartment projects, do not require such a large initial cash outlay because of unique leverage opportunities. The importance of this comparison lies solely in its ability to demonstrate the critical nature of tax rules to investment decisions.

APPENDIX

TABLE A–1
Investment in used machinery ($70,000 purchase price—$30,000 rehabilitation costs)

Year	Item	Non-discounted cash inflow or equivalent	Non-discounted cash outflow	Discounted cash inflow or equivalent	Discounted cash outflow
1	Initial investment		$100,000		$100,000
1	Investment credit ($50,000 maximum for used prop.)	$ 3,500		$ 3,500	
2	Excess cash generated by new investment	10,000		9,524	
2	Taxes saved on loss reported (after depreciation)	3,000		2,857	
3	Excess cash generated by new investment	10,000		9,070	
3	Taxes saved on loss reported	1,650		1,497	
4	Excess cash generated by new investment	10,000		8,638	
5	Taxes saved on loss reported	503		435	
5	Excess cash generated by new investment	10,000		8,227	
5	Taxes paid on gain reported		473		389
6	Excess cash generated by new investment	10,000		7,835	
6	Taxes paid on gain reported		1,302		1,020
6	Sale of investment	80,000		62,682	
6	Taxes paid on sale of investment		21,378		16,750
6	Recapture of investment tax credit		1,167		914
	Totals	$138,653	$124,320	$114,265	$119,073
			Discounted @ 5%		
	Net profit or (loss) after taxes	Non-discounted $14,333			($4,808)

Major tax rules applicable in this illustration;

a. Investment credit is available but to maximum amount because of used property and partial recovery required.
b. Maximum depreciation that can be claimed is 150 percent declining balance because property is used.
c. Entire gain on sale of investment will be ordinary income due to Section 1245.

TABLE A-2
Investment in new apartment dwelling

Year	Item	Non-discounted cash inflow or equivalent	Non-discounted cash outflow	Discounted cash inflow or equivalent	Discounted cash outflow
1	Initial investment.		$100,000		$100,000
1	Taxes saved on ($10,000) interest and property taxes during construction.	$ 6,000		$ 6,000	
2	Excess cash generated by new investment.	10,000		9,524	
2	Taxes saved on loss reported (after deprec.).	4,800		4,571	
3	Excess cash generated by new investment.	10,000		9,070	
3	Taxes saved on loss reported.	2,640		2,395	
4	Excess cash generated by new investment.	10,000		8,638	
4	Taxes saved on loss reported.	912		788	
5	Excess cash generated by new investment.	10,000		8,227	
5	Taxes paid on gain reported.		470		387
6	Excess cash generated by new investment.	10,000		7,835	
6	Taxes paid on gain reported.		1,576		1,235
6	Sale of investment.	80,000		62,682	
6	Taxes paid on sale of investment.		30,306		23,746
	Totals.	$144,352	$132,352	$119,730	$125,368
	Net profit or (loss) after taxes. . . . . . . Non-discounted	$12,000		Discounted @ 5%	($5,638)

Major tax rules applicable in this illustration:
a. Assumed that $10,000 of initial $100,000 investment could be deducted in first tax period as interest and/or property taxes.
b. Maximum depreciation that can be claimed is 200 percent declining balance because property is *new*, *residential* property.
c. Entire gain on sale of investment will be ordinary income due to Section 1250.
d. No portion of the investment is eligible for the investment credit.

TABLE A–3
Investment in oil well

Year	Item	Non-discounted cash inflow or equivalent	Non-discounted cash outflow	Discounted cash inflow or equivalent	Discounted cash outflow
1	Initial investment		$100,000		$100,000
1	Taxes saved on immediate deduction of intangible drilling and development costs	$ 48,000		$ 48,000	
2	Excess cash generated by new investment	10,000		9,524	
2	Taxes paid on gain reported (after depletion)		3,360		3,200
3	Excess cash generated by new investment	10,000		9,070	
3	Taxes paid on gain reported		3,360		3,048
4	Excess cash generated by new investment	10,000		8,638	
4	Taxes paid on gain reported		3,360		2,902
5	Excess cash generated by new investment	10,000		8,277	
5	Taxes paid on gain reported		3,360		2,764
6	Excess cash generated by new investment	10,000		7,835	
6	Taxes paid on gain reported		3,360		2,633
6	Sale of investment	80,000		62,682	
6	Taxes paid on sale of investment		24,000		
	Totals	$178,000	$140,800	$153,976	18,805
					$133,352
	Net profit or (loss) after taxes....... Non-discounted		$37,200	Discounted @ 5%	$20,624

Major tax rules applicable in this illustration:

a. Assumed that $80,000 of initial $100,000 investment could be deducted in first tax period as intangible drilling and development cost.

b. Percentage depletion is allowed and claimed in each year—22 percent of $20,000.

c. No portion of the investment is eligible for the investment credit. (This assumption is questionable.)

d. Entire gain on sale of investment will be long-term capital gain due to Section 1231.

9

The nontaxable transactions

In chapter 2, we noted that realization is a necessary condition to the recognition of a profit for income tax purposes. In addition, we observed there that virtually any change in the form or the substance of a property or property right may be sufficient to constitute realization as far as the tax laws are concerned. This chapter examines a number of special statutory exceptions to the general rule that income must be recognized for tax purposes as soon as it has been realized. These special exceptions are commonly referred to as the nontaxable transactions.

The importance of the nontaxable transaction to business management derives from the fact that postponement of the date on which a tax is due allows a taxpayer to keep a larger amount of capital at work for him for a longer period of time. Other things being equal, this increases the absolute amount of capital which an entrepreneur can accumulate and manage over a lifetime. For example, if a taxpayer invested in a particular property which has substantially increased in value, he may be reluctant to dispose of that investment even though he is *not* satisfied with its present financial performance and even though he can identify several better investment opportunities right now. If this taxpayer were to dispose of his initial investment, he would immediately have to pay an income tax on the entire unrealized gain, and he would then be able to reinvest only the after-tax proceeds in the new opportunity.

To illustrate the importance of the tax factors to an investment decision, consider the situation in which an investor has a tax basis of $10,000 in an asset presently worth $110,00 and which is generating an annual $6,600 income (that is, a 6 percent return based on present worth). If the taxpayer is in a 35 percent marginal tax bracket, as far as the gain on this investment is concerned, he would have to pay an income tax of $35,000 if he were to dispose of the old property. After paying the income tax, the investor would have only $75,000 to reinvest in a new property. Accordingly, the new investment would have to provide an annual return of more than 8.8 percent before it could be considered preferable to the initial investment (i.e., $6,600 divided by $75,000 equals .088). Investment opportunities which would yield a return of 7, 8, or even 8.5 percent would have to be rejected in favor of the extant 6 percent return simply because of the tax consequences. The increase required in the new return depends importantly on: (1) the absolute amount of the unrealized (or "paper") gain; (2) the marginal tax rate which would be applied to that gain; and (3) the present return on the investment. In general, the larger the amount of the paper gain, the higher the marginal tax rate, and the higher the present return, the greater the increase that will be required to make the change.

If one understands how important these tax factors are to investment decisions, it is easy to understand why knowledgeable business managers and investors are most interested in the nontaxable exchange provisions of the Code. Before we begin to examine any of the specifics of the several statutory provisions, however, we need to consider a few characteristics common to all of the nontaxable transactions.

COMMON CHARACTERISTICS OF
NONTAXABLE TRANSACTIONS

The detailed requirements of each of the several statutory provisions that authorize a nontaxable transaction vary substantially. Some of the provisions are mandatory if the prescribed conditions are met while others are elective under all circumstances. Some apply to gains only; others apply equally to gains and losses. Some demand a direct exchange—that is, a barter transaction involving no cash—whereas others allow a taxpayer to pass through a temporary cash position providing that he completes the reinvestment within a prescribed time period. In spite of the many differences, all of the nontaxable transactions commonly share a "boot" requirement, a transfer of tax basis, and a time constraint. In this first section of Chapter 9, we will consider these common characteristics so that the subsequent discussions of specific provisions can proceed with minimal attention to the general characteristics.

Potential need to recognize some gain

The term "nontaxable transaction" is commonly used to refer to transactions that are partially taxable as well as those that are wholly free from any immediate income tax. To be entirely free of any income tax, a taxpayer involved in a nontaxable transaction generally cannot *receive* anything except *qualified property*. Observe that a taxpayer *may* be able to *give* nonqualifying property and still not be subject to tax; he simply cannot receive such property. Exactly which property will pass as a qualifying property varies from one nontaxable exchange to the next; in all nontaxable exchanges, however, it is common to refer to any nonqualified property as boot. Cash is, of course, the most frequently encountered form of boot. Finally, observe that the tax consequences to one party to a transaction need not be determined by the tax consequences to the other party to the same transaction. In other words, a single transaction may create wholly taxable ordinary income for one party and be a wholly nontaxable transaction for the other party to the same transaction.

The fundamental concepts common to nontaxable exchanges that have been stated thus far can be illustrated by use of a simple diagram, as in Figure 9–1. Knowing nothing further about the transaction than

FIGURE 9–1

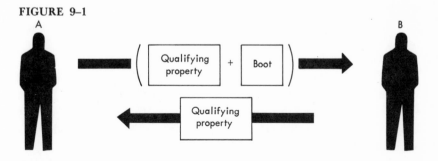

what is shown in the preceding illustration, we can safely make the following tax conclusions:

1. The transaction generally *cannot* be wholly tax free to B because he received boot.

190

2. The transaction may be wholly tax free to A even though he gave boot.
3. A's tax consequences are not necessarily affected by B's.
4. B's tax consequences are not necessarily affected by A's.

The need to recognize taxable income in any transaction is always dependent upon the presence of a gain. To determine whether or not a gain is present, we must apply the tax rules stated beginning on page 91. Although the rules stated there were worded in terms of capital assets, they are equally applicable to all assets. A taxable profit is simply the difference between (a) the fair market value (FMV) of everything received in a transaction and (b) the adjusted tax basis of everything given up in that same transaction. No taxpayer ever needs to recognize for income tax purposes more gain than he has realized. To give meaning to these sentences, let us return to our simple diagram and add some assumed values to that illustration, as shown in Figure 9–2. In this modified illustration, A's gain realized

FIGURE 9–2

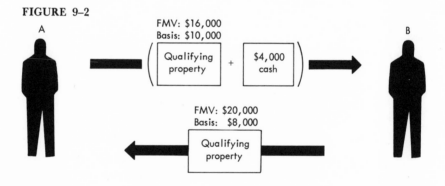

is $6,000; that is, $20,000 in value was received (we call this the "amount realized") and $14,000 in tax basis was given up ($10,000 in qualifying property and $4,000 cash); hence, $20,000 − $14,000 = $6,000. By applying the same determination method, we find that B's gain realized is $12,000 (i.e., $20,000 − $8,000). If this particular transaction qualifies under one of the special statutory provisions that will be examined later in this chapter, it means that A would *not have to recognize any of the $6,000 gain that he had realized*. If the same transaction also qualifies as a nontaxable exchange for B, it means that B *must recognize only $4,000 of the $12,000 gain realized* because of the boot.

Observe again, however, that a taxpayer need never recognize more gain than he has realized. In other words, if in this transaction B's adjusted tax basis in the property given to A had been $18,000 instead of $8,000, then B's realized and recognized gain is reduced to $2,000 notwithstanding the fact that B received $4,000 cash. Although this rule is often confusing to the uninitiated taxpayer first encountering the nontaxable exchange rules, his problem is really one of being caught up in words rather than in complexity. Note what would have happened if B had simply sold his qualifying property to someone for $20,000 cash. If his basis were $18,000, he would report only a $2,000 taxable income. Why, then, should the tax answer be different if instead of selling the property for cash a taxpayer trades it for another property plus cash? Obviously it should not be different—and that is what the rule stated accomplishes. The fact that there may be more cash than gain realized in an exchange simply means that the taxpayer is getting a partial return of capital as well as realizing a profit on the exchange.

Transfer of basis

The apparent intent of the law in all nontaxable exchanges is to provide for only a postponement of an income tax rather than a permanent forgiveness of that tax. The postponement is accomplished through related provisions which require that a taxpayer assume a "carryover" tax basis in any property acquired in a nontaxable exchange. The law assumes that sooner or later the taxpayer will dispose of any property in a taxable transaction and that he will, at that time, report as taxable income the difference between the value received and the basis carried over from the prior property. In the case of an individual taxpayer, this may be an invalid assumption since individuals often die with appreciated property. You will recall from the discussion in Chapter 5 that a deceased taxpayer's heirs take as their tax basis the fair market value of property at the date of the decedent's death or, possibly, six months later. Thus, if a taxpayer can exchange his properties in only qualified nontaxable exchanges until the time of his death, he and his heirs will effectively escape income taxation on the appreciation in value. The carryover basis rule is effectively made inoperative if the property acquired in a nontaxable exchange can be retained until the taxpayer's death. If a taxable disposition is made before the taxpayer's death, however, the carryover basis rule attempts to insure the recognition of the "correct" amount of gain or loss on the several transactions combined.

To demonstrate the effect of the carryover basis rules, let us return, to the facts assumed in connection with Figure 9–1. If this transaction qualifies under one of the nontaxable exchange provisions of the Code for both A and B, we can determine that A's tax basis in the property received would be $14,000. That is, A would take as his tax basis the basis he had in the property he gave up in this nontaxable transaction. Because he had $10,000 adjusted basis in the qualifying property given to B, and because he gave B an additional $4,000 in cash (and cash always has a tax basis equal to its face value), A's adjusted basis in the property received is deemed to be $14,000. B's tax basis is somewhat more difficult to determine.

Remember that as the problem was originally worded B was required to recognize $4,000 of the $12,000 gain realized in this exchange. This means that B must report on his next tax return an additional taxable income of $4,000 and that he must pay an income tax on that amount. Because B has to recognize that income and pay that tax, he also obtains the right to increase his tax basis in the property received by that same amount. In other words, B can increase his tax basis from $8,000 to $12,000. However, B must also divide the new and larger tax basis between the boot (cash) and the qualifying asset received in the transaction. The law always assumes that cash has a basis equal to its face value; hence B must allocate $4,000 in basis to the cash leaving him with a continuing $8,000 basis in the new property he acquired in the exchange.

The reasonableness of the carryover basis rules can be demonstrated by further assuming that each taxpayer sold his newly acquired property shortly after completing the exchange. If there were no further change in the value of any properties, this would mean that A could sell his property for $20,000. Since A's carryover basis is $14,000, he would have to recognize income of $6,000 at the time of the sale. Because A did not recognize any of the $6,000 gain realized at the time of the initial exchange, this carryover of basis yields a correct result considering the two transactions together. If there were no further changes in value B would have to recognize $8,000 on any subsequent sale. This again is a correct solution, considering both exchanges, since B initially recognized $4,000 of the $12,000 gain realized at the time of the first exchange and no further change in values transpired before the second sale.

In some circumstances, it becomes rather difficult to determine the adjusted basis of property acquired in a nontaxable exchange, especially if a single exchange involves both qualified and nonqualified property and the nonqualified property is something other than cash. In general, however, a taxpayer can most easily determine a correct adjusted tax basis for property acquired in a nontaxable transaction by use of the following formula:

Fair market value of non-cash property received
less gain realized but *not* recognized on the exchange
equals the adjusted basis of the property received.

Returning to our earlier illustration and applying the above formula to each taxpayer, we can confirm our prior calculations as follows:

	Taxpayer A	*Taxpayer B*
Fair market value of non-cash property received.	$20,000	$16,000
– gain not recognized on the exchange	6,000	8,000
= adjusted basis of property received	$14,000	$ 8,000

These results are consistent with the determinations made earlier.

If the property involved in a nontaxable transaction is a capital asset, it sometimes is important to determine a date basis as well as a cost basis because holding period requirements may determine how a gain is taxed. For all capital assets acquired in a nontaxable exchange, the law usually provides that the taxpayer can "tack" together the two holding periods. Thus, if a taxpayer held the original capital asset for 4 months and 10 days and the subsequent capital asset for 3 months and 8 days, and the second asset was acquired in a nontaxable transaction, the taxpayer would be assumed to have held the second asset for a total of 7 months and 18 days at the time of the taxable disposition.

Time constraints

Most of the nontaxable exchange provisions require that a taxpayer go directly from one investment into a second investment in a barter transaction. A few nontaxable exchange provisions, however, allow a taxpayer to move indirectly from one investment, through a temporary cash state, into a second investment and still avoid the recognition of gain in the interim. In the latter provisions, the Code stipulates a maximum time period for the reinvestment. If the taxpayer does not meet the time requirements he must then recognize the gain or loss following the traditional rules. The exact time requirements stipulated for each different provision will be noted, along with other details, in the next section of this chapter.

SPECIFIC NONTAXABLE EXCHANGE PROVISIONS

The most important nontaxable exchange provisions in the Code, in terms of their impact on business behavior, are those dealing with transactions between corporations and corporate shareholders. These are among the most complex provisions in the entire tax law. Consequently, the discussion which follows again must be superficial in coverage. Hopefully, this brief discussion will permit the reader to appreciate the general constraints that are operative as well as the golden opportunities that are available. In addition to several corporation-corporate shareholder transactions, we will examine the nontaxable exchange provisions covering productive use and investment properties; involuntary conversions from condemnation proceedings, fire, storm, shipwreck, and other casualties; sales of the taxpayer's primary residence; and investments in low-income housing.

Exchange of productive use or investment properties

Code Section 1031 provides that a taxpayer will not recognize taxable gain or loss on the exchange of ". . . property held for productive use or investment in trade or business or for investment (not including stock in trade or other property held primarily for sale, nor stocks, bonds, notes, choses in action, certificates of trust or beneficial interest, or other securities or evidence of indebtedness or interest) . . . solely for property of a like kind to be held either for productive use in trade or business or for investment." The reader should observe that this provision: (1) requires a direct exchange before it is operative; (2) applies equally to gains and losses; and (3) is mandatory, not elective. In other words, if a taxpayer trades one qualifying property for another, the tax law provides that he can not recognize gain or loss using the usual rules even if he wants to do so, and that the carryover basis rules will automatically apply. The importance of this observation is often important in loss situations: if a taxpayer desires to recognize a tax-deductible ("paper") loss on a productive-use or investment property, it is imperative that he sell the property in one transaction and separately purchase the desired property in a second transaction. If he directly trades for the second property, his loss will go unrecognized and the higher tax basis of the old property will be carried forward in the new property.

Words and phrases such as "productive use," "investment," "trade or business," "held primarily for sale," "solely," and "like kind" create obvious definitional problems in applying this Code section. Perhaps the first critical observation is to note that even though the section purports to deal with investment properties, the most common forms of investment properties are specifically ruled out of consideration by the parenthetic phrase. That is, stocks, bonds, notes, and securities cannot be treated as investment properties for purposes of this section. If an investor were to directly exchange 100 shares of General Motors common stock for shares with an equivalent value in another corporation, Code Section 1031 would not be authority to defer the income tax recognition of any paper gain or loss that had accumulated between the date of purchase and the date of the exchange. Indeed, under these circumstances, the taxpayer would have to report the gain or loss realized just as if he had sold the GMC shares for cash and subsequently purchased the other corporation's stock for cash.

Section 1031 does apply to almost all real and depreciable properties used in a trade or business as well as to other investments. It applies, for example, to such assets as machinery and equipment, factory buildings, warehouses, and parking lots used in a trade or business as well as to farm lands, speculative investments in apartment houses, oil wells, and art objects. The section would not be applicable to an exchange of a personal residence or a private automobile because these properties constitute neither an investment nor a productive-use property. Even though the portion of the Code provision quoted earlier would seem to require that there be no boot in a qualifying Section 1031 exchange—that is, the quoted portion requires that the exchange be *solely* for property of a like kind—other sections of the Code modify the apparent stringency of this rule and provide that the recipient of boot must report as taxable income the lesser of the gain realized or the boot received.

The most troublesome phrase in Section 1031 has proved to be the like-kind requirement. At the present time, a taxpayer can exchange almost any form of productive-use or investment property for any other form of productive-use or investment property and still qualify the exchange as a nontaxable transaction so long as either both properties are real properties or both are personal (nonreal) properties. It does not seem to change the tax consequences if one property is developed real estate and the other is undeveloped, or if one property is used in a business and the other is held as an investment. Thus, the exchange of undeveloped ranch land for a midtown apartment building would qualify as a nontaxable transaction (realty for realty), whereas the exchange of an airplane for an apartment building could not qualify (personalty for realty). The exchange of an airplane for apartment furnishings (personalty for personalty) could qualify so long as both were either used in a trade or business or held as an investment. One major exception to the general rule just stated was codified in the 1969 Tax Reform Act. That statutory change specifically disallows the exchange of livestock of different sexes from like-kind treatment under Section 1031.

In many Section 1031 exchanges only one party to the exchange is affected by the existence of the nontaxable exchange rules. For example, if a car used entirely for business is traded for a new model through an automobile dealer, only the taxpayer giving up the old car and acquiring a new one is affected by the nontaxable exchange provisions. Both the used and the new car would constitute inventory (or "stock in trade") for the auto dealer and, therefore, the exchange could not be even partially nontaxable for him. On the other hand, if a dentist and a farmer were to exchange a city duplex (which the dentist had owned as an investment) for some farm land (which the farmer had been tilling in his business), the nontaxable exchange provisions would apply to both taxpayers involved in the exchange. Incidentally, this provision is equally applicable to individual, corporate, and fiduciary taxpayers.

To illustrate how this section might apply to an actual situation, let us review the tax results that would accompany an exchange of 100 acres of mountainous timber land owned by ABC Corporation for a large corner lot in Silver City owned as an investment by Tom Jones, a local attorney. Assume that both ABC and Jones agree that the fair market value of the timber tract is $200 per acre and that the city lot is worth $30,000. To complicate matters a little more, assume also that Jones has an outstanding mortgage of $18,000 on his lot and that ABC Corporation agrees to assume that mortgage. Under these assumed facts, Jones's interest in the city lot is currently worth only $12,000, while the timber land is worth the full $20,000; thus, Jones would be expected to give ABC Corporation $8,000 boot. Before we can proceed to determine the tax results, we must know what adjusted basis each taxpayer has in the property traded. Let us assume that Jones's basis in the city lot is $21,000 and that ABC Corporation's basis in the timber land is $3,000.

The determination of the tax consequences in nontaxable exchanges is often facilitated by a simple visual presentation of all critical facts. In order to restate the facts of this illustration, let us utilize Figure 9–3, a diagram similar to the one introduced earlier in this chapter.

FIGURE 9–3

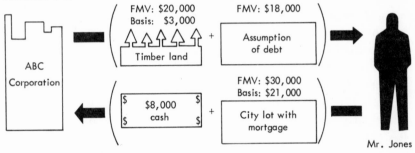

The introduction of a mortgage is the only new addition to the former diagram. For purposes of a like-kind exchange the assumption of a mortgage is tantamount to giving the debt-relieved taxpayer an equivalent sum of cash. In this illustration, therefore, ABC's assumption of Jones's $18,000 mortgage will be treated just as if ABC Corporation had paid Jones $18,000 cash.

The pertinent tax results can now be summarized as follows:

For ABC Corporation–
Amount realized ($30,000 lot plus $8,000 cash)	$38,000
– adjusted basis given ($3,000 in land plus $18,000 in debt)	21,000
= gain realized on the exchange.	17,000
– gain recognized (due to receipt of $8,000 cash boot)	8,000
= gain realized but not recognized	$ 9,000
Fair market value of non-cash property received	$30,000
– gain realized but not recognized	9,000
= adjusted tax basis in city lot received	$21,000

For Tom Jones–
Amount realized ($20,000 land plus $18,000 debt transferred)	$38,000
– adjusted basis given ($21,000 lot plus $8,000 cash).	29,000
= gain realized on the exchange.	$ 9,000

Because the transfer of the $18,000 mortgage from Jones to ABC is treated just like an equivalent amount of cash, Jones must recognize his entire $9,000 gain in the period he makes this exchange. Since Jones must recognize his entire gain realized, his basis in the property received becomes its fair market value, or $20,000.

Even though the reader may feel uncertain of several of the calculations, he should understand the few really basic tax results demonstrated in this illustration: first, he should understand that the transfer of a mortgage or other debt is treated as if the debtor had received an equivalent sum of cash in the exchange and used that sum to pay his prior obligation; second, he should understand that even though both taxpayers in this transaction exchanged qualifying property the effect of Section 1031 applied to only one party because the amount of boot received by the other party was larger than the gain he realized; third, the reader should understand that a taxpayer receiving a partial tax shelter because of a nontaxable exchange provision has a substitute (or carryover) basis in the property he receives. In this illustration, ABC's tax basis in the city lot becomes $21,000 which represents a carryover of the former basis ABC had in the timber land plus an additional $18,000 in basis which it obtained by assuming the mortgage against the city lot. As this illustration demonstrates, the economic importance of the right to engage in a nontaxable exchange obviously varies from one situation to the next. Other things being equal, the greater the amount of the unrealized gain, the more important it is for a taxpayer to arrange a nontaxable transaction.

Nontaxable transactions between a corporation and its shareholders

Transactions between a closely held corporation and its stockholders are often of more significance in terms of legal form than they are in terms of economic substance. For example, when a taxpayer incorporates a business that he has operated for a number of years as a sole proprietorship, the act of incorporation is of very little economic importance to anyone so long as all of the new corporation's stock is issued to the former proprietor. Under these circumstances, it seems entirely reasonable to suspend the usual rules requiring that any unrealized gains or losses be recognized for income tax purposes on the date of incorporation. The rationale for extending nontaxable exchange benefits to transactions between giant corporations and minority shareholders is much more difficult to explain. Nevertheless, under the proper circumstances, both classes of transactions can be brought within the purview of the nontaxable transaction rules.

Forming a corporation. Code Section 351 provides that no gain or loss shall be recognized for income tax purposes if one or more persons transfer property to a corporation solely in exchange for the stock or securities of that corporation *and* the person or persons transferring the property own 80 percent or more of the voting control of the corporation after the transfer. The importance of this provision is that it allows taxpayers to create new corporations without immediate tax consequences as long as those who transfer property to the new corporation own 80 percent of the corporation's stock after the transfer and they receive no "boot." Once again, if all the conditions are satisfied, this tax result will follow whether the taxpayer wants it to or not. If a taxpayer desires to engage in a taxable transaction, he has three options: (1) he can make certain that his transaction is arranged as a sale rather than as an exchange of property for stock and/or securities; (2) he can make certain that sufficient boot is distributed to guarantee his right to recognize the gain he desires to recognize; or (3) he can make certain that the transferors of property own less than 80 percent of the transferee corporation's stock.

In any exchange to which Section 351 applies, the usual carryover basis rules also apply. Observe, however, that the effect of a nontaxable transfer to a corporation is to double the aggregate tax basis. The transferor of property in a wholly nontaxable Section 351 transaction will transfer his former tax basis in the property transferred to the new stock or securities that he receives; at the same time, the corporate transferee also acquires that same tax basis in the properties that it receives. This doubling of basis can be illustrated simply as in Figure 9–4 in a before and after comparison.

Under some circumstances, a taxpayer is well advised to attempt a nontaxable incorporation; under other circumstances, he might seek to achieve a taxable one. In the previous illustration, for example, Taxpayer A might prefer to purchase his stock in A Corporation for cash if asset 1 were a plot of undeveloped land with a tax basis of $10,000 and a fair market value of $310,000. After A purchases his stock for cash, A Corporation might subsequently purchase A's land for $310,000. If the form of these two transactions can be sustained, A may assure his right to report a $300,000 capital gain on the sale of the land. If A had transferred the low basis land into the cor-

FIGURE 9–4

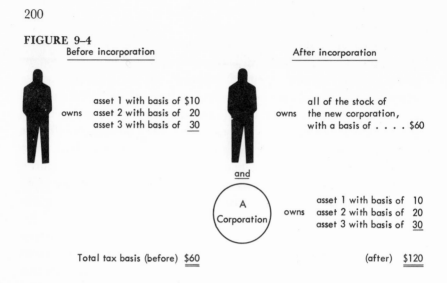

Before incorporation

owns asset 1 with basis of $10
asset 2 with basis of 20
asset 3 with basis of 30

After incorporation

owns all of the stock of
the new corporation,
with a basis of $60

and

A Corporation owns asset 1 with basis of 10
asset 2 with basis of 20
asset 3 with basis of 30

Total tax basis (before) $60   (after) $120

poration and the corporation had proceeded to develop that land, the entire profit recognized by A Corporation—including the $300,000 pre-transfer appreciation in value—would have to be reported as ordinary income. As suggested in Chapter 6, the desirable tax result can usually be achieved but only if the taxpayer makes each of his moves very carefully.

Reorganizing a corporation. The officers of an extant corporation sometimes decide that the corporation can achieve its objectives better if it can be reorganized in some way. For example, the corporate officers may decide to divide one corporation into two or more corporate entities to allow each to pursue a different business. Alternatively, the corporate officers may try to add economic strength to a financially distressed corporate organization by arranging a reorganization that would decrease the amount of outstanding debt and increase the amount of the stockholders' equity by the same amount. Under still other circumstances, the officers of one corporation may desire to acquire another corporate organization or all of its assets. Such a corporate acquisition can be accomplished in any of several ways; it can be accomplished by merger, by consolidation, by acquisition of all of the second corporation's operating assets, or by acquisition of sufficient stock of the second corporation to make that corporation a subsidiary of the acquiring corporation. Each of these corporate reorganizations can be accomplished as a nontaxable transaction if all parties to the transaction fully comply with the intricate rules of Subchapter C of the Internal Revenue Code.

The general requirements of the corporate reorganization provisions follow the characteristics common to all nontaxable exchanges described earlier in this chapter, except for the fact that corporate reorganization provisions usually apply to both parties to the transaction if they apply to either one. If the reorganization is to be accomplished wholly tax-free, the parties to the reorganization usually can exchange only qualifying property. A limited amount of boot is allowed in certain corporate reorganizations but not in all of them. In the latter group of transactions, the only form of qualifying property is stock or securities in corporations which are party to the reorganization.

To demonstrate the importance of the corporate reorganization provisions, let us consider the case of an assumed Adam Smith who owns 100 percent of the stock of Smith Industries, Incorporated. Smith, who is approaching retirement age, has decided to dispose of his interest in Smith Industries. Initially, Smith thought that he might sell his entire interest to a local investor group which had expressed an interest in his company. Smith discovered, however, that such a sale would be almost prohibitively expensive in terms of the income tax. He had formed his corporation many years ago with invested capital of $100,000. During the intervening years, this small corporation had grown until today it is worth in excess of $5 million. If Smith were to sell his stock, he would trigger an immediate income tax of something like $1.75 million, leaving him with $3.25 million to reinvest. Instead of selling, therefore, Smith agrees to exchange all of his stock in Smith Industries for stock in Giant Conglomerate Corporation of America. If everything is properly arranged, this means that the exchange will proceed without tax consequences to Adam Smith, Smith Industries, or Giant Conglomerate Corporation. This result will be possible even if Smith ends up owning only, say, 1 or 2 percent of the outstanding stock of Giant and even if Smith Industries constitutes only a small part of Giant Conglomerate Corporation. In this situation, the economic transformation achieved by Adam Smith is much more than one of legal form alone. Before the nontaxable exchange, Smith owned and operated his own business; after the exchange, he can rest easily with his small interest in a giant enterprise which is engaged in a multitude of diverse economic endeavors. Even though the realization of economic gain in this illustration is as complete as it can ever possibly be, the tax laws authorize the total deferral of any income tax if all of the Code requirements are met. In this area even the tax experts fear to tread alone. Before a corporate reorganization is finalized, most tax experts and corporate officers will insist upon an advanced ruling on all tax consequences by the Treasury Department. If Treasury issues an adverse ruling, or if it will issue no ruling, the original reorganization plans are almost invariably called back and modified or dropped. The tax consequences often are so substantial for so many people that no corporate officer or tax advisor is willing to risk the potential liability of proceeding in the face of an adverse ruling, even if they are of the opinion that the ruling is incorrect and would not be upheld by a court.

The fact that corporate reorganizations can proceed as nontaxable exchanges has had a tremendous impact on our economy. In the past 20 years in particular, corporate stocks and securities almost became a second form of money. Stocks and securities were as good as money only because they could, under the right circumstances, be exchanged tax-free. Empires were built, and sometimes lost, through corporate mergers and acquisitions alone. Very little of this merger activity would have been possible had the tax laws not provided nontaxable exchange opportunities. If a corporation or its shareholders had to recognize all prior appreciation in value for income tax purposes before proceeding with a corporate reorganization, reorganizations would be economically impractical.

The reader should now be in a position to understand why, on several previous occasions, the author could state that the double tax often was not a major consideration in the life cycle of the closely held corporation. In most closely held corporations the owners currently extract (with only a personal income tax) whatever amount of income they need for personal consumption in the form of salaries, interests, and rents during their years of active interest in corporate affairs. All corporate income in excess of the owners' personal needs is accumulated within the corporate shell where it is reinvested and expanded through new and larger business investments. If the owner does not die sooner, and if he does not desire the control of his corporation to pass to another member of his family, he typically allows his firm to be reorganized as part of a larger venture in a nontaxable transaction. Finally, then, the stock of either the original company or of the merged organization is passed through the taxpayer's estate, where it is purged of the potential income tax liability by the step up in basis given the heirs. After the death of the taxpayer, the heirs can sell the stock and recognize no income or loss because their basis equals the fair market value at the date of the decedent's death. Thus the accumulated corporate income is finally "realized" by the family in a taxable transaction that has little or no tax consequence because of the basis rules. Because corporate (business) reorganizations are of such great importance, the next chapter will consider in greater detail the pertinent tax factors.

Liquidating a corporation. The liquidation of a corporation typically can be accomplished tax-free as far as the corporate entity is concerned, but, under most circumstances, a liquidation necessitates the recognition of taxable gain or loss on the part of the recipient shareholders. The need of the shareholder to recognize some gain on the liquidation of a corporation means, quite obviously, that it is often much more expensive taxwise to get out of a corporate form of business organization than it is to get into the corporate form in the first place. For this reason, a taxpayer should never take lightly a decision to incorporate. The inconsistency of the tax rules can be demonstrated simply as in Figure 9–5. The gain or loss realized by the stockholders

FIGURE 9–5

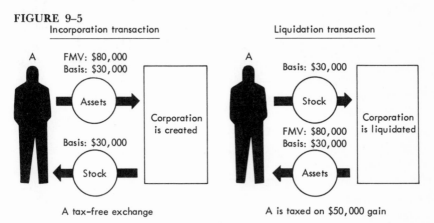

on the liquidation of the corporation can be classified either as ordinary income or as capital gain. If the corporation is not a collapsible corporation, the gain realized by the shareholders typically will be classified as a capital gain.

Involuntary conversions

If a taxpayer's property is involuntarily converted into cash or other property by action of a condemnation proceeding, a casualty, or a theft, the taxpayer usually is free to treat the involuntary conversion as a nontaxable transaction as long as it resulted in a gain and the taxpayer reinvests the proceeds received in a similar property within a prescribed time period. The proceeds received in an involuntary conversion typically are either a condemnation award or insurance proceeds, both of which are commonly paid in cash. Section 1033 gives the taxpayer an option: he is free to report the gain realized on an involuntary conversion under the usual tax rules if he desires to do so; if he does not, he may treat the gain as the gain realized on a nontaxable exchange if he will replace the property destroyed with a similar property within two years after the end of the year in which the gain was realized. If the taxpayer does not reinvest the entire proceeds in a similar property, the amount retained is treated as boot. Interestingly, the option to treat an involuntary conversion as a nontaxable transaction does not extend to losses; they must be reported in the year realized.

To illustrate the tax rules applicable to involuntary conversions, assume that a taxpayer had the following assets destroyed by fire; that the insurance company made reimbursements in the amounts indicated; and that the taxpayer reinvested the amount shown in a similar property within the prescribed time period.

Asset	Adjusted basis	Insurance proceeds	Amount reinvested
#1.	$10,000	$15,000	$17,000
#2.	20,000	26,000	24,000
#3.	30,000	37,000	28,000
#4.	40,000	30,000	n.a.

The gain realized on asset #1 is, of course, $5,000 ($15,000 − $10,000). If the taxpayer elects, however, he need not recognize any of the $5,000 gain realized because he reinvested all of the insurance proceeds, and more, in a similar property. Assuming that he elects not to recognize the gain realized, his basis in the replacement property will be $12,000; that is, a carryover basis of $10,000 from old asset #1 plus the *extra* $2,000 cash ($17,000 reinvested less $15,000 insurance proceeds) invested in the similar property.

The gain realized on asset #2 is $6,000 ($26,000 − $20,000). Because the taxpayer retained $2,000 of the insurance proceeds ($26,000 received − $24,000 reinvested), he must recognize $2,000 of the $6,000 gain realized. The taxpayer may, however, elect to defer recognition of the remaining $4,000 gain realized. Assuming that the taxpayer does elect to defer recognition of that $4,000, his basis in the replacement property will be $20,000 ($24,000 fair market value of the new property less $4,000 gain not recognized).

The gain realized on asset #3 is $7,000 ($37,000 − $30,000) Because the taxpayer invested only $28,000 in the replacement property—that is, he retained $9,000 in cash—he must recognize the entire gain of $7,000. The basis of his new property then becomes its cost, $28,000.

The involuntary conversion of asset #4 resulted in a $10,000 loss. The taxpayer has no option but to report that loss in the year of the involuntary conversion. It is immaterial if the taxpayer reinvests any or all of the insurance proceeds from asset #4; the loss must be recognized immediately. If replacement is made, the basis of any new property will be its cost.

Surprisingly, perhaps, a most difficult aspect of applying Section 1033 has been in the determination of what constitutes a qualifying replacement property. The Code requires that it be "similar or related in service or use" to the property destroyed. The IRS and the courts have interpreted the statutory requirement rather narrowly. If the taxpayer desires to exercise his right to treat any gain from an involuntary conversion as a deferred gain, he must be very careful in selecting replacement properties. Because the law still is changing in this regard, no attempt will be made to summarize the kinds of replacements that will satisfy each of the many courts in the various jurisdictions. The need for expert assistance in making replacement investments is obvious.

Residence sales

If a taxpayer sells his primary residence at a gain, the usual rules would require that he immediately report the gain realized as a capital gain. If a taxpayer sells his primary residence at a loss, the usual rules deny him the right to any deduction since the property is purely a personal property. Section 1034 of the Code provides the taxpayer with some relief from the usual rules, but only if he sells his primary residence at a gain.

Section 1034 in effect allows a taxpayer one year during which he must replace a former primary residence with a new one if he wishes to defer the recognition of any gain realized on the sale of a former home. If a taxpayer builds a new home, the replacement period is extended to 18 months. If a taxpayer is called to active military duty, the replacement period is extended to 4 years. Within these prescribed time periods, a taxpayer may replace any form of primary residence with any other form and still avoid recognition of gain. For example, if both were in fact the taxpayer's primary residence, he could move from a ketch-rigged sailboat to a trailer house, or from a condominium to a country estate, and avoid the recognition of any gain on the sale of the former home. This provision is also worded to be mandatory if the conditions are satisfied. If a taxpayer desires to recognize the gain realized on the sale of a former home, he must either reinvest a sufficiently small amount in the new home or remain without a purchased home for longer than the prescribed time period.

If the taxpayer does not reinvest the entire cash proceeds from the sale of his former residence in a new home, the excess cash retained is again treated like boot. In this regard, the rules applicable to involuntary conversions are very much like the rules applicable to sales of a primary residence. To demonstrate their comparability, let us assume numbers with residence sales that are identical to the numbers assumed earlier for involuntary conversions, and then compare the tax results of the two situations.

Case	Adjusted basis of old home	Amount realized on sale of old home	Cost of new residence
#1	$10,000	$15,000	$17,000
#2	20,000	26,000	24,000
#3	30,000	37,000	28,000
#4	40,000	30,000	n.a.

Because the analysis of the tax results is so similar to the earlier discussion, it will not be repeated here. In summary form, the critical tax results of each of the above "cases," assuming that all time requirements are satisfied, are shown in the table below.

Case	Gain or (loss) realized on sale of old home	Gain or (loss) recognized on sale of old home	Adjusted tax basis of new home
#1	$ 5,000	$ 0	$12,000
#2	6,000	2,000	20,000
#3	7,000	7,000	28,000
#4	(10,000)	0	n.a.

The only difference between the tax results for involuntary conversions and for residence sales concerns case #4. There, because the loss realized on the sale of a personal asset is not deductible, the tax result differs from the case of the involuntary conversion—in which instance a tax deduction always is authorized.

Special rules are applicable to residence sales made by taxpayers who are 65 years of age or older. The special rules authorize the senior citizen to *exclude* part or all of any gain realized on the sale of a primary residence in addition to the more general right to treat the sale of a residence as a nontaxable transaction if gain is realized and a replacement is made on a timely basis. For tax planning purposes, it is important that every taxpayer realize that he may be entitled to a special *exclusion* if he waits and sells his home after his 65th birthday. It would be especially unfortunate if a taxpayer sold his home at a sizable gain shortly before he became eligible for that special exclusion. Because it is of limited applicability, however, we will not discuss the details of that special provision here. Readers who are approaching 65 years of age and who own homes which have appreciated in value should be especially careful in timing their home sales wisely.

Low-income housing

The newest of the nontaxable exchange provisions stems from the Tax Reform Act of 1969. This special provision is contained in Section 1039 which allows a taxpayer one year in which to reinvest proceeds from the sale of certain low-income housing if he wishes to avoid the recognition of gain. Before the recognition of the entire gain can be postponed, the sale must be made to a qualified party (generally an occupant or tenant); the sale must be approved by the Secretary of Housing and Urban Development; and the entire proceeds from the sale must be reinvested in another qualified housing project. Retention of any portion of the sales proceeds will be treated as boot and cause the recognition of some portion of the gain realized.

In Chapter 8, we noted the special 60-month amortization provision which also can be applied to investments in certain low-income housing. The opportunity to obtain a quick recovery of an initial investment plus the right to obtain a tax-free rollover of the proceeds realized on the sale of such an investment may increase investments in low income housing. Obviously, that was the hope and intent of Congress. The only major tax stumbling block that remains for the investor is the fact that the gain realized on a disposition that cannot be treated as a nontaxable transaction is likely to be classified as ordinary income under Section 1250. The only way the investor can convert the entire gain into long-term capital gain is through retention of an investment in some low-income housing for a period of 16 years and 8 months or longer. Retention of such an investment for more than ten years guarantees some capital gain, assuming that the final sale results in a gain rather than a loss. The greater the time period beyond ten years, the larger the ratio of capital gain to ordinary income that can be reported. If the taxpayer utilizes the tax-free rollover of Section 1039, the holding period for the initial investment will add to each subsequent reinvestment. If a taxpayer is willing to commit himself to a long-range program of investments in low-income housing, the tax laws will serve to increase the probabilities that such an investment will be profitable.

Other nontaxable exchanges

This discussion does not exhaust all the nontaxable exchange provisions in the Code. Section 1035, for example, authorizes a tax-free exchange of insurance policies under prescribed conditions. Section 1036 authorizes a nontaxable exchange of stock for other stock in the same corporation (which guarantees the tax-free character of any stock split). And Section 1037 authorizes the reacquisition of real property on a tax-free basis under certain circumstances. These and other nontaxable exchange provisions will not be discussed here either because they are of limited applicability, or because they are of minimal importance to most tax-planning opportunities. In the few remaining pages of this chapter, we will consider briefly several planning considerations of more general importance.

PLANNING CONSIDERATIONS IN NONTAXABLE TRANSACTIONS

Many taxpayers seem to be remotely aware of the nontaxable exchange provisions and yet they seem not to take adequate advantage of them. Perhaps their reluctance is attributable to some misunderstanding of the more practical aspects of completing a nontaxable exchange successfully. For example, the taxpayer may believe that he must personally locate another investor who is willing to trade properties before he can successfully engage in a tax-free rollover of a productive use or investment property. If that belief were factually correct, there would indeed be few meaningful tax opportunities available. Fortunately, many tax-free exchanges can be arranged through the use of a property broker in what is known as a three-cornered exchange.

Three-cornered exchanges

A taxpayer who owns a substantially appreciated productive-use or investment property generally should spend more of his time and effort in locating a desirable replacement property, and less of his time and effort in locating a potential buyer for the property that he wishes to sell, if he wants to maximize the tax opportunity available. After the taxpayer has located an appropriate replacement property, he should proceed to contact a property broker to play the necessary intermediary role in a tax-free exchange. That is, the taxpayer requests the broker to purchase the property which the taxpayer wants to acquire, and, following such a purchase by the broker, the taxpayer and the broker will exchange properties. This, of course, leaves the broker with the appreciated property that the taxpayer wanted to sell. Because selling such properties constitutes their business, brokers are quite willing to make such arrangements if they can see a reasonable profit in the deal for themselves. The taxpayer may be quite willing to pass along a small portion of his profit to the broker because it allows him to achieve his investment objectives at a minimal tax cost. The sequential steps of the three-cornered exchange can be diagramed as in Figure 9–6. If all parties take sufficient care in arranging the details of these separate transactions, Taxpayer A can achieve his investment objectives tax free. The arrangements between A and B are especially critical. If the tax authorities can determine that B only acted as an agent of A, the plan will fail and A will be treated as if he personally purchased property C for cash. Taxpayer A also must be careful in his dealings with C. If A proceeds too far into the negotiations with C, so that the sale is all but finalized before the broker is introduced into the deal, some courts have found that A actually purchased property C even though the legal papers show that the sale technically was made to B rather than to A by party C. For those who know the rules and who document their way care-

210

FIGURE 9-6

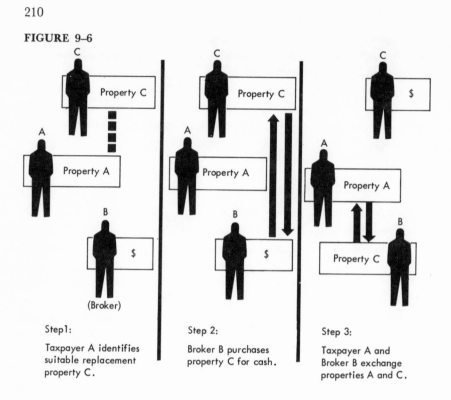

Step 1:

Taxpayer A identifies
suitable replacement
property C.

Step 2:

Broker B purchases
property C for cash.

Step 3:

Taxpayer A and
Broker B exchange
properties A and C.

fully, however, the three-cornered exchange can be a useful technique in minimizing the tax consequences of semi-routine business transactions.

Mortgaged properties

Taxpayers sometimes reject the use of a tax-free exchange, believing that the existence of a mortgage on a property will in effect be treated as boot and, therefore, for all practical purposes, convert an apparently tax-free transaction into a wholly taxable one. This danger was adequately demonstrated in the illustration on page 198. What was not explained there, however, is the fact that the tax authorities will not treat the transfer of a mortgage as an equivalent of cash to the extent that two mortgages offset each other.

If the two taxpayers in the illustration on pages 197 and 198 understood the tax rules, they would have arranged a slightly different transaction from the one proposed there. Specifically, ABC Corporation might first arrange to borrow $18,000 against 150 acres of its timber land. This would, of course, give ABC $18,000 cash tax-free since borrowing money is not deemed to constitute realization even if property is mortgaged in the process. Then ABC Corporation and Attorney Jones might proceed to exchange the city lot, with its $18,000 mortgage, for the 150 acres of timber land, which also carries an $18,000 mortgage. Under these revised conditions, neither party would have to recognize any taxable income on the exchange because the two mortgages exactly cancel each other out. Thus, Mr. Jones ends up with 150 acres of timber land (rather than 100 acres) and a $15,000 mortgage, but he need not pay any income tax on the $9,000 gain which now remains entirely unrecognized. Jones's tax basis in the 150 acres would be $21,000—a carryover basis from his old city lot. ABC Corporation, under the revised circumstances, ends up with $10,000 more cash than it had before, 50 acres less timber land, and the right to ignore $8,000 in taxable income that had to be recognized in the previous arrangement. ABC Corporation's basis in the city lot would be $4,500, a carryover basis from the 150 acres of timber land. (Since ABC's tax basis in 100 acres was $3,000 it is assumed that its basis in 50 contiguous acres would be another $1,500.)

Role of intent

Each of the nontaxable exchange provisions contains potential tax traps for the unwary taxpayer. For example, before a taxpayer can properly defer the recognition of a gain realized on the sale of his home, he must be able to establish that the home sold was in fact his *primary residence*. If the taxpayer were to try and apply that provision to the gain realized on the sale of a summer cottage on the coast, it probably would not be sustained. If a taxpayer has more than one home, determining which place constitutes the primary residence turns largely upon the role of intent. The number of days spent at each location may be indicative of intent but such a simplistic criterion need not control in any particular disposition. The point is that a taxpayer must sometimes take great care in documenting his intent if he wishes to retain his right to claim that a particular transaction is a nontaxable one.

One case history in this regard seems especially instructive. A California taxpayer decided to dispose of a particular investment property. At the moment he could not identify a satisfactory replacement property, but a buyer was anxious to purchase the property which he wished to sell. In order not to lose the sale, the taxpayer agreed to make an exchange with a broker which would allow the anxious buyer to acquire his property. The property accepted in return was not what the California taxpayer really wanted and this fact was adequately documented in correspondence between the taxpayer and the broker. Everyone wanted it well understood that, as soon as an appropriate property could be located, the broker was to acquire that property and trade for the one temporarily accepted by the California taxpayer. Before too long, the taxpayer found his desired investment property and the second exchange was promptly completed. Much to everyone's surprise, however, the tax authorities found that the series of exchanges did not satisfy the requirements of Section 1031. The IRS argued that the California taxpayer never intended to hold the intermediate property as either a productive use or an investment property. It was held only as an expedient to attaining certain tax results. The taxpayer's own letters proved his intent and the IRS position was sustained by the courts. As this case demonstrates, a nontaxable transaction can very easily be converted into a taxable transaction by taxpayers who proceed without giving sufficient attention to every detail.

Corporate reorganizations

FOR REASONS EXPLAINED in Chapter 9, the tax rules authorizing a tax-free corporate reorganization are among the most important provisions in the entire Code. They are also, unfortunately, among the most complex provisions in the tax law. What follows in this chapter is an introduction to this important and fascinating section of the American way of taxation. The typical business executive should expect to find here just enough information to help him begin to understand the major tax opportunities and problems that must be given detailed attention in the actual acquisition or disposition of any corporate business venture. Related problems of securities regulations and financial accounting requirements must remain outside the scope of this book.

This chapter is divided into three major sections. The first section is devoted to definitional distinctions among the several forms or types of corporate reorganizations. The second section investigates the most important code sections that come into operation whenever any type of corporate reorganization is found to exist. The third section includes a brief discussion of five of the more common problem areas often associated with corporate reorganizations.

BASIC DEFINITIONS

Section 368(a)(1) of the Internal Revenue Code defines six different types of corporate reorganization. Other sections provide the operative consequences. If any particular business rearrangement cannot be fitted into one of these six definitions, the reshuffling of corporate ownership and/or corporate properties' generally will be treated like any other transaction and thus be subject to the usual tax rules explained in Chapter 2.

In the financial press, the six types of corporate reorganization are commonly known as Types A, B, C, D, E, and F—a derivation of their tax heritage. Subparagraph A of Section 368(a)(1) defines the "type A" reorganization; Sec. 368(a)(1)(B) defines the "type B" reorganization, and so on. Because this terminology has been generally accepted, and because it facilitates reference to some otherwise cumbersome descriptive phrases, we shall utilize this reference throughout this chapter.

Type A reorganization

The type A reorganization involves the merger or consolidation of two or more corporate entities under state law. If one of the old entities survives the reorganization, it is known as a merger; if neither old entity survives and a new entity is born, the reorganization is referred to as a consolidation. In skeletal form the typical merger can be depicted as in Figure 10–1. The specific merger transaction involves

FIGURE 10–1

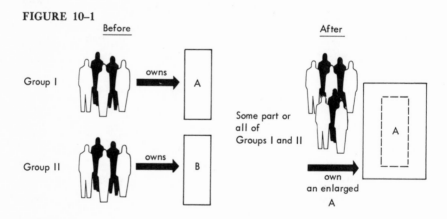

the exchange by Group II of all their B stock for A stock or other property; the transfer of all assets from Corporation B to Corporation A; and the dissolution of Corporation B.

The type A reorganization is popular in part because the Code imposes no restrictions on the form or the amount of compensation that can be used by Corporation A to effect the merger. The acquiring corporation can, for example, purchase for cash the shares of B owned by dissident stockholders, or it can issue its own bonds or preferred stocks rather than its own common stock to certain former shareholders of Corporation B. Only judicial doctrines of uncertain scope are applied to distinguish between a routine sale and a type A reorganization in borderline cases.

Although the type A reorganization has minimal restrictions on the amount and form of consideration that can be utilized, it sometimes is rendered ineffective by the fact that it generally requires the approval of a stipulated majority of both corporations' shareholders before it can be accomplished. In addition the acquiring corporation generally inherits all of the acquired corporation's potential problems as well as its possible benefits. Consequently, if contingent liabilities, for example, are of major significance in a given situation, a type A reorganization may be quickly ruled out of contention for wholly nontax reasons.

Type B reorganization

The type B reorganization is defined as the acquisition of control (meaning 80 percent of the voting power and value of the stock) by one corporation over another corporation, with acquisition achieved *solely* by the exchange of voting stock for voting stock. If any consideration other than voting stock is used to effect the transfer, it cannot be a type B reorganization. Nevertheless a "creeping" type B acquisition—that is, one spread over a reasonable period of time and involving *unrelated* transactions, some of which may have included cash—is possible under the proper circumstances. In other words, it is not mandatory that the 80 percent control be achieved in a single stock-for-stock transaction but, if it is not achieved in that manner, the classification of the final acquisition as a tax-free reorganization may be open to challenge. If the acquiring corporation obtains less than an 80 percent control over the acquired corporation, the transaction cannot be a type B reorganization under any circumstances. The net result of a type B reorganization is the acquisition of a subsidiary corporation by a parent corporation. In skeletal form it can be diagramed as in Figure 10–2. The specific transaction in a type B

FIGURE 10–2

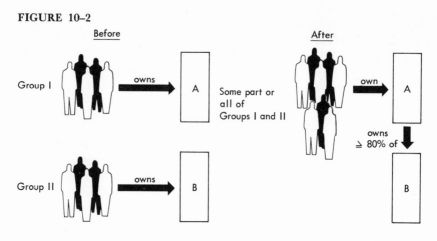

reorganization involves only the exchange of B stock for A stock by part or all of Group II.

A comparison of Figures 10–1 and 10–2 emphasizes one very important difference between the type A and the type B reorganization. In the latter, both corporations are kept alive. This means, of course, that any liabilities of Corporation B generally do not extend to the assets of Corporation A. It also means that any unique value that Corporation B may have—such as a well-known name, customer goodwill, a scarce franchise, or any other privilege—can be permanently retained by Corporation A, indirectly through its control over B. Type B reorganizations may also be preferred over other types because of lesser appraisal rights given dissenting shareholders, or because the shareholders of the acquiring corporation may not have to be consulted before this reorganization can be effected. These specific rules are part of our securities laws.

The major restricting condition of the type B reorganization is the strict voting-stock-for-voting-stock requirement. Even apparently routine concomitants of a normal reorganization—such as fractional shareholders' rights, reorganization legal and accounting expenses, debt assumptions, and contingent exchanges—have sometimes raised havoc with this one requirement. In general the IRS and the courts have taken a narrow interpretation of the restricting code provision, and all tax planners must exercise extreme caution in this area.

Finally, the reader should observe that it is entirely possible for the acquiring corporation to liquidate its new subsidiary shortly after acquiring it in a type B reorganization. In that event the economic effect is, for all practical purposes, the same as a statutory merger.

The form and the sequence of the events which transpire, however, will determine which (if any) form of reorganization has occurred. If an acquisition fails to satisfy at least one of the definitions contained in Sec. 368(a), the transaction generally becomes a wholly taxable one.

Type C reorganization

The type C reorganization is one in which the acquiring corporation obtains *substantially all* of the properties of another corporation in exchange for its own, or its parent corporation's, voting stock and (possibly) a limited amount (not more than 20 percent in value) of other consideration. In skeletal form the assets-for-stock merger contemplated in a type C reorganization can be depicted as shown in Figure 10–3. The specific transaction in this situation involves the

FIGURE 10–3

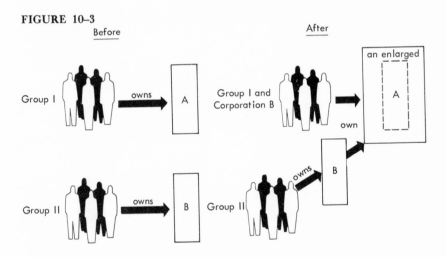

transfer of assets, and very often of liabilities as well, from Corporation B to Corporation A in exchange for Corporation A's voting stock and, possibly, a limited amount of cash or other property.

The most troublesome requirement of the type C reorganization has proved to be the substantially-all requirement. If Corporation B initially owns some assets that Corporation A does not wish to acquire, great care must be taken in the manner and the timing of the disposition of the unwanted assets if the subsequent asset-for-stock exchange is to withstand an IRS challenge as a valid type C reorganization. If a corporation is nearly insolvent, a type C reorganization may also prove difficult to arrange because the acquired corporation has few assets that can be acquired. In this situation, most of the assets belong to the corporation's creditors, and, therefore, any acquiring corporation will find it nearly impossible to acquire "substantially all" of the insolvent corporation's properties.

The boot relaxation rule—that is, the provision authorizing up to 20 percent of the consideration in some form other than voting stock of the acquiring corporation or its parent corporation—can also be troublesome in certain circumstances. If any consideration other than voting stock is utilized in a type C reorganization, then the liabilities assumed by the acquiring corporation must also be treated as part of the boot. Because the assumed liabilities often exceed 20 percent of the value of the assets in a reorganization exchange, the opportunity to utilize any consideration other than voting stock may be severely limited. An error in the valuation of properties might also prove fatal to a type C reorganization which attempted to take advantage of the boot relaxation rule. If the original valuation of the properties transferred for voting stock proved to be in excess of their real fair market value, and the value of the properties transferred for other consideration proved to be greater than originally estimated, then the 20 percent limitation might be exceeded and the exchange fail to qualify under the type C requirements.

As is emphasized in the skeletal diagram of the classic type C reorganization, above, one important result of this type of business rearrangement is the creation of a holding company (Corporation B in the diagram.) Note that because B was required to transfer substantially all of its assets to Corporation A, it is left with little or nothing but A stock. Under these circumstances, it is not surprising to discover that Group II commonly will liquidate Corporation B and distribute the A stock to its shreholders following a type C reorganization. When this happens, the economic result is again tantamount to a type A merger, but the form of the transaction and the sequence of the events are distinct and failure to comply with all of the requirements of one or the other will again normally result in a fully taxable transaction rather than in a nontaxable corporate reorganization.

Type D reorganization

The type D reorganization literally encompasses two essentially dissimilar business rearrangements. It can apply to the transfer of substantially all of the assets of a corporation to *its own* subsidiary corporation if this asset transfer is followed by the liquidation of the transferor (parent) corporation. The net effect of this form of the type D reorganization is to put a new corporate shell around an old corporate body, which is essentially the equivalent of a type E or F arrangement. Alternatively, a type D reorganization may apply to the division of an existing corporation into two or more corporations. Because the latter of these two alternatives is by far the more important and common variety, we will restrict our attention to the divisive form. In skeletal form, the simplest divisive type D reorganization can be illustrated as in Figure 10–4. The specific transactions in this divisive

FIGURE 10–4

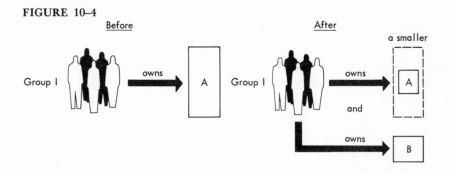

type D reorganization involve the transfer of some part of Corporation A's assets to a new *or* an existing Corporation B in exchange for B's stock and the distribution of this B stock by Corporation A to all or some portion of its shareholders (that is, to Group I but not necessarily pro rata to the members of that group). If the distribution of the B stock is made to only some part of Group I, and if this distribution is made in exchange for all of their shares in Corporation A, the "after" diagram would have to be modified to look like that in Figure 10–5.

Before a corporate division can be effected as a tax-free type D reorganization, certain other code requirements must also be satisfied. Among the most important collateral requirements is the one in Sec. 355 stipulating that both surviving corporations must be engaged in the active conduct of a trade or business that had been conducted by the now-divided corporation (or Corporation A, in our diagram) for no less than five years preceding the division. Suffice it to observe here that the meaning of the phrase "trade or business," and the outer

FIGURE 10–5

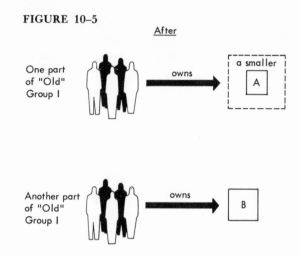

After

One part
of "Old"
Group I   → owns → a smaller A

Another part
of "Old"
Group I   → owns → B

boundaries of the "five-year rule," have been the source of many disputes between taxpayers and the IRS. Litigation in this area is commonplace and only the bravest or most foolish entrepreneur would attempt to draw his own conclusions as to the meaning of the requirements without competent advice.

The requirement that the shares of the second entity be distributed in a divisive type D reorganization can be satisfied in any one of three ways. Returning to our earlier diagram, if the old Group I shareholders surrender none of their stock in Corporation A when they receive the B shares, the division is properly called a "spin-off." If some part or all of some owners' shares in Corporation A are surrendered on the receipt of the B stock the division is known as a "split-off." Finally, if the now-divided corporation transfers all of its assets to two or more corporations (say, for example, to Corporations B and C) and is itself liquidated, the division is called a "split-up."

The type D reorganization is very useful in separating warring factions of stockholders of a single enterprise. It also may be useful in isolating the more risky trades or businesses in separate corporate shells. This can also be accomplished, of course, by the easier creation of a subsidiary corporation under Sec. 351 if the stock of the risky entity is not to be distributed. Historically, the divisive type D reorganization also was of importance in dividing what was essentially one business into two or more corporations to gain the added advantage of another corporate surtax exemption. As explained earlier, on pages 41–42 however, that possibility is no longer viable.

Type E reorganization

The type E reorganization encompasses the recapitalization of an existing corporation. The precise definitional boundaries of a "recapitalization" are admittedly elusive. In general, the phrase refers to a reshuffling of the outstanding stocks and bonds of a single corporation in terms of their amounts, priorities, maturity dates, or other features. The exact transactions involved in an E reorganization may involve the exchange of (1) "old" stocks for "new" stocks; (2) "old" bonds for "new" bonds; (3) "old" bonds for "new" stocks; or (4) "old" stocks for "new" bonds. Each of these alternatives presents slightly different tax possibilities. In general only the movement *from* an equity (or stock) interest *to* a creditor (or bond) interest creates major tax problems. The stock-for-bonds exchange may be treated as essentially equivalent to a dividend and be taxed accordingly.

The type E reorganization is commonly associated with a corporate insolvency. Corporations in financial difficulties often are reorganized in a way that, hopefully, will shore up their financial structure and stave off bankruptcy. In terms of tax-planning opportunities, the E reorganization is of limited importance.

Type F reorganization

A mere change in identity, form, or place of organization is a type F reorganization. It, too, has little tax-planning importance. To say that a code provision is not of much importance for tax planning is certainly not to suggest that such a provisoin is void of tax importance. Note, for example, that if it were not for the type F reorganization, a stockholder could be taxed on the difference between the present fair market value and his tax basis in shares of stock in a corporation that decided for good business reasons to reincorporate in another state.

As noted earlier, if a particular business reorganization satisfies any one of the six definitions of Section 368(a)(1), the usual tax result is a nontaxable transaction and a carryover tax basis. The seller of a successful business, which has significantly increased in value over the years, generally has a strong preference for a nontaxable disposition. The buyer, on the other hand, often prefers to make a business acquisition in a taxable manner. Tender offers and prices paid, therefore, may vary substantially depending on how the details of the transaction are arranged.

TAX CONSEQUENCES

Code Sections 354 and 361 are the provisions that guarantee nontax treatment to the various parties to a corporate reorganization. Sections 356 and 357 make an otherwise nontaxable transaction partially or wholly taxable in the event that boot is involved in the transaction. Finally, Sections 358 and 362 demand a carryover tax basis in the event of a nontaxable reorganization. In general, the effect of these several separate code sections is comparable to those detailed in Chapter 9 for less complex nontaxable transactions.

Recognition of gain or loss

Stockholders and security holders are granted immunity from the usual tax rules by Sec. 354 only to the extent that they exchange stock and securities of a corporation that is a party to a reorganization for stock and securities of another corporation that is also a party to that same reorganization. (For purposes of this section, the word "securities" refers to long-term debt.) If a stockholder receives shares in a corporation that is not party to that reorganization, he will be treated as receiving boot in an amount equal to the fair market value of those shares. Furthermore, the dollar value of securities that can be received tax-free usually is limited to the dollar value of securities surrendered. In other words, even in a corporate reorganization, a taxpayer typically cannot move upstream from an equity to a creditor interest without imposition of an income tax. A few years ago the hybrid or "Chinese" securities issued in some of the more glamorous corporate acquisitions caused major problems with tax definitions. Because of the combined forces of a depressed market and tighter security laws and accounting rules, as well as some changes in the tax laws, the era of extremes in equity-flavored investment units may already have passed.

Corporations frequently transfer operating assets and other properties in type A, C, and D reorganization transactions. Such a corporate transferor is protected by Sec. 361 from the need to recognize any gain in the transaction so long as those assets are transfered pursuant to a plan and to another corporation that is a party to the reorganization and so long as it receives in return only the stock or securities of that corporation. If property other than qualifying stock or securities is received, the corporation generally may avoid paying a corporate income tax on such boot if, in pursuance of the plan of reorganization, it distributes such boot to its shareholders. Incidentally, Sec. 361 also denies the transferring corporation the right to recognize (i.e., to deduct) any loss realized in a reorganization-related transfer of properties.

Treatment of liabilities. Corporate reorganizations frequently include the transfer of liabilities as well as assets between entities. Generally Sec. 357 provides that the assumption of a liability will not be treated as boot or money received by the party being relieved of the debt if the transaction would otherwise be tax-free. Two exceptions to this general rule should, however, be noted. In the event of (1) a transfer of liabilities either created to avoid the federal income tax or to accomplish nonbusiness objectives, or (2) an assumption of liabilities in excess of the tax basis of properties transferred, the debt-relieved corporation must treat the assumed liabilities as the equivalent of cash boot. No ready operational definition of the several critical words and phrases can be stated briefly. Suffice it to observe that this is one aspect of a planned business acquisition or disposition that a qualified tax advisor will investigate carefully before recommending action to his client.

Treatment of boot. If any party to a corporate reorganization receives additional consideration—that is, if he receives any property other than that authorized to be received tax-free by Sec. 354 or 355—he must recognize taxable income equal in amount to the lesser of (*a*) the boot received or (*b*) the gain realized. For a review of the meaning of the phrase "gain realized," the reader might return to Chapter 5; in broad terms, it is the difference in amount between the "amount realized" and the adjusted "basis" of the assets surrendered. If taxable income must be recognized, it can be classified as either ordinary income or capital gain depending upon all facts and circumstances surrounding the transaction. Loss cannot be recognized even if boot is received.

Basis rules

Taxpayers involved in wholly nontaxable corporate reorganizations usually take a carryover tax basis in any assets received by operation of Sec. 358 or 362. Returning to our earlier diagram of a type A statutory merger, for example, the Group II stockholders would simply transfer whatever tax basis they had in their "old" Corporation B stock to their "new" Corporation A stock. In the type C reorganization diagram, Corporation A would simply assume whatever tax basis Corporation B had previously had in the assets transferred and Corporation B would take that same tax basis in the Corporation A stock it had received.

As noted in Chapter 9, the idea of the carryover basis is to achieve a temporary postponement rather than a permanent forgiveness of the pending income tax. Theoretically, the temporarily deferred gains and losses will be realized *and recognized* whenever the newly acquired properties are later disposed of in a more "normal" (taxable) transaction. Also, as explained earlier, however, the temporary postponement is often converted into a permanent avoidance of the income tax for individual taxpayers because of the fact that inherited properties take an income-tax-free step-up in basis in the hands of the heirs.

If boot is received and gain must be recognized in an otherwise nontaxable transaction, the parties to the reorganization may be able to increase their tax basis by the amount of the gain recognized. The taxpayer receiving boot, however, must also decrease his tax basis by the amount of boot received. Because the amount of gain recognized is often equal to the amount of boot received, the increase authorized by the gain recognized is exactly offset by the amount of boot received and the net effect of the two rules just stated is (for the recipient of boot) a return to his prior basis. For the party giving the boot, however, an increase in basis usually results. Fortunately, business managers can let their tax advisors worry about the many details associated with the actual application of these tax basis rules. The good manager should always remember that a proper allocation of tax basis among the assets received may spell the difference between a profitable and an unprofitable exchange. In most circumstances, the selling taxpayer wants to allocate so as to maximize capital gains, whereas the buying taxpayer wants to allocate so as to maximize future tax deductions in as short a period as possible.

SPECIAL PROBLEMS

Corporate reorganizations often involve literally hundreds of taxpayers and millions of dollars worth of properties. It is little wonder, therefore, that the tax rules in this area are complex and the problems legendary. To close this brief review of reorganizations, we will examine just five of the more common special problems briefly.

Unwanted assets

An acquisition-minded corporation may desire to obtain something less than all of the assets of a business being offered for sale. As a consequence, the overly anxious seller may be tempted to make a hasty disposition of any unwanted assets. He must exercise great care to make such a disposition at a minimal tax cost. If, for example, the officers of the selling corporation were to distribute the unwanted assets to the corporation's shareholders to facilitate a subsequent merger, the likely result would be an ordinary dividend taxed at ordinary rates for the recipient stockholders. If a stock redemption were involved, the distributing corporation might also discover that it too had to recognize a taxable income because of the distribution of property to the shareholders. A sale of any unwanted assets to a third party could be equally costly if not prearranged properly. Under some circumstances, a corporation may be able to separate the "wanted" and the "unwanted" properties in two or more corporations via a tax-free type D reorganization before consummating a merger of the wanted-property corporation. In this event, however, a type C reorganization probably could not be arranged even for the desired-asset corporation because of the "substantially-all" requirement. A type A or B reorganization, however, might be successfully arranged under these circumstances. Both competent advice and an advance ruling from the Treasury Department would be warranted under these conditions.

Net operating losses

Profitable corporations at one time actively sought to acquire essentially worthless corporate shells solely because, by acquiring such corporate shells, they could also acquire the right to claim the acquired corporation's accumulated net operating loss deductions against their own taxable income. Interestingly, the most worthless corporate shells—that is, the ones with the greatest accumulation of losses—brought the highest price. The tax rules have been substantially modified during the past 20 years to preclude much success in this way today. Generally, the net operating loss deductions carried forward will be allowed as a tax deduction to the acquiring corporation if and only to the extent that the old (or acquired) business produced profits after its purchase. The rules that determine exactly how much and in what manner an acquired business can be modified without destroying a loss carryforward deduction are legion. In addition, the accounting conventions that allocate revenues and expenses among several divisions of a single enterprise are at best rough approximations. Consequently, trading in corporate shells with accumulated net operating losses is not impossible; it simply is not an amateur's game.

Contingent acquisitions

Buy-sell agreements are sometimes drawn up as conditional contracts. For example, the number of shares of stock to be issued to the selling corporation or to its stockholders may be made contingent upon the profit performance of the acquired business for the next several years. Contingencies commonly raise numerous and difficult tax problems. Initially, contingent consideration may create the possibility of boot. If the only additional consideration that can be received is more shares of qualifying stock, if the portion of the shares held in reserve is reasonable in relation to the total number of shares to be transferred, and if the entire transaction must be finalized within a reasonable number of years, then such a contingency usually will not constitute boot. Determining a tax basis for any shares disposed of during the period of the contingency, however, is less easily resolved. If the acquiring corporation retains the right to back out of an acquisition, or if it retains the right to rescind the transaction under specified circumstances, the tax problems multiply rapidly. Fortunately, the tax stakes in these arrangements are typically so great that they are given proper attention before it is too late to correct any problems inherent in the arrangement.

Liquidation-reincorporation

A reincorporation that follows closely on the heels of a corporate liquidation can easily be converted into a *taxable* reorganization by the IRS and the courts. If this result were not possible, a taxpayer might be tempted to accumulate all temporarily "excess" income within a corporate shell without any payment of dividends. Then, when the owner had need of the accumulated assets, he could liquidate the corporate entity and receive the funds at the cost of a capital gain tax rather than paying an ordinary income tax on any dividends. If the owner wished to continue the essential business, he could immediately transfer the necessary operating assets back into a new corporation and begin the accumulation process all over again. The accumulated earnings and profits account of the old corporation would have been wiped clean in the liquidation, and the new corporation could open with a clean slate. Does this sound too good to be true? Usually it is! Unless the owners of the reincorporated business are a significantly different group from the old owners, or unless the new corporation is engaged in a significantly different business from the prior corporation, the courts are likely to sustain an IRS contention that the liquidating distribution was really an ordinary dividend distribution and that the new corporation has inherited all attributes of the predecessor corporation.

Certainly a bailout of accumulated corporate income at the price of only a capital gains tax to the shareholders remains a viable alternative. The wise business manager will simply make certain that he does not inadvertently take actions that not only destroy this possibility but also serve to convert what could have been capital gains into ordinary income.

Debt-financed acquisitions

Many business managers have sold their corporations for the long-term debt of an acquiring corporation. Because such a sale is ordinarily a taxable transaction, the seller may discover that he can get a better price for any of several reasons. One factor increasing the price in a debt-financed acquisition is the fact that the buyer can deduct part of his purchase price as interest during the years he is paying for the new property. In addition, the buyer gets a new and higher basis in the assets purchased, and thus he can look forward to larger tax deductions in the future years than he could have, had the sale been arranged in a nontaxable manner. Such a sale was often tolerable for the seller because he could elect to defer the tax recognition of any gain realized by virtue of the installment sale provisions of the Code. (See Chapter 12 for a discussion of the installment sale.) In many cases, the tax recognition was deferred for as long as 20 years or longer by the terms of the debt. If the seller discovered that he required additional funds in the interim years, he was always free to sell some portion of the acquiring corporation's debt and pay his tax on only the portion of the bonds sold.

The Tax Reform Act passed by Congress in 1969 reduced the popularity of the debt-financed acquisition for two important reasons. First, the installment sale provisions of Sec. 453 were modified so as to preclude the deferral of the recognition of gain if the seller receives demand notes, coupon bonds, or any other security that is readily tradable in an established market. Second, the acquiring corporation may be denied the right to deduct interest on debt obligations issued after October 9, 1969, to acquire another business directly or indirectly. The latter revision, Sec. 279, is applicable only for interest in excess of $5 million and then only under specified circumstances. Needless to say, the few readers of this book who engage in such hefty acquisitions can also obtain ready reference to the other pertinent details. For smaller acquisitions, dealing with unlisted securities, debt-financed acquisitions remain one of the several options available.

Family tax planning

THE FEDERAL GIFT TAX and the federal estate tax, although secondary in importance to the federal income tax, strongly influence the way in which individuals dispose of their assets. These two taxes apparently were enacted both as a revenue-producing device for the government and as a method of achieving wealth redistribution within the nation. Neither objective has been achieved very effectively. In a recent year the two taxes combined provided the federal government with approximately $3.5 billion in revenues, which was less than 2.5 percent of the total tax revenues collected that year. All studies that have attempted to determine the effect of the gift and estate taxes on wealth redistribution have concluded that these taxes have had a very limited impact.

In this chapter, we will review in general the provisions that determine the tax liability imposed by the gift tax and the estate tax as well as the more common methods utilized by taxpayers in avoiding and minimizing them. The chapter is divided into three sections. The first section deals with the gift tax; the second, with the estate tax. The final section attempts to integrate the income, estate, and gift taxes into a simple family-tax-planning model that can help a person decide not only how much to give (and how much to retain), but also which properties to give (and which properties to retain).

THE FEDERAL GIFT TAX

The federal gift tax is an excise tax imposed anytime a taxpayer exercises his right to make a gratuitous transfer of property. The gift tax is a liability of the donor (the person making a gift), not of the

229

donee (the person receiving a gift), unless the donor explicitly makes the gift subject to a condition that the donee pay the gift tax. Subject to a few exceptions to be explained momentarily, the gift tax applies to all gratuitous transfers made after June 6, 1932. It applies equally to all forms of property: real and personal property; business, non-business, and purely personal-use property; tangible and intangible property; and to present interests as well as to future interests in property. In other words, if a taxpayer today makes an irrevocable transfer of a future interest in a property to a person not yet born, the transfer is immediately subject to the gift tax even though the economic impact of the transfer of property rights may not be realized for many years. The problems encountered in valuing a future interest in property are sometimes substantial. Suffice it to note here that valuation may involve the need to determine a discounted present value of an estimated earnings stream based on the life expectancy of several parties to a gift. Observe also that a transfer must be irrevocable before the gift tax will apply. If a person prepares his last will and testament, or if he names a beneficiary to a life insurance policy, such action will not constitute a gift because the taxpayer generally retains the right to modify his present intention at any time in the future. Finally, the reader should understand clearly that the gift tax has essentially nothing to do with the income tax. For example, the interest on state and local government bonds is exempt from the federal income tax. A gift of either a state bond or the interest from such a bond, however, would be wholly subject to the federal gift tax.

Basic provisions

The determination of a gift tax liability proceeds conceptually in a manner very similar to that used to determine an income tax liability. The broad outline of the gift tax calculation can be stated as follows:

> Gross value of all gifts made
> less exempt gifts and deductions
> _____
> equals taxable gifts
> times tax rate
> _____
> equals gross tax liability
> less tax credits (prior payments)
> _____
> equals net tax payable.

Translating real world events into such a simplistic formula is subject to the usual number of definitional and calculational problems. We shall examine here only a few of the more common problems and opportunities.

Gross gifts. The determination of a dollar value to represent the "gross value of all gifts made" typically involves two major kinds of problems. One set of problems involves the specification of exactly which transfers will be deemed to constitute a gift (as opposed to a nongratuitous transfer); the second set of problems involves the determination of the fair market value of those transfers found to be gratuitous. The former problem is generally resolved by the intent of the taxpayer.

Code Section 2412(b) provides that any transfer of property ". . . for less than an adequate and full consideration in money or money's worth . . . shall be included in computing the amount of gifts made." The intent of the section is apparent, but its application is sometimes difficult. If a person makes a foolish deal—that is, if he unwittingly sells a property worth $50,000 for $30,000—the Code would seem to require that he pay a gift tax on his miscalculation, in this instance on $20,000. In practice, the IRS is not that cruel. Instead of trying to apply the Code requirement literally, the IRS tries to determine the intent of the taxpayer. If he entered into an arm's length transaction in the ordinary course of business, the transaction will not be subject to a gift tax. If the transaction is one between related parties, or if the IRS has any other reason to suspect that the transaction is not a bona fide sale or exchange, it may attempt to tax the difference between the fair market value given and the consideration received as a gift.

In unusual circumstances, a gift tax may also become payable through the inadvertent or unintended action of a taxpayer. In these circumstances, the taxpayer may not have given any conscious thought to his making a gift, but his actions in fact accomplish such a result. Suppose, for example, that a father and his adult son began raising a herd of cattle in a joint venture. Under these circumstances, it would not be unusual for the father to create solely from his personal funds a joint bank account for the use of both him and his son in the cattle venture. Without formalizing their agreement, the two men may generally understand that the proceeds of the venture will be split equally between the two and that both are free to draw upon the bank account for personal as well as business needs if necessary. The potential gift element in such an arrangement is easiest to see if we will assume that: (1) both men contribute an equal amount of effort to the operation; (2) after 10 years the cattle business exactly breaks even; (3)

neither party ever used the bank account for personal needs; and (4) the two finally split the balance in the account when they terminated their joint venture. Under these extreme assumptions, it is clear that the father effectively made a gift to his son of one half of the amount he initially placed in the joint bank account. When the simplifying assumptions are removed and the venture is allowed to make a profit or loss in various years, when the relative contributions of the two are unequal in terms of personal effort as well as capital, and when the account is used for personal as well as business needs, the determination of the amount of the gratuitous transfer is much more difficult to make. Theoretically, however, it is necessary that the gratuitous transfer be separated from any nongratuitous transfer in this arrangement and that the former quantity be made subject to the federal gift tax.

After a taxpayer has identified his gratuitous transfers, it is necessary to determine their fair market value on the date of the gift. If the transfer is one of a total present interest—that is, the donee receives an immediate rather than a deferred value of an entire property—only the normal problems of valuation are present. Even the "normal" problems of valuation are substantial for all properties not regularly traded on an open market, and occasionally they are substantial even for properties that are widely traded. In settling disputed values, the courts commonly refer to such ephemeral criteria as a willing buyer, a willing seller, a free market, and full knowledge—assumed conditions that do not exist even in the most active markets of a man-made world more accurately characterized by substantial ignorance than by full knowledge. Nevertheless, the valuation process must go on and when taxpayers and government authorities cannot agree the parties can only turn to the judicial system for an arbitrated settlement of their differences.

If a taxpayer transfers less than a total interest in a property, new and even more difficult problems of valuation are encountered. For example, a taxpayer may make a gift of the income from a property to person A for his lifetime, a gift of the same income stream to person B for his lifetime but to take effect only after the life of person A, and finally a gift of the remainder interest in the property to person C. Before the gift-tax consequences can be determined, we must know the value of the gifts made to persons A, B, and C. Obviously such valuations can only be made with certain presumptions about the size of the income stream over a period of years, a discount rate, and a mortality table of expected human lives. In these instances, the Code specifies the use of designated actuarial tables. Any attempt to investigate problems of valuation would lead us far afield of the objectives of this book. We will, therefore, assume that such valuation problems can somehow be solved and proceed with the more direct tax consequences.

Exempt gifts and deductions. The taxpayer may subtract "exempt gifts and deductions" from the gross value of all gifts made to determine his taxable gifts. Exempt gifts and deductions fall into four categories: (1) a $3,000 exclusion per donee each year; (2) a $30,000 lifetime exemption; (3) all gifts to non-profit religious, charitable, literary, scientific, or educational organizations and to the U.S. government and its political subdivisions; and (4) a marital deduction generally equal to one half the value of any property given the taxpayer's spouse.

The $3,000 individual exclusion is an annual exclusion that makes the vast majority of gifts nontaxable events. Note that any individual can give an unlimited amount of property away without a gift tax if he is willing to give it to enough different people. Also note that, over a lifetime, a rather large sum can be given tax-free to any one individual if the taxpayer will begin early to take advantage of his annual exclusion. Over 50 years, for example, a man could transfer $150,000 to a child or grandchild without incurring a gift tax if he would but make the maximum $3,000 tax-free gift each year. Gifts of future interests are not eligible for this annual exclusion.

The $30,000 lifetime exemption is in addition to the annual exclusion and is affected only when a taxpayer makes gifts that exceed $3,000 in one year to any individual. It is not affected by gifts to charity. To illustrate the relationship between the annual $3,000 exclusion and the $30,000 lifetime exemption, consider the series of gifts suggested below. The illustration is based on the assumption that all gifts are gifts of present interests and that the taxpayer had no prior record of any gifts in excess of $3,000 per donee in any one year.

Year	Gifts to daughter	Gifts to son	Remaining lifetime exemption	Taxable gifts
1972	$ 3,000	$ 3,000	$30,000	$ 0
1973	10,000	5,000	21,000	0
1974	0	10,000	14,000	0
1975	10,000	5,000	5,000	0
1976	10,000	10,000	0	9,000

In 1973, $7,000 given to the daughter and $2,000 given to the son combine to reduce the donor's remaining lifetime exemption from $30,000 to $21,000. In 1974, no portion of the gift to the son can be offset by the donor's failure to make a gift to the daughter; rather, the lifetime exemption again must be reduced by $7,000. Even though this taxpayer would not have to pay a gift tax until 1976, he would have to file a gift tax return in each of the three prior years because his gifts in those years exceeded the $3,000 annual exclusion.

Although gifts to religious, charitable, literary, scientific, and educational institutions generally are exempt from the gift tax, such gifts must be reported and then deducted on the gift tax return if they exceed $3,000 to any one donee in any one year. A taxpayer often desires to retain a property for as long as he and/or his spouse shall live but to guarantee the passing of the property to a charity upon their deaths. In these circumstances, the taxpayer can either make an appropriate provision in his will, or he can make an immediate and irrevocable gift of the remainder interest to charity. The tax treatment of a charitable remainder interest is dependent upon special rules that will not be considered here.

The tax rates. The tax rate applied to all taxable gifts is determined according to a progressive rate schedule specified in Code Section 2502. The present rates are stated in Table 11–1. The reader should observe that this one progressive rate schedule is applicable to the total taxable gifts made during a person's lifetime. Thus, the gift tax liability for gifts made during any one year depends upon the aggregate value of all taxable gifts made during the taxpayer's life, not just upon the gifts made in one year. The difference between the gift tax and the income tax is striking in this regard. Regarding the income tax, every taxpayer starts over at the lowest possible marginal rate each year; spreading taxable income equally over time serves to minimize the aggregate income tax liability. Except for the annual $3,000 exclusion provision, spreading gifts over time is of no benefit for gift-tax purposes.

Tax credits. In order to determine the net gift tax liability for any single reporting period, a taxpayer must first determine his gross tax liability on all taxable gifts made during his life (as explained above), and then he may subtract from that gross tax liability the sum of all gift tax payments made in prior periods. The prior gift tax payments constitute a tax credit for the current period. Only by utilizing

TABLE 11–1
1973 Gift tax rates

If taxable gifts are		The amount of the gross tax liability is			
Over	But not over	A basic amount	Plus	A marginal rate times	The amount over
$ 0	$ 5,000	$ 0	+	2.25%	$ 0
5,000	10,000	112.50	+	5.25%	5,000
10,000	20,000	375	+	8.25%	10,000
20,000	30,000	1,200	+	10.50%	20,000
30,000	40,000	2,250	+	13.50%	30,000
40,000	50,000	3,600	+	16.50%	40,000
50,000	60,000	5,250	+	18.75%	50,000
60,000	100,000	7,125	+	21.00%	60,000
100,000	250,000	15,525	+	22.50%	100,000
250,000	500,000	49,275	+	24.00%	250,000
500,000	750,000	109,275	+	26.25%	500,000
750,000	1,000,000	174,900	+	27.75%	750,000
1,000,000	1,250,000	244,275	+	29.25%	1,000,000
1,250,000	1,500,000	317,400	+	31.50%	1,250,000
1,500,000	2,000,000	396,150	+	33.75%	1,500,000
2,000,000	2,500,000	564,900	+	36.75%	2,000,000
2,500,000	3,000,000	748,650	+	39.75%	2,500,000
3,000,000	3,500,000	947,400	+	42.00%	3,000,000
3,500,000	4,000,000	1,157,400	+	44.25%	3,500,000
4,000,000	5,000,000	1,378,650	+	47.25%	4,000,000
5,000,000	6,000,000	1,851,150	+	50.25%	5,000,000
6,000,000	7,000,000	2,353,650	+	52.50%	6,000,000
7,000,000	8,000,000	2,878,650	+	54.75%	7,000,000
8,000,000	10,000,000	3,426,150	+	57.00%	8,000,000
10,000,000	...	4,566,150	+	57.75%	10,000,000

this tax credit arrangement can a progressive tax over a lifetime be achieved with more frequent reporting periods.

An illustration

In order to illustrate the basic provisions of the federal gift tax, let us determine the gift tax liability for an imaginary taxpayer who makes the gifts detailed below. The illustration assumes that the taxpayer had made no taxable gifts prior to 1972 and that all gifts are

Year	Gifts to daughter	Gifts to son	Gifts to charity	Remaining lifetime exemption	Taxable gifts
1972	$10,000	$ 3,000	$ 5,000	$23,000	$ 0
1973	10,000	17,000	10,000	2,000	0
1974	20,000	20,000	10,000	0	32,000
1975	10,000	10,000	30,000	0	14,000

of present interests. The taxpayer in this illustration would have to file a gift tax return in each of the years 1972 through 1975 because his gifts in each year exceeded the $3,000 annual exclusion per donee. The taxpayer would not, however, have to pay a gift tax until 1974. Since December 31, 1971, gift tax returns must be filed on a quarterly basis. That is, the taxpayer must file at the end of the calendar quarter in which his gifts first exceed the $3,000 annual exclusion or in which he makes a gift of any future interest in property. If a taxpayer's gifts to charity are the only gifts which exceed the $3,000 limitation, no gift tax return is required until the fourth calendar quarter.

In terms of the formula suggested earlier, this taxpayer's gift tax computation could be summarized as follows:

Year	Gross gifts current year	Current exemptions and deductions	Aggregate taxable gifts	Aggregate gross tax liability	Aggregate tax credit	Current net tax liability
1972	$18,000	$18,000	$ 0	$ 0	$ 0	$ 0
1973	37,000	37,000	0	0	0	0
1974	50,000	18,000	32,000	2,520	0	2,520
1975	50,000	36,000	46,000	4,590	2,520	2,070

The taxable gifts reported in 1975 are the sum of the taxable gifts made in 1974 plus those made in 1975, or $46,000. The gross tax liability is determined on this $46,000 base, and the credit for the gift tax paid in prior years (here, $2,520) is deducted from the gross tax liability to determine the net tax payable for the current year. A taxpayer, obviously, must maintain records of gifts made throughout his lifetime in order to complete the gift tax return in any single year.

Planning considerations

The gift tax is exceedingly easy to avoid. If a taxpayer does not want to incur this tax, all that he has to do is refrain from making any gifts. In practice, therefore, tax planning relative to the gift tax usually relates to the determination of the lesser of two evils. The taxpayer will accept the need to pay a gift tax whenever doing so reduces some other tax by an amount greater than the gift tax he incurs. The general constraints to be considered in making such a determination will be considered in the final section of this chapter.

Systematic giving. Taxpayers with substantial amounts of property should begin a systematic pattern of giving as early in life as possible if they want to minimize the aggregate tax they or their heirs must pay. In some situations, a taxpayer may believe that nontax considerations are more important than tax savings, and the actions of such a taxpayer should be guided accordingly. A taxpayer who believes that childhood wealth leads to laziness, unhappiness, or family strife, for example, would be well advised to forgo any tax savings in the interest of a better quality of human existence. For those who do not believe that early wealth contributes to a less meaningful existence, however, systematic giving can be beneficial.

A systematic pattern of giving assures the taxpayer that he will take maximum advantage of both the $3,000 annual exclusion and the $30,000 life-time exemption. Observe that both of these tax-minimizing provisions are applicable to every taxpayer. Thus, if a husband and wife want to maximize the gift-tax opportunities, they can make all gifts jointly so long as both parties consent to this special treatment. If they do consent, the annual exclusion for the couple increases from $3,000 to $6,000 per donee and the lifetime exemption increases from $30,000 to $60,000. A consent to make gifts jointly must be in writing and filed on a timely basis with the IRS.

A systematic pattern of giving may also serve to reduce the estate tax slightly. Gifts made within the three years preceding the death of a taxpayer generally are treated as gifts made in contemplation of death and, as such, they are effectively called back and the value of the property included in the estate and made subject to the estate tax. If a taxpayer has established a systematic pattern of lifetime giving, however, the heirs can more easily defeat the statutory presumption that gifts made in the three years preceding death were made in contemplation of death. By defeating that presumption, the size of the estate and the estate tax are reduced accordingly.

Charitable gifts. A taxpayer may have many good reasons for making a gift to charity. Most importantly, charitable gifts allow an individual to support personally those eleemosynary institutions and activities he believes to be the most deserving. There also are at least four important tax reasons for making charitable gifts. Two tax reasons are related to the income tax and a third is associated with the estate tax. Further aspects of these tax consequences will be discussed in the next two sections of this chapter. For the moment we need only note that a charitable gift can be made without incurring a gift tax.

Gifts to political parties. The gift tax provisions make no special mention of gifts made to political parties. Presumably, therefore, gifts in excess of the $3,000 annual exclusion and the $30,000 lifetime exemption (or $6,000 and $60,000, respectively, in the case of gifts made jointly by a husband and wife) would be subject to the gift tax. According to a recent report in the *Wall Street Journal,* the Republican Party may have found a way around the potential gift tax for larger gifts. That report alleges that a number of separate committee funds with different names were created for the common purpose of electing Republican candidates in the November 1972 elections. Campaign literature suggested an appropriate division of gifts among the several committees for large contributors. If the existence of the multiple entities is challenged in the courts, on the grounds that there was no real substance to the separation of the funds and that they should be treated as a single entity on the judicial authority of substance over form, some gift tax may yet be payable by taxpayers making large contributions. If the creation of multiple entities to receive gifts for this common cause is not challenged in the courts, or if it is challenged and the challenge fails, the reader might consider the application of this form of entity splitting in other situations where a gift tax could apply.

Cross gifts. Several years ago one imaginative taxpayer tried to avoid the gift tax provisions in a somewhat unique way. He arranged an agreement with close friends whereby each of them would make gifts of $3,000 to designated persons. By pooling their individual rights to a $3,000 annual exclusion per donee, the taxpayer hoped to be able to increase effectively his own ability to give more to a limited number of people without a gift tax. The basic idea of cross gifts is illustrated simply in Figure 11–1. Under this plan Taxpayers A, B, and C would each designate three individuals to whom they wish to make tax-free gifts each year; in this illustration, the donees are designated a1, a2, a3, b1, b2, and so on. Each of the three would make the maximum tax-free gift to each of the nine donees. The effect of a three-man agreement is obviously to triple the maximum tax-free gift from $3,000 per donee to $9,000 per donee. If successful, the idea could be expanded with larger numbers of participants to the agreement. In this case the court found, however, that the transfers were not gifts since there was consideration exchanged by each party to the agreement: that is, the promise of the other parties to make a reciprocal transfer. Although the rationale for the tax result is confus-

FIGURE 11-1

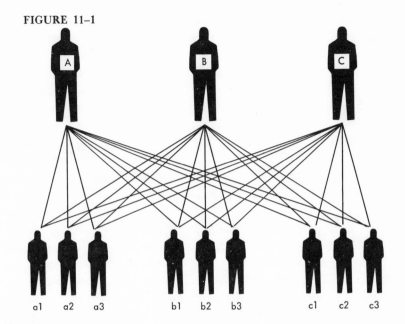

a1   a2   a3   b1   b2   b3   c1   c2   c3

ing, the court apparently decided that the extra amounts would not be eligible for the annual exclusion because they were *not* gifts and that the same extra amounts would be subject to the gift tax because they were gifts! The theory of substance over form seems to be a more adequate explanation of the conclusion than the definitional nuance suggested by the court.

Serial gifts. Under certain circumstances, a taxpayer may desire to transfer a particular property to a donee, but the transfer of the entire property at one time may be made expensive because of the gift tax rules. Suppose, for example, that after exhausting their $60,000 lifetime exemption a couple jointly desired to transfer a specific property worth $90,000 to their son. If they made the complete transfer in a single year, the transfer would be subject to a gift tax on $84,000. Instead of arranging the transfer as a gift, the couple might consider selling the property to the son with the initial payment to be made in the form of 15 interest-free $6,000 promissory notes, with one note maturing in each of the next 15 years. Each year the couple might forgive the son the $6,000 note due that year and thus avoid any gift tax on the transfer. This possibility raises several interesting tax questions for both the parents and the son. For example, the form of the initial transfer might be disregarded and the transfer treated as a gift rather than a sale under the substance-over-form rule. If the form of the transaction is sustained, it could create taxable income for the parents, even though they receive no cash and attempt to report the alleged sale of an installment basis. The tax basis of the property to the son, for income tax purposes, will depend upon how he is deemed to have acquired it: one set of basis rules applies to property acquired by gift and another set to purchased property. (See Chapter 5 for a statement of the different basis rules.) Although this serial gift notion creates several interesting tax problems, it has been used successfully in the minimization of gift taxes.

THE FEDERAL ESTATE TAX

The federal estate tax is an excise tax that is imposed when an individual transfers his property rights at death. The estate tax is *not* a tax on property as such, but a tax on the right to transfer property at death. In other words, the estate tax is not a tax on ownership as such, but a tax on the transfer of ownership rights occasioned by the death of a property owner. Observe also that the estate tax is not an inheritance tax on the right to receive property. Although the estate tax does reduce the net size of the estate transferred, it is a tax on the deceased taxpayer's estate, not on the recipients' rights to receive. Because the federal estate tax is a tax on the right to transfer property at death, the initial determination essentially must be an inventory process. That is, in order to determine the estate tax it is first necessary to determine exactly what properties a person owns at the time of his death.

Basic provision

The final determination of an estate tax liability proceeds conceptually as follows:

> Gross value of the estate
> less exemptions and deductions
> _____
> equals taxable estate
> times tax rate
> _____
> equals gross tax liability
> less tax credits
> _____
> equals net tax payable.

Once again it is the translation of real-world events into this simple formula that creates the problems of compliance and the opportunities for tax avoidance. The estate tax and the gift tax share a major common problem in valuation—both taxes demand that an explicit dollar value be specified for certain property rights whether or not the properties are ever actually sold or exchanged. If the tax collector and the taxpayer cannot agree on a valuation, the courts must resolve the differences in opinion. We shall again assume that such valuations can be made, in one way or another, so that we may concentrate our attention on the tax problems specifically.

Gross estate. If we ignore the problems of valuation, the major problems remaining in the determination of a gross estate are those of discovery and identification. All property owned by the decedent at the moment of his death must be included in his estate. This includes real and personal property, tangible and intangible property, and business as well as purely personal-use property. Code Section 2033 states it this way: "The value of the gross estate shall include the value of all property to the extent of the interest therein of the decedent at the time of his death."

One of the common definitional problems encountered in determining an estate tax involves property that is jointly owned. The law recognizes several different forms of joint ownership including joint tenancy, tenancy in common, tenancy by the entirety, and community property. Under some forms of joint ownership, the value of the entire property must be included in a deceased taxpayer's estate; under other forms of ownership, only a fractional share is included. The dower and curtesy rights of a wife or husband can also be factors in the determination of a taxpayer's gross estate. And under yet other circumstances, a person may have to determine whether or not the value of a gross estate must include property over which the deceased person held certain "powers of appointment." These and many other problems can only be noted in passing. Solution of them in any specific circumstance may require many hours of work by a qualified attorney.

More generally, we can observe safely that the gross estate typically will not include property that a taxpayer has given away prior to his death. The major exception to this conclusion involves transfers in contemplation of death, a special situation noted earlier in this chapter. As explained there, a gross estate usually must include the value of any gifts made in the three years prior to the decedent's death, unless the heirs can prove that the gift was not made in contemplation of death. Gifts made by a healthy person, for example, would usually not be deemed to be gifts in contemplation of death if the donor died in an airplane crash or other unavoidable accident shortly after making the gift.

If a gift is intended to reduce the size of an estate, the taxpayer must take care to complete the gift in every respect. For example, if a taxpayer simply names a beneficiary for an insurance policy, he will not be deemed to have made a gift of that policy and the face value of the policy must be included in his gross estate. This conclusion is based upon the premise that the taxpayer retains the right to change beneficiaries at any time and that something more than the naming of a beneficiary will be required to substantiate the conclusion that the insured person actually made a gift of an insurance policy. It is possible for a person to make a gift of an insurance policy, or of anything else, prior to his death, but this act requires more than a simple statement of good intentions.

A taxpayer's rights in an annuity, pension, or profit-sharing plan also may present unusual problems in estate tax determinations. Whether or not such rights must be included in the gross estate depends upon how the rights were acquired (by purchase or through employment), how the plan is worded, who the employer was, and what options had been exercised prior to death. The number of possible alternatives is far too large to permit a restatement of the several different results here. Taxpayers with substantial estates should make certain long before their death that such contracts are arranged in the most favorable way.

After the executor or administrator of an estate has determined which properties must be included in a deceased taxpayer's gross estate, he turns his attention to problems of valuation. In the case of the federal estate tax, the executor generally can elect to value all properties at either the date of the decedent's death or six months after his death. Usually, he will select the value on the date which will yield the lower aggregate valuation and, therefore, the lower estate tax. As explained in Chapter 5, however, the heirs' tax basis in inherited properties is also determined by this election of the executor. Under unusual circumstances, an executor may opt for a higher valuation for estate-tax purposes because the income-tax advantages, in higher tax basis, gained by the heirs more than outweigh the additional estate tax.

Exemptions and deductions. The estate tax, like every other tax, has a list of exemptions and deductions that serve to reduce the size of the tax base. The most important deductions and exemptions for estate-tax purposes are: (1) a deduction of all debts against the estate or against the deceased taxpayer; (2) all funeral expenses and the administrative expenses of settling the estate; (3) a specific $60,000 exemption; (4) a marital deduction, generally equal to 50 percent of the adjusted gross estate, for property that passes to the surviving spouse; and (5) most contributions to charitable organizations. Each of these deductions is in turn subject to special interpretations and application in particular circumstances. We can only note in passing the broad outlines of each item.

The authorized deduction of all debts against the gross estate in the determination of the taxable estate means, of course, that the federal estate tax is imposed on the *net* value of the taxpayer's property, not on its gross value. A taxpayer who purchases a $300,000 property on a contract requiring a $50,000 down payment and assumption of a $250,000 mortgage shortly before his death would not be increasing the size of his taxable estate by making such an acquisition. This result is in direct contrast with the usual property tax based on gross values. As noted earlier, the estate tax is not a property tax, even though valuation of property owned is the first step in the tax-determination process.

The deduction authorized for administrative expenses includes the executor's commission, attorneys' fees, court costs, and all costs associated with selling property and otherwise managing the estate after the taxpayer's death and prior to the property distribution. The right to deduct funeral expenses serves similarly to reduce the estate tax base to the net value of property that a deceased person could actually pass to family or other heirs before giving consideration to the estate tax itself.

The $60,000 specific exemption serves to remove all small estates from the federal estate tax. In effect, it means that any net estate of less than $60,000 will automatically be free of this particular tax. Several states impose a state inheritance tax on estates of less than $60,000. Therefore an estate may be subject to an inheritance tax even if it is not subject to an estate tax.

The 50 percent marital deduction is intended to equate the tax results of persons living in non-community-property states with those living in community-property states. The community-property laws in effect provide that one half of everything accumulated during a marriage belongs equally to each partner to the marriage. This presumption serves, of course, to reduce the size of the estate that passes at the time of the primary wage-earner's death. The marital deduction tends to correct the potential inequity that otherwise would apply to residents of the common-law states.

Finally, the law authorizes a deduction for property transferred to a nonprofit religious, charitable, scientific, literary, or educational organization or to the U.S. government or one of its political subdivisions. In general this deduction is limited to present interests in property. A remainder interest—that is, an interest that will mature on the death of a designated person at some time in the future—may be deductible, however, if the charitable remainder is in a farm or a personal residence. Other special rules apply to the deduction of charitable gifts made in trust.

The tax rates. The tax rate applied to the taxable estate is determined according to a progressive rate schedule specified in Code Section 2001. The present estate tax rates are given in Table 11–2. By comparing Table 11–1 and Table 11–2, the reader can observe that the gift-tax rates tend to be approximately 75 percent of the estate-tax rates on an equivalent tax base. Both taxes cease to be progressive beyond $10 million. The highest marginal rate applicable to the gift tax is 57.75 percent; the highest marginal rate applicable to the estate tax is 77 percent. These observations become critical to certain tax-planning opportunities which will be explained later.

Tax credits. The federal estate tax authorizes tax credits for: (1) any federal gift tax paid on property that was also included in the gross estate; (2) state inheritance taxes, subject to certain limits and adjustments; and (3) prior federal estate taxes paid on properties included in more than one estate within a ten-year period. Each of these tax credits, as well as a possible foreign death-tax credit, is intended to reduce the multiple taxation of a single tax base. We noted earlier the possible need to include gifts made in contemplation of death within the value of the gross estate. This means, of course, that a single property transfer may be subject to both the federal gift tax and the federal estate tax. In order to avoid the multiple taxation of this one property transfer, the estate tax authorizes the tax credit for the gift tax paid (or payable) on the same property. The combined effect of (a) the inclusion of property transferred in contemplation of death with the gross estate and (b) the gift-tax credit is to tax such a transfer at the higher of the two tax rates.

TABLE 11–2
1973 Estate tax rates

If the taxable estate is		The amount of the gross tax liability is			
Over	But not over	A basic amount	Plus	A marginal rate times	The amount over
$ 0	$ 5,000	$ 0	+	3%	$ 0
5,000	10,000	150	+	7%	5,000
10,000	20,000	500	+	11%	10,000
20,000	30,000	1,600	+	14%	20,000
30,000	40,000	3,000	+	18%	30,000
40,000	50,000	4,800	+	22%	40,000
50,000	60,000	7,000	+	25%	50,000
60,000	100,000	9,500	+	28%	60,000
100,000	250,000	20,700	+	30%	100,000
250,000	500,000	65,700	+	32%	250,000
500,000	750,000	145,700	+	35%	500,000
750,000	1,000,000	233,200	+	37%	750,000
1,000,000	1,250,000	325,700	+	39%	1,000,000
1,250,000	1,500,000	423,200	+	42%	1,250,000
1,500,000	2,000,000	528,200	+	45%	1,500,000
2,000,000	2,500,000	753,200	+	49%	2,000,000
2,500,000	3,000,000	998,200	+	53%	2,500,000
3,000,000	3,500,000	1,263,200	+	56%	3,000,000
3,500,000	4,000,000	1,543,200	+	59%	3,500,000
4,000,000	5,000,000	1,838,200	+	63%	4,000,000
5,000,000	6,000,000	2,468,200	+	67%	5,000,000
6,000,000	7,000,000	3,138,200	+	70%	6,000,000
7,000,000	8,000,000	3,838,200	+	73%	7,000,000
8,000,000	10,000,000	4,568,200	+	76%	8,000,000
10,000,000	...	6,088,200	+	77%	10,000,000

The tax credit allowed against the federal estate tax for taxes paid as state inheritance taxes serves to provide all states with a minimum revenue from inheritance taxes. If an individual state did not provide such a tax, its residents would obtain no personal benefit since the federal estate tax would be increased accordingly. On the other hand, if an individual state attempted to increase its own state inheritance tax substantially beyond the maximum federal tax credit, it would stand a real chance of losing its more wealthy citizens to another state. The few states that have attempted to impose significantly higher inheritance taxes have found that state residency is often a mobile condition, especially for the most wealthy taxpayers.

The tax credit allowed for successive federal estate taxes on specific properties included as part of more than one taxable estate within a single ten-year period is intended to reduce the potential cumulative effect of the estate tax. The amount of this credit is directly related to the time interval that has elapsed between the deaths of the various owners. If two years or less have elapsed since the property was last passed through a taxable estate, the tax credit is 100 percent of the previous estate tax; if two to four years have elapsed, the credit is equal to 80 percent of the prior tax; if four to six years, it is 60 percent; if six to eight years, 40 percent; and if eight to ten years, 20 percent. No tax credit is allowed if the property last passed through a taxable estate more than ten years earlier. As a practical matter this tax credit is of rather limited importance because most people with substantial property typically arrange their personal affairs to insure that property will not pass through a taxable estate in anything short of 50 to 100 years under ordinary circumstances.

Planning considerations

The federal estate tax cannot be permanently avoided, because death remains a certainty for everyone, unless a taxpayer is willing to renounce his United States citizenship and become a citizen and resident of a non-estate-taxing country. If a taxpayer dies intestate (that is, without a will), the laws of his state of residency will determine how property is divided among potential heirs. In general, a person's property will be divided between his surviving spouse and children, if any. If no children or spouse survives the taxpayer, the property usually will pass to any grandchildren. If there is no surviving spouse, child, or grandchild, the property typically will be divided among siblings. The exact rules are commonly referred to as the laws of decent and distribution, and they vary from one state to the next. If a taxpayer prepares a valid will prior to his death, he may, within certain limits, distribute his properties in any manner he sees fit. The most powerful estate tax avoidance technique available to wealthy taxpayers is usually the creation of one or more generation-skipping trusts by the terms of the taxpayer's will.

Generation skipping. The aggregate estate tax for a family unit obviously will be minimized over several years if the taxpayer leaves his property to the youngest possible heir, other things being equal. Assuming a normal life expectancy for all potential heirs, a taxpayer might even attempt to leave his property to yet unborn descendants in order to minimize the estate-tax liability that would attach to properties passed through several generations of the family. The greatest problem with that solution is, of course, the fact that most taxpayers are unwilling to ignore blindly the potential financial needs of all intervening generations in the interest of saving an estate tax or two. A wealthy taxpayer might, however, be tempted to risk a minimal distribution to the intervening generations if there were no better alternative available to him. The better alternative usually lies in the property concept known as the life estate.

A taxpayer can provide most adequately for his surviving spouse, his children, and even his grandchildren through the creation of a trust naming them life beneficiaries of the trust income. This means that the designated life tenants have the right to enjoy the income from such property—subject, possibly, to the discretion of an appointed trustee—for so long as they shall live. Their rights do not include the right to dispose of the property itself, again subject to the possible right of a trustee to invade the trust corpus under specified conditions of need. The tax magic of this property arrangement is that when the surviving spouse, children, and grandchildren die, none of the original taxpayer's property is left to be included in their respective estates. They had only the rights of a life tenant, rights that totally expire with their lives. Because they have no residual property rights, no values are included with their gross estates.

If it were not for the rule against perpetuities, a very wealthy person might attempt to leave his entire estate to all heirs to be held only as life tenants and thereby avoid any further estate tax on his accumulated wealth. The rule against perpetuities requires, however, that some individual be named as a remainderman. The remainderman is a person in whom total property rights will vest after all intervening life estates have run their course. The rule against perpetuities further requires that the remainderman be a person born within 21 years after the life of a person who is living when the trust is created. This rule generally allows a taxpayer no less than three generations to receive the benefit of accumulated property without the imposition of a second estate tax. Thus, it is not unusual for 100 years to pass before a single property becomes subject to an estate tax for the second time.

Deathbed gifts. A taxpayer who has never taken advantage of his right to make gratuitous dispositions of property at gift tax rates, which are lower than estate tax rates, has one final opportunity to achieve a tax saving by making a deathbed gift. This peculiar situation results from a combination of two basic rules explained earlier. Specifically, tax savings result from the fact that (a) the estate tax is based on the net value of the estate, after giving consideration to all debts, and (*b*) the estate can claim a tax credit against the estate tax for the amount of any gift tax payable on gifts found to be made in contemplation of death.

To illustrate this tax-saving opportunity, we shall consider the effect of a $4 million deathbed gift by a taxpayer with a net taxable estate of $14 million before the gift. If this taxpayer does nothing to dispose of his property before death, his estate tax will amount to $9,168,200, leaving his heirs with $4,831,800 to be distributed from the net after-tax estate. If the taxpayer makes a death-bed gift of $4 million, his estate tax will be determined as follows:

Gross estate (including deathbed gift)	$14,000,000
less "new" liability for gift tax (see note below)	1,378,650
Revised taxable estate	$12,621,350
Gross estate tax liability	$ 8,106,640
less gift tax credit............................	1,378,650
Net estate-tax liability	$ 6,727,990
Value of property left in estate (after gift).............	$10,000,000
Less gift plus estate taxes (total)	8,106,640
Equals value of property distributed in estate.............	$ 1,893,360
Plus value of property given away at death..............	4,000,000
Total value distributed by deceased taxpayer.............	$ 5,893,360
less value he could distribute with no gift	4,831,800
Equals net increase in distribution due to the deathbed gift of $4 million...........................	$ 1,061,560

Note: This gift-tax liability is based on the assumption that the entire $4 million gift will be taxed as the first taxable gift of the deceased taxpayer.

The tax saving of $1,061,560 can be determined more directly, as follows. The creation of the gift tax liability, due to the deathbed gift, increased the debts of the deceased taxpayer by $1,378,650. This additional debt effectively saved the estate $1,061,560 (that is, 77 percent of $1,378,650) and cost the estate nothing because a full credit was allowed against the estate tax for the gift tax payable. As this illustration demonstrates, even deathbed gifts can be used to save taxes in extreme circumstances. If a taxpayer will plan ahead, however, much more tax can be saved for him through a systematic pattern of lifetime giving.

INTEGRATING THE INCOME, ESTATE, AND GIFT TAXES

In the final analysis, there are only two things a person can do with property that he accumulates beyond his consumption needs.

He can either retain property as part of his own estate until his death or give it to someone before his death. Each of these alternatives can be further broken down into two further possibilities for tax purposes. Relative to the property a taxpayer retains, either he can leave that property in its present form (or, possibly, he can use it only in nontaxable exchanges), or he can dispose of it in a taxable transaction and reinvest the proceeds prior to his death. Relative to the property a taxpayer gives away, he can give it either to a friend or relative, or to a charitable organization. In summary, then, the wealthy taxpayer seems to be faced with two fundamental questions: a "how much" question and a "which" question. In other words, the taxpayer must first decide how much property to give away (and how much to keep) and then select from his many properties those he should give (and those he should keep). If the only factors to be considered in this decision were tax factors, a relatively simple decision model could be constructed to help him with the decisions. In the real world, of course, nontax factors may well govern actual decisions. The taxpayer simply should be aware of all tax considerations before he makes his final decisions.

How much to give; how much to keep

All other things being equal, the wealthy taxpayer ought to divide his total estate between gifts and retained properties in such a way that the marginal tax rate applied to his last dollar of gift would be equal to the marginal tax rate applied to the last dollar passed through his estate. Carried to the extreme, this rule would say that a taxpayer ought to give his entire estate to a charitable organization because in that way he could reduce his marginal tax rate on both counts to zero. We will reject this extreme conclusion on the presumption that few people will be so motivated by tax considerations. For purposes of our immediate discussion, let us assume that a taxpayer has given to charity as much as he desires to give and that he now is concerned only with the gifts-to-family-and-friends versus retention-of-property question. The decision rule suggested earlier will be a satisfactory guide as far as tax considerations are concerned. That is, the taxpayer ought to give until the marginal tax rate on the last dollar given would be equal to the marginal tax rate applied to the last dollar of value passed through the estate.

To illustrate this decision rule, let us return again to consider an imaginary taxpayer who has accumulated a net taxable estate of $14 million and has not made any gifts beyond his $3,000 annual exclusion and the $30,000 lifetime exemption. At least three years prior to his death, this taxpayer ought to consider giving away properties valued at no less than $10.5 million, if he wants to minimize his tax consequences. That conclusion is based upon the fact that the taxpayer will pay an estate tax of more than 57.75 percent (the highest marginal tax rate for gifts) if he allows anything more than $3.5 million to pass as a part of his taxable estate. A division of $10.5 million in gifts and $3.5 million in a taxable estate would result in a total tax liability of approximately $6.4 million ($1.543 million in estate tax and $4.855 million in gift tax). This tax result is approximately $2.8 million less than would result if the taxpayer allowed the entire estate to pass without making gifts. It also is lower than any alternative division of gifts and retention of assets he might consider. It is interesting to note that this decision rule says that no one should ever allow more than $3.5 million to pass from him to his heirs in the form of a *taxable* estate. For those with larger accumulations of properties, gifts must be the order of the day.

As a practical matter, the decision rule suggested here is overly simplified because there is a time preference penalty attached to the gift tax that is not adequately expressed in this rule. The gift tax is payable immediately, or nearly so, whereas an estate tax can be deferred until after the death of a taxpayer—sometimes it can even be paid in a ten-year installment. The practical application of the suggested decision rule is further complicated by the fact that a marital deduction may serve to decrease the size of an estate substantially *if* a spouse outlives the taxpayer. Thus, a gross estate of over $6 million might be reduced to $3 million by the marital deduction alone. The decision rule is stated in terms of the *taxable* estate and *taxable* gifts and those quantities are, of course, the net quantities which remain after all authorized deductions have been subtracted from the gross value of properties owned. Sometimes, as in the case of the marital deduction, a taxpayer will not be able to determine the amount of his authorized deductions accurately until the date of his own death, since his spouse might precede him in death.

For taxable estates of between $60,000, the minimum estate subject to the estate tax, and $13.5 million, the taxpayer must consider alternative divisions of property to discover the most desirable solution. Although the preferable tax result can be stated in terms of a relatively sophisticated mathematical formula, most readers will more readily understand a random approach to finding the preferred solution. For a taxpayer with a net taxable estate of $3 million, for example, we can readily determine by reference to Tables 11–1 and 11–2 the tax effect on the following alternative divisions of property:

		Marginal tax bracket	
Value left in estate	Value given away	Estate tax (percent)	Gift tax (percent)
$3,000,000	$ 0	53	0
0	3,000,000	0	39.75
2,000,000	1,000,000	45	27.75
1,000,000	2,000,000	37	33.75
750,000	2,250,000	35	36.75
500,000	2,500,000	32	36.75

This simple comparison tells us that something approximating a $750,000 taxable estate combined with $2,250,000 in inter-vivos gifts (that is, gifts made during life) should provide a minimum tax. Other similar comparisons can be constructed for any other estate value to determine the preferred distribution of properties between gifts and estates. For smaller estates the exclusions and deductions become increasingly important. In the case of an estate of $300,000 to $400,000, for example, a careful use of the annual gift exclusion plus the lifetime exemption, combined with a marital deduction, usually can serve to render the entire estate free of either the federal estate or gift tax.

What to give; what to keep

A taxpayer who is convinced of the wisdom of giving away some of his accumulated wealth prior to death must further consider the problem of selecting taxwisely those properties he should give away and those he should retain. For purposes of this decision, primary reference should be made to the relationship between the tax basis of the properties owned and the fair market values of those same properties. In general, any one of three conditions may exist:

1. The fair market value of the property may be substantially greater than the tax basis of the property;
2. The fair market value of the property may be essentially equal to the tax basis of the property; or

3. The fair market value of the property may be substantially less than the tax basis of the property.

If all other considerations are equal, the taxpayer would generally find that the preferred dispositions are as follows:

Potential use of property	FMV > basis	FMV ≈ basis	FMV < basis
Use as source of investment capital.	No	2nd choice	1st choice
Keep (but do not use in a taxable transaction) and pass thru estate	1st choice	2nd choice	No
Give to family or friends.	2nd choice	1st choice	No
Give to charity	1st choice	2nd choice	No

A taxpayer's reasons for preferring this disposition of properties are closely related to the basis rules reviewed in Chapter 5.

Remember that a potential or "paper" loss cannot be passed to another person as a tax deduction because of the basis rules. If a depreciated property is given to anyone, the donee takes as his basis (for the determination of loss) the fair market value of the property on the date of the gift. Thus, if the donee sells the depreciated property shortly after he receives it, the loss accumulated prior to his holding period will be lost forever as far as taxation is concerned. If a depreciated property is retained and passed through the taxpayer's estate, the heir takes the fair market value of the property on the date of the deceased taxpayer's death, or six months later, as his tax basis. Thus, if the heir sells the depreciated property shortly after he receives it, the loss accumulated prior to the deceased taxpayer's death is again lost forever for tax purposes. This means that every taxpayer should always realize all tax deductible losses on his own account before death. Failure to realize such losses permanently dissipates their potential income-tax-saving value. Deathbed sales of depreciated properties are always recommended from a tax standpoint.

Substantially appreciated properties are best retained by a taxpayer and passed through his estate. This method of disposition results in a permanent forgiveness of the income tax on the value appreciation because the heirs get the step-up in basis. The estate tax will still be payable on the fair market value of the property retained, but that adds nothing at the all-important margin. The taxpayer will have to pay an estate tax if he keeps any property at all beyond the authorized deductions and exemptions. Thus, keeping appreciated properties is to his greatest advantage from a tax standpoint. Alternatively, a taxpayer can use appreciated properties as a preferred source of charitable gifts. These tax advantages will be explained shortly.

Ideally, a taxpayer will make his noncharitable gifts from properties which have a fair market value just slightly higher than their tax basis. The reason for selecting these properties for family gifts is again attributable to the basis rules for property acquired by gift. Remember that if the FMV > basis, the donee takes as his tax basis the donor's basis increased by the amount of the gift tax paid by the donor. The increase for the gift tax cannot, however, increase the tax basis in excess of the fair market value on the date of the gift. Thus, property with a slightly appreciated value is preferred. The following tabulation of possible basis under different conditions illustrates this conclusion:

Case	Donor's basis	Fair market value on date of gift	Gift tax paid	Donee's basis for determining gain	Donee's basis for determining loss
A	$100,000	$120,000	$15,000	$115,000	$115,000
B	100,000	110,000	15,000	110,000	110,000
C	100,000	90,000	15,000	100,000	90,000

The only case in which the taxpayer obtains full benefit of the tax rules is in case A, where the donee can increase his tax basis by the full amount of the gift tax paid. In case B the donee gets some but not all of the benefit of the gift tax. In case C the potential benefit of the tax is permanently lost since the donee can never add the tax to his basis, even if the property given to him should increase in value to more than the donor's cost sometime after the date of the gift. A taxpayer can also maximize his tax advantage by paying particular attention to which gifts he gives first in any calendar year because they are the gifts to which no gift tax usually will attach.

We noted in the previous section that a wealthy taxpayer usually is well advised to give away a substantial portion of his property before death because of the difference in the marginal tax rates applicable to gifts and to estates. Taxpayers following this general prescription will often discover that they have exhausted their property with essentially equal tax basis and fair market value before they have disposed of the preferred amount of property. Under these circumstances, the taxpayer should look next to appreciated property as a source of gifts to family and friends. If the donor anticipates that the donee will sell the property, he should also consider the marginal tax bracket of the recipient when making gifts. Because the donee takes a carryover basis, the donor should give the most appreciated properties to the taxpayer in the lowest marginal tax bracket. This selective giving will minimize the tax consequence for the family as a whole. If the donor, for personal reasons, wants the donee to keep a property (and not to sell it), he might consider giving the most appreciated property to the donee in the highest tax bracket because that selection will minimize the after-tax value of the gift to the donee. The lower the after-tax value the less the chances are that the donee will sell the property, based at least on purely investment criteria.

Charitable gifts

The combined effect of several tax rules is to allow a wealthy tax-payer to support his favorite eleemosynary institutions and activities at a minimum economic cost. Before we can determine the actual cost of charitable giving, it is necessary to introduce the income tax provisions pertinent to the charitable contribution deduction. In general, the Code authorizes an individual taxpayer to deduct, for income tax purposes, contributions made to charitable organizations up to a maximum of either 50 percent or 30 percent of the taxpayer's adjusted gross income. The 50 percent limit applies to contributions of cash made to public charities; the 30 percent limit applies to contributions of capital gain properties to public charities. Contributions made in excess of these limits in any one year can be carried forward and deducted in subsequent years. Contributions made to private charitable foundations have been subject to more stringent rules since the Tax Reform Act of 1969. Because private charitable foundations are no longer of primary importance to tax planning, none of these rules will be discussed here.

The act of making a gift is *not* deemed to constitute realization for income-tax purposes. This means that a taxpayer with an appreciated property can avoid any income tax by giving away his appreciated property. If the gift is made to a charitable organization, the charity can sell the property and avoid any recognition of gain because of its general exemption from the income tax. A charitable gift thus serves to avoid for everyone concerned the income tax implicit in an appreciated property. As noted earlier in this chapter, charitable gifts are also authorized deductions in the computation of both the gift tax and the estate tax. The act of making a charitable gift of an appreciated property thereby serves to reduce a taxpayer's income tax and his estate tax without increasing his gift tax.

The measure of a charitable contribution deduction depends upon the class of property given. Contributions made in cash are measured simply by the amount of cash given. Contributions of property which, if sold, would produce a long-term capital gain are measured by the fair market value of the property on the date they are given. Contributions of property which, if sold, would produce ordinary income (including short-term capital gains) are measured by the basis of the property given, unless the fair market value is lower than basis, in which case the fair market value becomes the measure of the deduction.

Translating the many related tax rules that apply to charitable contributions into practical advice, a taxpayer should consider giving *only* appreciated capital gain properties to his favorite charities. The correctness of this conclusion can be demonstrated by a comparative analysis. The comparison presented below is based on the assumptions that the contributing taxpayer: (1) is in a 70 percent marginal tax bracket as far as ordinary income is concerned; (2) is in a 35 percent marginal tax bracket as far as long-term capital gains are concerned; (3) does not exceed the annual limits for the charitable contribution deduction; (4) makes all gifts to public charities; and (5) would have sold the same properties in a taxable transaction had he not given them to the charity. Because of the assumptions implicit in these

Amount to be given (FMV)	Form of gift	Tax basis of property given	Income tax saved due to contribution deduction	Income tax saved due to nonrecognition of gain	Net real economic cost
$110,000	Cash	$110,000	$77,000	$ 0	$33,000
110,000	L.T.C.G. property	10,000	77,000	35,000	(2,000)
110,000	Ordinary income property	10,000	7,000	70,000	33,000

calculations—that is, the assumptions that the taxpayer is in the highest possible marginal tax bracket for both ordinary income and long-term capital gains, and the assumption that the donated property was a very highly appreciated property—we can determine that under some extreme conditions a taxpayer is economically better off to give his long-term capital gain property to charity than he is to sell it in the open market himself! In this illustration, the taxpayer would be able to keep only $75,000 of the proceeds if he had sold the capital gain property on the open market. That is, the $110,000 realized on the sale less the $35,000 long-term capital gains tax would leave the taxpayer with $75,000 in his pocket. If the taxpayer gave the same property to a charity, his income tax liability would be reduced by $77,000, that is 70 percent of $110,000. Because a tax reduction of $77,000 is $2,000 better than a $75,000 after-tax sale proceeds, this taxpayer actually would prefer the gift to the sale alternative.

For the vast majority of the taxpayers in the world, the extreme assumptions made here are unrealistic. Nevertheless, the tax effect on the cost of giving may be substantial. To illustrate a more likely result, let us make the same calculations for a taxpayer: (1) in a 50 percent marginal tax bracket as far as ordinary income is concerned; (2) in a 25 percent marginal tax bracket as far as long-term capital gains are concerned; (3) whose charitable contributions do not exceed the annual limitations; and (4) who would have sold the same properties in a taxable transaction had he not given them to the charity. The real economic cost of a charitable contribution is

Amount to be given (FMV)	Form of gift	Tax basis of property given	Income tax saved due to contribution deduction	Income tax saved due to nonrecognition of gain	Net real economic cost
$10,000	Cash	$10,000	$5,000	$ 0	$5,000
10,000	L.T.C.G. property	4,000	5,000	1,500	3,500
10,000	Ordinary income property	4,000	2,000	3,000	5,000

determined by the marginal tax bracket of the donor and the amount of the unrealized gain in the donated property. The higher the marginal tax bracket and the greater the unrealized gain, the lower the economic cost of making a charitable gift. In this illustration, we can see how the tax effect has allowed a taxpayer to make a $10,000 contribution to his favorite charity at a real economic cost to him of only $3,500.

Both of the last two illustrations actually overstate the real economic cost of making a charitable contribution because the act of making the gift also serves to reduce the size of the donor's taxable estate and thus his estate tax. Any refinement of the illustrations to include a measure of this additional tax saving would have to be based upon too many assumptions to have much practical value. The important conclusion, however, is that a substantial charitable gift may sometimes be made at a relatively low real after-tax cost to the donor.

Successful family tax planning obviously involves the careful consideration of personal objectives as well as income, gift, and estate tax provisions. Most successful tax plans involve a substantial lead time if they are to be implemented property. The use of life estates, placed in trust prior to a taxpayer's death, may serve to decrease the family income-tax liability as well as the donor's gift and estate tax liabilities. The careful integration of the many pertinent considerations involves full cooperation on the part of all parties. Any individual who has accumulated a significant amount of property should give serious consideration to discussing his personal situation with a qualified advisor. Personal experience of the author suggests that first-generation wealth is typically least interested in tax consequences. In other words, "the man who made it" is least concerned about what taxes might do to his accumulated estate. Second-, third-, and fourth-generation wealth are often much more willing to modify personal fortunes to minimize the tax cost for everyone.

Accounting method options

CODE SECTION 446 provides the general accounting method requirements that must be satisfied by every taxpayer. This Code Section is subdivided into five subsections which are lettered (a) through (e). Subsection 446(a) states that a taxpayer must compute his taxable income on the same method of accounting as he uses in keeping his regular books. Subsection (b) gives the Secretary of the Treasury authority to designate a particular accounting method if either the taxpayer has no regular method or the method he uses does not clearly reflect income. Subsection (c) proceeds to list several methods that may be used, including a cash method, an accrual method, and a modified cash method prescribed by Treasury regulations. Subsection 446(d) allows a taxpayer to use more than one method of accounting if he is engaged in more than one trade or business. And, finally, subsection (e) requires a taxpayer to obtain the prior consent of the commissioner if he desires to change his method of accounting. Collectively, these requirements are sufficiently flexible to permit every taxpayer a maximum opportunity to select the most favorable method of accounting. Except for an occasional refusal to authorize a change in accounting methods, the statutory requirements have been interpreted rather liberally. Thus, it is doubly important for every taxpayer to make his initial selection wisely.

In addition to selecting one general method of accounting for each trade or business, a taxpayer must select many specific accounting procedures and conventions to be utilized in implementing a single method of accounting. The number of alternative accounting procedures and conventions is substantially larger than the number of generally accepted accounting methods. Each election can have a significant impact on the tax liability ultimately reported for any taxpayer. In this chapter, we shall consider some of the more important planning aspects of the various accounting methods and conventions. The first portion of the chapter will be concerned with general methods of accounting; the second portion, with more specific accounting procedures and conventions. The Code contains over 50 elections that must be made within the first tax year of any taxable entity and several hundred additional elections which can be made in any year in which they are applicable to a taxpayer. A number of these elections are essentially equivalent to an alternative accounting procedure. We shall consider here a few of the more important tax accounting elections.

GENERAL METHODS OF ACCOUNTING

The most commonly known methods of accounting are the cash receipts and disbursements method, usually called the "cash method", the accrual method, and the completed contract method. For tax purposes, a fourth method of accounting, called the installment method, has been accepted both for general use and for reporting specific transactions. The income reported by a taxpayer in any single year will differ importantly under each of these accounting methods. Although the aggregate net differences will tend to be reduced over a long period of time, they still are important for tax purposes because of the time preference value of money. The longer a taxpayer can defer a tax liability, other things being equal, the smaller the real economic cost of the tax.

The cash method

The vast majority of individual taxpayers report their taxable income on a cash method of accounting. This means, of course, that they report their items of gross income in the year in which they receive cash or other property and that they report deductions in the year in which they pay for a deductible expense. The only financial records typically maintained by these taxpayers are a check book and an odd collection of cancelled checks, "paid" vouchers, sales receipts, and some miscellaneous notes and diary-type records. These documents along with the Form W-2 (the "Wage and Tax Statement" prepared by the taxpayer's employer) and the Forms 1099 (the "U.S. Information Returns" prepared by banks, savings and loan associations, dividend-paying corporations, and other payors of miscellaneous earnings) are somehow combined to provide the necessary information required to complete an individual tax return (Form 1040 or 1040A) by April 15 each year.

Most service-oriented businesses, including the professions of medicine, dentistry, law, and accountancy, also report their taxable income on a cash method. In these instances, however, it is common to find a more complete and accurate set of financial records. Farms, restaurants, gasoline stations, and other businesses that combine a service orientation with sometimes large capital investments typically report on a modified cash basis of accounting. Most of their modifications are attributable to capital investments in fixed assets that can only be capitalized and depreciated over a useful life.

Specific limitations. The only general restrictions historically placed on the cash method of accounting have been those for capital improvements and for businesses in which the sale of merchandise is a material income-producing factor. The prescribed treatment of capital investments was explained in Chapter 8. In businesses in which merchandise is important, the law usually requires an adjustment to the cash method of accounting for changes in year-end inventories. If this adjustment were not mandatory a taxpayer could very easily reduce his reported net income by increasing his stock of inventory and increase his reported net income by depleting his normal inventory. The effect of the required adjustment is to change only the computation of the tax deduction for the cost of merchandise sold from a strict cash basis to an accrual basis of accounting. The deduction for the cost of merchandise sold must be made as follows:

Cost of merchandise on hand at first of year
Plus cost of merchandise purchased during the year
Equals cost of merchandise available for sale
Less cost of merchandise on hand at end of year
Equals the tax-deductible cost of merchandise sold

In other words, a cash-basis taxpayer can deduct only the amount shown on the last line of the above formula, not the amount shown on the second line of that formula, as his cost of goods sold. The remaining elements of taxable income can generally be reported on a cash receipts and disbursements basis. This is what the Treasury Regulations refer to as a modified cash basis of accounting.

In addition to the general restrictions for capital expenditures and for the cost of goods sold, a number of special restrictions on the cash method of accounting have been imposed by the IRS and the courts in particular instances. For example, we noted in Chapter 6 that a cash-basis taxpayer must report capital *losses*, but not capital gains, in the year a sale is made even though he does not receive the proceeds of the sale until the following accounting period. The rationale for this special administrative interpretation is unknown.

For more obvious reasons, the IRS and the courts require that a cash-basis taxpayer report extraordinary transactions on a cash-equivalent basis rather than on a literal cash basis. If they had not made this interpretation, all barter-type transactions would remain tax free for all cash-basis taxpayers. Quite obviously, that temptation would be too great to resist. Given our present tax rates, the nation could be turned into a semi-barter economy overnight by any contrary interpretation of a cash basis of accounting. In effect, this means that even if a taxpayer reports his recurring salary, dividends, interest, professional fees, rents, royalties, and other items of routine income on a cash basis, he cannot report his sale of an investment or "capital-type" asset on that same cash basis. In the latter instance, the authorities will require that the taxpayer determine the fair market value of any assets received and that he then report his taxable income on something of a cash-equivalent basis. If a cash-basis taxpayer desires to defer the recognition of income from an extraordinary transaction until he actually receives cash, it is necessary for him either to comply with the special tax provisions for installment sales or to fall within the nontaxable exchange provisions of Chapter 9. The installment sale provisions will be discussed later in this chapter.

Advantage of the cash method. Except for the specific limitations just observed, a taxpayer reporting his taxable income on a cash receipts and disbursements basis has a tremendous ability to control the timing of many tax-critical events. The importance of proper timing has been noted throughout this book. In Chapter 6, for example, we noted how the proper timing of year-end security transactions can critically change the amount of tax payable on particular capital gains and losses. In Chapter 3 we noted how a taxpayer might maximize his use of the standard deduction by the careful timing of his personal or "other itemized" deductions.

There are literally hundreds of other circumstances in which a cash-basis taxpayer can change his tax liability by changing the date on which he does certain things. A taxpayer who has earned an unusually large income in a particular year can help to reduce the marginal tax rate which would be applied to his income by either deferring additional income or by accelerating the payment of all tax deductible items. A professional man may, for example, defer the mailing of his bills to clients during the last month of his high income year and thereby discourage many clients from paying until early in the next accounting period. Alternatively or concurrently, a taxpayer in a high income year might lay in an unusually large stock of expendible supplies and deduct them by making a timely payment. A farmer, for example, could purchase extra feed, fertilizer, or seed near the year end. Another taxpayer might prepay interest or property taxes, or make early charitable contributions, if he needs more tax deductions in the current year. If an extraordinary sale is made at a large profit near the year's end, the sale may be arranged as an installment sale and the first payment deferred until the next year. These general ideas apply equally well to any taxpayer who has some basis for predicting a substantially smaller taxable income in a subsequent accounting period. Just the opposite kind of action would be recommended for any taxpayer anticipating a substantial increase in taxable income.

In a limited number of extreme circumstances, the IRS and the courts may disallow an otherwise authorized tax deduction claimed by a cash-basis taxpayer on the grounds that the item seriously distorts the reported income of the taxpayer. In the case of "excess investment interest," the Treasury Department recently convinced Congress to pass restrictive legislation. The effect of the new statutory provision is to disallow a deduction for interest expense incurred on a loan made to finance investments that do not produce much in the way of ordinary taxable income. This statutory disallowance of interest will not apply until the interest expense exceeds $25,000 plus the ordinary income produced by the investments. Taxpayers borrowing such large sums of money undoubtedly have sufficient expert assistance to alert them to the potential tax problem. Taxpayers with more limited ambitions and opportunities should simply remember that the IRS *may* be able to deny an otherwise legitimate cash-basis tax deduction if that deduction seriously distorts taxable income in a given year. The potential hazard of disallowance notwithstanding, the taxpayer reporting income on a cash method of accounting retains a maximum opportunity for successful tax planning.

The accrual method

The accrual method of accounting is utilized by virtually all large corporate businesses. Most professional accountants would insist that only an accrual method of accounting can determine a meaningful income figure, at least for purposes of financial reporting. The essence of the accrual method of accounting is the belief that revenues (or gross income) should be recognized when *earned,* regardless of when cash is received, and that expenses should be matched against the revenues they produce and thereby be deducted in the year the correspondent revenue is recognized, not in the year in which the expenses happen to be paid. Professional accountants admittedly have problems in deciding exactly when some revenues have been earned and in determining the causal relationship between certain expenditures and the correspondent revenues. They have other problems in measurement relative to both revenues and expenses. Nevertheless, most practicing accountants agree on the general procedures utilized in measuring income on an accrual basis. In recent years, the Accounting Principles Board has attempted to reduce the number of acceptable alternative procedures that can be applied in common situations. A successor organization, the Financial Accounting Standards Board, is expected to continue this trend toward uniformity in reporting standards for financial reporting purposes. Although accrual accounting for tax purposes is occasionally at variance with accrual accounting for financial purposes, there is more similarity than difference between the two concepts.

Required usage. We noted in the introduction to this chapter that Code Section 446(a) requires a taxpayer to compute his taxable income on the same method of accounting as he uses in keeping his regular books. This means that for all practical purposes most large corporations have no realistic option but to report taxable income on an accrual method of accounting. A few medium-sized businesses have managed to convince the courts that they are satisfying the Code requirements by keeping a set of reconciling adjustments between accrual basis books and cash basis tax returns. A few other institutions, most notably banks, have managed to continue to report their taxable incomes on a cash basis. With these exceptions, however, most taxpayers will find that it is preferable to keep their routine books on a cash basis if they desire to report income for tax purposes on a cash basis. If cash basis books are adequately maintained, it is relatively easy for an accountant to convert a cash basis income determination to an accrual basis one any time the need arises. If, for example, a bank or other credit institution demands an accrual basis income statement from a cash basis taxpayer, a certified public accountant usually can prepare such a statement at a minimum cost so long as a good set of cash basis records has been maintained. Arranging affairs in this way minimizes the risk that an accrual basis method of tax reporting may be demanded by the IRS under the requirements of Code Section 446(a).

Special limitations. Even if a taxpayer maintains his regular books and files his tax return on an accrual method of accounting, there typically will be a number of differences between specific items as reported on the financial statements and the tax return. Most of the significant differences can be traced to Code provisions that were enacted to achieve particular economic or social objectives. The rapid amortization provisions and percentage depletion are just two examples of such differences. Other differences can be attributed to administrative considerations peculiar to taxation. The Code, for example, does not generally authorize the deduction of estimated future expenses that are reported currently for financial accounting. Even though the traditional explanation for this difference is made in terms of the large revenue losses for the government, a more realistic explanation is the fear that acceptance of such estimated amounts as an authorized tax deduction would lead to widespread disagreement between the taxpayer and the tax collector. To the maximum extent possible, the trend over the past several years has been to reduce the areas of potential disagreement, even if that has meant a revenue loss for the government. The acceptance of accelerated guideline lives for depreciation purposes, and the acceptance of the repair allowance concept as part of the asset depreciation range system, are two recent cases in point. In yet other situations, the differences between accrual method accounting figures for tax and for financial accounting purposes can be explained on a where-withal-to-pay concept. The nontaxable exchanges, explained in Chapter 9, have no counterpart in financial accounting. The apparent difference is in no small measure related to the fact that a taxpayer has no dollars with which to pay a tax, even if he has a substantial realized gain, when he enters into a nontaxable transaction. In select situations, Congress has found this sufficient reason to permit the deferral of the tax liability. In financial accounting there is no comparable reason for deferring the recognition of income and, therefore, accounting typically recognizes all gains and losses as soon as they have been realized.

In addition to these general differences between the accrual method of accounting as it is utilized for financial and for tax purposes, the Code provides some very special limitations in unusual situations. Section 267, for example, disallows any tax deduction for the loss realized on a sale or exchange of property between certain related taxpayers. The disallowance is applicable for tax purposes, no matter how real the sale transaction might be in legal or economic terms, if the stipulated Code conditions are satisfied. Another subsection of that same Code provision disallows the deduction of certain expenses *accrued* by a taxpayer for the benefit of a related cash basis taxpayer, if the accrued liability is not paid within two and one-half months after the close of the accrual basis taxpayer's year. The reason for this special provision is most easily understood in the context of a closely held corporation that reports its taxable income on an accrual method of accounting. If the statutory prohibition did not exist, the owner of the corporation could declare a salary payable to himself and thus obtain an immediate tax deduction for his accrual basis corporation. As a cash basis taxpayer, the owner would not have to report any taxable income from such a salary until he decided to have his corporation make a payment on the accrued liability for his own salary. The owner-operator could obviously defer any recognition of taxable income until a most convenient year and still have the benefit of the immediate tax deduction in his corporate entity. The effect of the two and one-half month rule is to allow the taxpayer a maximum one-year time lag between any deduction by the accrual basis taxpayer and the recognition of income by the cash basis taxpayer who are related to each other. Even though the rule limits the potential advantage of this idea, it does not preclude the possibility of a substantial tax saving under the proper circumstances.

Considerations in electing the accrual method. The large incorporated business has little alternative but to keep its records, tax as well as financial, on an accrual basis. The smaller business, on the other hand, has a viable option. Perhaps the greatest disadvantages associated with the accrual method of accounting for tax purposes are: (1) the reduction in the taxpayer's control over the timing of both gross income and tax deductions; (2) the extra cost and complexity commonly associated with a complete accrual accounting system; and (3) the potential need to recognize taxable income prior to the receipt of cash with which the taxpayer can pay his tax liability. Most of the advantages associated with an accrual method of accounting are financial rather than tax related. The greatest advantage probably is the increase in the accuracy of the income measurement, which, hopefully, permits the manager to operate a business more effectively. Lesser advantages accrue for tax purposes (1) because of the relative ease of taxpayer compliance, once an accrual accounting system is maintained, and (2) because of the ability to make the one-time accelerated tax deduction for debts owed to a related taxpayer reporting on the cash basis.

The completed contract method

Construction projects which require longer than a single accounting period for completion usually can be reported under one of two alternative methods of accounting. These methods are the percentage-of-completion method and the completed-contract method. The latter of the two methods is the more widely utilized. Under a completed contract method of accounting, no item of gross income or tax deduction is authorized until the entire contract has been completed. Prior to completion, the taxpayer effectively records all advance receipts and disbursements in a suspense accounting which is finally cleared when each project is finished.

A major reason for electing the completed contract method of accounting for tax purposes is the obvious fact that it defers any tax liability on a profitable contract until the last possible moment. A second and equally pragmatic reason for preferring a completed contract method of account for long-term projects is the fact that it minimizes the number of estimates that have to be made. This, in turn, minimizes the number of potential disputes between the taxpayer and the IRS. Finally, the completed contract method defers the tax liability until the time a taxpayer has the greatest financial capacity to pay the tax due. Each of these reasons contributes significantly to the popularity of this accounting method in industries characterized by extended building, installation, and construction projects.

The most serious disadvantage of the completed contract method of accounting is its tendency to bunch income and losses into years on an irregular basis. This bunching is especially disadvantageous when a progressive tax rate schedule is applied to taxable income. Although income averaging serves to reduce the severity of the tax distortion for individual taxpayers, it is a less than perfect solution and it is wholly ineffective in loss years. A corporate taxpayer typically will be less affected than an individual taxpayer by the bunching of income both because of the relative absence of progression in the corporate tax rate schedule and because of the more limited number of adjustments that have to be made to convert a negative taxable income into a deductible net operating loss. Large corporations may also be less affected by bunching because of the greater number of contracts negotiated. If an approximately equal number of equally profitable projects are completed each year, bunching tends to disappear. One final reason for rejecting the completed contract method of accounting is the fact that it defers a deduction for any loss incurred until the last possible year.

The installment method

The installment method of accounting may be either a general method used by dealers in property or a special method selected for casual sales of property by a taxpayer reporting his more routine taxable income on some other method of accounting. Under both circumstances the fundamental idea is to defer the recognition of taxable income until the receipt of cash. The taxpayer must determine a gross profit ratio for the authorized installment sale(s) and then apply this ratio to each cash collection to determine the amount of gross income that he must recognize. For example, if a taxpayer sold a property with an $80,000 adjusted tax basis for $100,000, he would have realized a $20,000 gross profit on the sale. Thus, the taxpayer's gross profit ratio would be 20 percent ($20,000 gross profit divided by $100,000 sales price) and, if the sale qualified as an installment sale, he would recognize only 20 percent of any collections on this sale as taxable income in each year.

Dealer sales. Dealers in both real and personal property may elect to report their taxable income on an installment basis. In the case of personal property sales, the dealer's gross profit ratio generally is computed as a single percentage for an entire year. Collections are separated by the year of sale and the appropriate percentages are applied to collections to determine the gross income to report in any one year. Special provisions are made for repossessions, transfers of debt, imputed interest, etc. In the case of real estate sales, the taxpayer cannot receive more than 30 percent of the sales price in the year of the sale if the installment method of accounting is to be utilized. If the sales contract involves a capital asset and it does not provide for at least 4 percent simple interest, the law will impute interest at the rate of 5 percent. In some situations, this imputation can reduce the sales price sufficiently to disallow an intended installment sale of real property because the cash received in the year of the sale exceeds 30 percent of the reduced sales price, even though it did not exceed 30 percent of the original contract price.

Casual sales by nondealers. Taxpayers reporting their recurring taxable income on either a cash or an accrual method of accounting may elect to report casual sales of property on an installment basis if all of the conditions set forth below are satisfied. Most importantly, the installment method may be utilized for casual sales only if the taxpayer receives payments of less than 30 percent of the selling price in the year of sale and if payment is made in two or more installments. Just as in the case of dealer sales, the casual sale of a capital asset must provide for interest at the rate of 4 percent or more per annum. Failure to make a provision for sufficient interest will result in the imputation of interest and risk the loss of installment sale privileges because of the 30 percent limitation. Casual sales of personal property—that is, of non-realty—are further limited to sales involving $1,000 or more.

Planning considerations. The major advantage of the installment method of accounting for the dealer is the fact that it defers the recognition of the income tax as long as possible. For the individual taxpayer concerned with the casual sale of property, the installment sale has additional possible advantages. If the taxpayer anticipates a reduction in his marginal tax rate in the future, perhaps because of retirement, it is especially important for him to consider utilization of the installment sale provision. In this instance the tax is not only deferred as long as possible, it is also taxed at the lowest possible marginal rate. On the other hand, a taxpayer looking forward to a substantially increased taxable income in the future should probably avoid an installment sale even if this means an earlier payment of the tax. The increase in the marginal tax rate could very easily offset any time preference value of a tax deferral.

The $50,000 annual limitation on the amount of long-term capital gains eligible for the 25 percent alternative tax may also provide a good reason for seeking to arrange an installment sale. By spreading a larger long-term capital gain over an appropriate number of years, an individual taxpayer can reduce the effective marginal tax rate on the gain from 35 percent to 25 percent and, at the same time, achieve the benefit of the deferred tax liability. If the taxpayer can provide a minimum interest (4 percent) and substitute a higher sales price for the additional interest factor in the sale contract, he can effectively convert additional ordinary income into long-term capital gain. This possibility was explained earlier, on pages 108–9. In summary, the installment sale must be remembered both as a potential general method of accounting and as a specific accounting procedure that can be elected on a casual sale of property.

ACCOUNTING PROCEDURES AND CONVENTIONS

The number of alternative accounting procedures and conventions is substantially greater than the number of alternative general methods of accounting. We noted in Chapter 8, for example, that the Code authorizes a number of accounting procedures to determine the cost allocations common to depreciation. The acceptable depreciation procedures include a straight-line, sum-of-the-years digits, 125-percent, 150-percent, and 200-percent declining balance alternative. Earlier in this chapter, we also observed the need to determine the deduction for the cost of goods sold on an accrual basis, without regard for the taxpayer's usual method of accounting. We did not observe there, however, that the cost-of-goods-sold determination can be made under any of several alternative inventory costing conventions including FIFO (first-in first-out), LIFO (last-in first-out), weighted-average, moving-average, retail-sales, and specific identification. Each of these accounting conventions or procedures will yield a different taxable income in anything other than a perfectly static economy.

Inventory costing conventions. Time and space constraints preclude any detailed examination of each of the inventory costing conventions just noted. The reader should be aware, however, that the selection of an inventory costing convention may have a substantial impact on the amount of taxable income that he must recognize. During a period of rising prices, it generally is to the taxpayer's advantage to utilize a LIFO costing technique because, as the name implies, the assumption under that costing convention is that the very last goods to be purchased during a year were the first to be sold! During a period of rising prices, the last goods to be purchased are the most costly. If we assume that the most costly goods were the first to be sold, we are in effect charging the highest priced goods to the tax deductible cost of goods sold and charging the least expensive goods to the ending inventory, a nondeductible asset. During a period of falling prices, the FIFO costing technique would yield the largest tax deduction and the lowest inventory valuation. The other inventory costing techniques tend to yield an intermediate measure of both the cost of goods sold and the ending inventory. If a taxpayer desires to use the LIFO method of inventory costing for tax purposes, he may also be required to use it for financial accounting purposes. And if a taxpayer desires to change from one inventory costing convention to another, he must obtain the consent of the commissioner and make an appropriate adjustment to his reported taxable income in the year of change.

The unit of account. The basic unit of account selected for any single element of a larger accounting system may have a substantial impact on the income reported by that system in a given year. The phrase "unit of account" refers to the lowest common denominator in any accounting classification. Relative to an automobile, for example, the unit of account may be each specific car, some portion of a car, say, the motor, or an entire fleet of cars. Relative to a building, the unit of account may vary from the building as a single physical structure to literally thousands of component parts (such as wiring, plumbing, roof, elevators and escalators, carpeting, furnishings), or, alternatively, to a cluster of buildings which share a common purpose. The selection of the most desirable unit of account for tax purposes may be especially important because that selection may affect the eligibility of an item for the investment credit; the maximum amount of depreciation which may be applied to it; the selection of an estimated useful life; and the classification of related expenditures as immediately deductible repairs or as nondeductible capital investments. The general problem of the unit of account is essentially equivalent to the problem relative to percentage depletion which we considered on pages 176 and 177. We noted there that it sometimes is desirable to combine more than one depletable property and to treat the combination as a single property. Under other circumstances, we observed that it is desirable to separate two or more properties and to treat them individually for tax purposes. Generally, the broader we make the unit of account the more likely we are to increase the estimated useful life. On the other hand, the broader the unit of account the more likely that we can treat a particular related expenditure as an immediately deductible repair and the less likely the need to recognize a gain on the disposition of some small element within the larger unit. The selection of the most tax-advantageous unit of account can only proceed on an item-by-item investigation.

Other convenient tax assumptions. In addition to selecting a most appropriate unit of account, a taxpayer typically may make certain other assumptions to further simplify his tax accounting system. A taxpayer of any size cannot, for example, calculate depreciation on a daily basis. He is buying, selling, and trading fixed assets throughout the year and he usually cannot afford to make separate depreciation determinations for each of the many transactions. Thus in addition to the right to group similar fixed assets into a single unit of account, the Code authorizes a taxpayer to make certain standard assumptions about the timing of all acquisitions and dispositions during a year. For example, a taxpayer may assume either (*a*) that all acquisitions occurred in the middle of the year, or (*b*) that all acquisitions during the first six months of the year occurred on the first day of the year and that all acquisitions made during the last half of the year occurred on the first day of the following year. The IRS usually will accept such an assumption if the taxpayer will follow it consistently. Once a convention is established the taxpayer can time acquisitions and dispositions in a most favorable manner.

Fiscal year. A year is the period commonly used to measure income for tax purposes. That year can be a fiscal year or a calendar year. Many taxpayers who own and manage their own business attempt to arrange a fiscal year for the business which is just slightly different from the tax year utilized by them as an individual. If a business is placed on a fiscal year ending January 31, and the owner-operator is on a calendar year, for example, the business can adjust its salary payments to the owner-operator in January with no tax consequences to the individual for an entire year. This ability to defer the tax liability for the income from a business for one entire year is tantamount to permanently excusing one year's income from taxation.

If a taxpayer wishes to modify the taxable year of any taxable entity, he generally must get the consent of the commissioner before he makes the change. It sometimes is easier to make an initial election wisely than to obtain the commissioner's permission to change. If a taxpayer obtains permission to modify a tax year, he generally must file a short-period return. In some situations, the adjustment procedure required in preparing a short-period return may result in an unusually large tax liability which can be corrected only if the taxpayer first pays the tax and then, at the end of his regular accounting period (prior to the change), he files a claim for refund based on actual results for the prior 12 months. A failure to file the refund claim on a timely basis may result in the taxpayer permanently losing his right to do so.

Records: good and bad. Every taxpayer should remember that in tax matters the presumption of the court, generally, is that the IRS is correct until proven wrong. This presumption for the government argues for a good accounting system. At one time in our history, a taxpayer could rely on the mercy of the court to grant him a reasonable allowance for any tax item that he could not prove. That doctrine was known popularly as the "Cohan Rule" because of a court case between the IRS and the famous entertainer, George M. Cohan, over certain entertainment expenses. In the recent past, the courts have exhibited an increasing reluctance to follow the Cohan Rule and taxpayers are well advised to keep the best possible records if they wish to obtain the most favorable tax result.

Small taxpayers in particular may be surprised to discover the reluctance of the IRS to accept what appear to them to be perfectly reasonable validation records. In the case of the charitable contribution deduction, for example, the IRS has sometimes refused to accept a cancelled check as sufficient evidence of the fact that a contribution has in fact been made. The reason for their hesitancy in this instance stems from a case in which a physician cashed a check each Sunday with his church treasurer for the alleged purpose of obtaining sufficient change to open his office on Monday morning. The taxpayer in fact used the check as evidence of an apparent charitable contribution. The ruse was discovered and the cancelled check suddenly lost much of its potential value as evidence of a valid tax deduction under some circumstances.

The need for good records is evident in many aspects of successful tax planning. As one final illustration, however, we might return to the world of the capital gain. Taxpayers who have purchased more than a single block of stock in a particular corporation, and who have allowed their stock certificates to remain in the custody of the brokerage house, have occasionally been surprised to discover that their intended long-term capital gain turned into a short-term capital gain because of a failure in communication. This has happened when an investor has simply instructed his broker to sell 100 shares of ABC Corporation common stock without designating which block of shares the broker is to utilize in completing the sale. If the broker inadvertently utilizes a certificate purchased within six months of the sale, and if the IRS discovers which block of stock was actually used to complete the sale, it will follow a specific identification inventory method and insist that the sale completed actually involved the sale of an asset held for less than six months, notwithstanding the fact that the taxpayer intended that the broker use an earlier acquisition to complete the sale.

Although it is almost impossible to overestimate the value of a truly good set of accounting records in income tax matters, it is very easy to underestimate the potential value of other records. In some situations, an IRS agent or a court will accept a purely personal (and often sloppily prepared) diary as evidence of certain tax-deductible expenditures. Although such personal records may be worthless in suspicious cases, they tend to corroborate other evidence of good faith and sometimes spell the difference between getting administrative agreement and going to court. The taxpayer should not destroy charge slips, guest lists, convention programs, and other evidence which may support a questionable tax deduction for travel, entertainment, or other business expenses. Guest logs are almost necessary to support some tax deductions for club memberships and other entertainment facilities. Even a good colored photograph may help to sustain the claim for a casualty loss deduction. A taxpayer sensitized to the many tax opportunities and pitfalls should also begin to comprehend the need for validation records, good or bad.

One-time elections. The Code contains more than 50 elections that pertain to newly organized businesses. A few of these provisions are worded in such a way that the taxpayer has a minimal opportunity to correct an initial "bad" decision. Code Section 248, for example, authorizes a corporation to amortize organization expenses over a period of 60 months or longer. If the corporate officers fail to make the election on a timely basis, however, none of the organization expenses can ever be deducted until the corporation is dissolved.

In Chapter 8, we noted the fact that a taxpayer can never extend an original estimated life to obtain a larger investment credit, if he uses a fixed asset for a period longer than he originally estimated. For this reason, a taxpayer may be inclined initially to estimate a useful life of at least seven years for all investment purchases that qualify for the investment credit. The taxpayer will discover, however, that he must use the same estimated life for both investment credit and depreciation purposes. Generally speaking the shortest possible life estimate is preferred for depreciation purposes. Thus, the taxpayer must make an important decision at the time he acquires any property eligible for an investment credit: Should he extend an estimated life to obtain the potential benefit of the larger investment credit, realizing that he may have to recapture part or all of that investment credit if he makes an earlier disposition, or should he minimize the estimated life to obtain the potential benefit of a larger depreciation deduction?

These are just two examples of important one-time elections. The details of each election are sufficiently intricate, and the methods of compliance are sufficiently peculiar, that further discussion of each is best left to the books written for those concerned with tax compliance rather than with tax recognition. The good business manager need understand only the importance of obtaining qualified help on a timely basis.

Income averaging. Individual taxpayers with an erratic income pattern will pay a larger income tax than will other taxpayers earning the same aggregate taxable income in equal amounts over several years. The reason for the difference is, of course, attributable to the progressive rate schedule used by individual taxpayers. In an attempt to minimize the extra tax due to an unusually large income in any single year, the Code authorizes an annual income averaging option for individual taxpayers. This option allows the taxpayer to compute his tax liability in a special way and, if that tax is less than the tax computed in the ordinary way, to pay the lower amount. The general formula utilized in this special tax computation is as follows:

Taxable income recognized in the current year xxxx
less 120 percent of the average taxable income recognized by the
   taxpayer in the four prior years (this four-prior-year average is
   called the average base period income). xxxx
difference is "averageable income" (income averaging can be
   elected only if averageable income is more than $3,000) xxxx

Determine, in the usual way, the tax liability on a taxable income
   equal to the sum of (*a*) 120 percent of the taxpayer's averaged
   base period income plus (*b*) 20 percent of his averageable income xxxx
deduct the tax, determined in the usual way, on a taxable
   income equal to 120 percent of the taxpayer's average
   base period income. xxxx
the difference is the ordinary tax on 20 percent of the
   taxpayer's averageable income xxxx
multiply this difference times 5 . . . . ×5
the product is the tax on averageable income xxxx
add the tax, determined in the usual way, on a taxable income
   equal to 120 percent of the taxpayer's average base period
   income. xxxx
the sum equals the alternative tax under income averaging xxxx

Special rules are provided for taxpayers who have not been married throughout the base period years, for foreign source income, for distributions from pension and other retirement funds, and for capital gains taxed under the alternative long-term capital gain tax rate. Taxpayers who did not furnish at least one-half their support in the four base period years are not eligible for income averaging, unless their support was furnished by their spouse. These and other special rules can modify the general formula suggested above. Even in the situation where income averaging may be elected, this statutory solution to the problem of bunched income is much less than a perfect solution. Perhaps its greatest deficiency is the failure to authorize income averaging in unusually low income years as well as in high income years. The amount of tax saved by income averaging proves, on close examination, to be rather capricious because it depends upon a unique interaction between no less than four distinct variables. Even though a detailed analysis of those variables must remain beyond the confines of this book, every taxpayer should be aware of the possibility of tax savings through income averaging in any year in which he recognizes an unusually large taxable income.

Common tax traps

TAX TRAPS often are as ruinous to tax planning as sand traps are to shooting par. In the game of golf, the traps at least are equally visible to all players. In the tax game, unfortunately, the traps may be hidden from the view of all but the most erudite players. These tax traps can be of economic, judicial, or statutory origin.

Economic traps are not unique to transactions which are characterized by unusual tax consequences. Nevertheless, transactions which embody a special tax advantage seem to be especially prone to chicanery. One expert, whose only business is the investigation of potential tax-sheltered investments, recently reported that no more than five percent of the proposals which he investigates are economically sound. Obviously, more than five percent of these investments are being sold to unwary customers. A possible thesis that might explain the commercial success—for their sellers, anyway—of tax-sheltered investments is the fact that prospective buyers get so involved in trying to understand the tax impact of the proposal that they fail to scrutinize the more mundane economic projections associated with it. An investment in a limited partnership about to construct a new apartment complex, for example, usually will be sold on the basis of tax losses coupled with positive cash flows that can only be explained in terms of rapid depreciation deductions; the immediate deduction of property taxes and interest expense during the construction period; a possible investment credit; and partnership tax rules. These tax complications may cause the potential investor to lose sight of the fact that the entire proposal can be no better than the economic projections embodied in it. If, for example, the occupancy rate or the projected rents are overestimated, or if the projected operating expenses are underestimated, the real economic impact of such an error generally will not be magically rectified by some obscure tax rule. In a limited number of situations tax rules actually do transform apparent economic losses into real economic gains; more commonly, however, tax rules serve only to mitigate the intensity of a real economic loss. Because economic traps are not unique to transactions with special tax consequences, we will dismiss them from further consideration. The successful business manager, however, will always consider economic risks before he begins to consider tax complications.

In this chapter, we will investigate some of the major tax traps which are either of judicial or statutory origin. Any result which does not prove to be the most desirable possible result because of a special tax rule may be classified as a tax trap. For example, offsetting short-term capital losses with long-term capital gains in a year when potential short-term capital gains are available may be considered a tax trap—so can claiming straight-line depreciation when rapid depreciation is authorized. Such a broad definition of tax traps proves to be unwieldy; it is, in fact, bounded only by the generous limits of man's ignorance. In order to make our task more manageable, we shall define tax traps to include only those judicial doctrines and statutory provisions which have been designed positively to limit, defeat, or destroy tax-planning ideas that otherwise would be viable.

JUDICIAL TAX TRAPS

Judicial tax traps may best be described as the few scattered black clouds dotting the generally clear horizon on a perfect summer day. Even the most experienced tax practitioner cannot predict with 100 percent certainty just when and where those black clouds may strike disaster on an unsuspecting taxpayer. Although it leaves much to be desired in terms of academic precision, perhaps the safest generalization in tax planning can be expressed in the words of an old Wall Street adage. That adage says that you can make money being a bull and you can make money being a bear, but you can never make money being a pig. Judicial tax traps have an uncanny way of striking the "tax pig." The most common judicial tax traps have been conveniently labelled "substance over form," "business purpose," and the "step transaction" doctrines.

Substance over form

The judicial notion that legal consequences should depend upon the substance of a transaction rather than upon its form is not unique to problems of income taxation. In tax matters, however, the consequences very often are critically different depending upon what one assumes to constitute the substance of the transaction. Furthermore, the form of a transaction usually is deemed to be indicative of its intended substance. In a closely held corporation, we know that the owner has good tax reasons for preferring to make all corporate distributions to owners as salaries, interests, or rents, rather than as dividends. What, then, is to prevent the owner-operating stockholder from declaring a particular corporate distribution to be one of the more tax-favored ones? In other words, can the owner-manager transform a potential corporate dividend into a salary simply by declaring his intention and recording that intention properly in the corporate records? Some recent decisions of the tax courts seem to suggest that some portion of the assets distributed by a closely held corporation to the owner-manager will be considered to constitute a dividend *even if the aggregate payment to the owner-manager does not exceed a reasonable compensation for the services which he has rendered to the corporation.* This conclusion has been applied thus far, however, only where the corporation had substantial earnings but a very poor dividend record. Whether or not the implication of these decisions will be upheld by the appellate courts on review remains to be seen. If they are upheld, those decisions will constitute a radical extension of the substance-over-form concept. Previously the danger that tax deductible salaries might be converted into nondeductible dividends existed only after salaries were found to be unreasonably large. It now appears that any time a profitable corporation fails to pay minimal dividends the courts may find that parts of some other distributions actually constitute dividends, at least in the case of closely held corporations. Certainly there is no statutory basis for the recent decisions; if there is any authority for them, it must derive from such judicial doctrines as substance over form.

A somewhat parallel question involves the need to distinguish between corporate debt and equity. In the closely held corporation there again are many good tax reasons for an owner to designate a major part of his capital investment as debt rather than labeling his entire investment as an equity interest. If the owner took sufficient care to provide all of the indications of debt, and if the debt-to-equity ratio was not stretched to grotesque proportions, the courts traditionally held that valid debt existed. In the more extreme cases, the courts found, on the judicial authority of substance over form, that some instruments which purported to be debt were in fact equity. The Tax Reform Act of 1969 included a new provision, Section 385 of the Code, giving the commissioner of the IRS wide authority to distinguish between corporate stock and debt for tax purposes. Although the commissioner has not yet exercised his new authority, the eventual Treasury Regulations will tend to reduce the need for judicial intervention in this aspect of income taxation in the future.

We have considered here only two specific illustrations of the judicial substance-over-form doctrine. It can, however, appear in relation to almost any tax problem. The more a taxpayer stretches the boundaries of reasonableness in applying tax rules, the more likely he is to encounter this judicial tax trap. On rare occasions the taxpayer may even attempt to utilize this judicial doctrine as an equity argument in his own interest. If, for example, a taxpayer clearly intended to do one thing but he failed to complete each and every technical detail required by statute to achieve his intended objective, he may try to convince the court that the substance of his actions should prevail over any minor oversight in form. Although there is nothing to preclude such an argument, the business manager ought to be aware of the fact that most judicial tax doctrines seem to be exclusive property of the IRS. In other words, as they are actually applied in tax cases, the judicial doctrines we are reviewing here seem typically to constitute a one-way street leading into a tax trap, not a two-way street which includes a convenient way to correct an unfortunate error committed by the taxpayer.

Business purpose

The judicial doctrine of business purpose says that a transaction will not be given any effect for tax purposes unless it also achieves a valid business purpose. Incidentally, saving taxes alone is not deemed to constitute a valid business purpose. This doctrine stems from the case of *Gregory* v. *Helvering,* which was first tried in 1932. In that case the taxpayer, Mrs. Gregory, fully complied with the letter of the tax law. She arranged, within a few days' time, a spin-off of some portion of her corporation's assets into a new, second corporation, a dissolution of this new corporation, a distribution of the assets held by the new corporation to her as sole owner, and a sale of the same assets to a third party. According to the law then in effect, the Revenue Act of 1924, the spin-off should have been a nontaxable transaction; the liquidation plus distribution of assets a taxable transaction that would produce a capital gain for Mrs. Gregory; and the sale of assets a taxable transaction but one that would produce no taxable income. The absence of any taxable income could be attributed to the fact that the assets had received a tax basis equal to their fair market value in the liquidating distribution (which had just been taxed as a capital gain) a day or two prior to their sale. The trial court, the Board of Tax Appeals in this case, agreed with the taxpayer's conclusion, saying, in effect, that it had no authority to do anything but interpret literally the tax laws Congress had passed. The Circuit Court of Appeals for the Second Circuit and the Supreme Court disagreed with the trial court and thereby created the business purpose doctrine. Translated freely, their decisions said that literal compliance with the tax law may not be sufficient; if a transaction has no valid business purpose other than saving taxes, it does not satisfy the intent of Congress and, therefore, should be given no effect. The critical result for Mrs. Gregory was that the court found that there had been a dividend distribution by the original corporation, to be taxed as ordinary income, rather than a liquidating distribution by the new corporation, to be taxed as a capital gain. The overlap between the judicial doctrines of substance-over-form and business-purpose was apparent in this case.

Perhaps one of the most intriguing aspects of all judicial tax traps is the fact that one is never certain just when the courts will elect to apply them. In 1956, the Circuit Court of Appeals for the Tenth Circuit, in the case of *Diamond A. Cattle Company* v. *Commissioner,* reached a decision in which it said: ". . . when Congress passes an act in language that is clear and unambiguous, and construed and read in itself can mean but one thing, the act must be judged by what Congress did and not by what it intended to do." Here the taxpayer was allowed to claim a tax privilege that Congress did not intend, notwithstanding the potential application of contrary judicial doctrines that were already well established.

Step transactions

A third judicial concept sometimes utilized by the courts to destroy otherwise effective tax-saving schemes concocted by taxpayers and their advisors is known as the step transaction doctrine. The effect of this judicial tax trap is to collapse a series of carefully arranged intermediate transactions into a single transaction and to look only at the substance of the net result to determine tax consequences. Although this judicial concept was not specifically mentioned in the *Gregory* decision, it could have been applied there as effectively as the business purpose test. Any tax-planning idea that relies upon the recognition of each and every detailed step of a complicated scheme that could be made in a much more direct manner, and that involves a minimal time span for its completion, runs a high risk of judicial intervention under one doctrine or another. The step transaction doctrine has been applied most frequently in corporate reorganization situations. Again, however, it has not been applied consistently. On some occasions, the courts have given full recognition to each carefully arranged movement in a grand tax minuet; on other occasions the courts refuse to see the beauty of it all. Even the seasoned opinion of the best legal counsel available may be uncertain of the outer boundaries of these judicial tax traps. In a social sense, their elusive quality may be their most redeeming feature.

STATUTORY TAX TRAPS

The life cycle of most unintended tax loopholes is characterized by four phases of development: (1) discovery; (2) successful application; (3) administrative, and sometimes judicial, intervention; and (4) legislative elimination. For purposes of this book we will define statutory tax traps to include only those Code provisions that have been enacted as the fourth and final phase of this life cycle. One might think of this collection of Code sections as the long fingers of Congress plugging the many holes in a leaking dike that is used to redirect resources from the private to the public sector. Among the sections we shall consider are the following:

Sec. 532. Corporations Subject to Accumulated Earnings Tax;
Sec. 542. Definition of Personal Holding Company;
Sec. 341. Collapsible Corporations;
Sec. 306. Disposition of Certain Stock;

Sec. 318.   Constructive Ownership of Stock; and

Sec. 482.   Allocation of Income and Deductions Among Taxpayers. The Code contains numerous other provisions that could properly be included within our limited definition of statutory tax traps. These, however, are some of the more important sections for tax planning generally and they are illustrative of the other sections. Tax practitioners are well acquainted with the details of most of these statutory tax traps. We will consider only their broad outlines for the benefit of the general manager.

The accumulated earnings tax

Because the corporate tax rate historically has been significantly lower than the personal tax rate on equivalent incomes for most wealthy individuals, the corporation has been used as a primary tax shelter by many taxpayers. This tradition, and its potential challenge in the near future, was explained in Chapter 4. Congress realized the potential abuse of the corporate rate shelter when it passed the initial income tax act in 1913 and thus included provisions for an accumulated earnings tax in that bill. The original idea was to ignore the corporate entity and tax the shareholder on his ratable share of the corporate income, whether distributed to him or not, if there was evidence of an accumulation of earnings beyond the reasonable needs of the business. That initial idea was dropped in 1921 when Congress created the present rules, which provide a wholly separate penalty tax imposed directly on the corporate entity under circumstances similar to those identified in the original bill.

Basic provisions. The major features of the present provisions, contained in Sections 531 through 537, are the imposition of a special tax at the rate of either 27.5 percent or 38.5 percent on unreasonably accumulated taxable income. The latter quantity is an adjusted version of the corporation's taxable income. The Code does include an accumulated earnings tax credit of $100,000, but this is an adjusted credit that must be reduced for accumulations of earnings in prior years. The 27.5 percent rate is applicable to the first $100,000 of accumulated taxable income in any year; thereafter the rate is 38.5 percent. Because the personal marginal tax rates never exceed 70 percent, the use of a corporate entity to accumulate income is seldom advisable if the accumulated earnings tax will be applied because the total tax of 75.5 percent (48 percent ordinary corporate tax plus a

27.5 percent accumulated earnings tax) will be greater than the worst possible tax that would be applicable if the income were received directly by the owners without the imposition of an intermediate corporate entity.

Before the IRS and the courts can impose the accumulated earnings tax, they must find that the corporation has been formed or availed of for the purpose of avoiding the personal income tax of the shareholders. As a practical matter, this means that the business manager should give primary consideration to recognizing those bits of evidence that lead a court to find that the forbidden purpose exists rather than worrying about the details of the actual tax calculation.

Unreasonable accumulations of earnings. Most authorities will find that there is no unreasonable accumulation of earnings within a corporation unless one or more of the following factors are present:

1. Substantial loans to major stockholders or other personal-benefit assets or agreements between the corporation and its principal stockholders;
2. An unusually high current ratio—that is, the ratio of current assets to current liabilities is much higher than that common to the industry—and either large cash balances or large investments in relatively risk-free assets; or
3. A minimal record of dividend payments coupled with closely held corporate stock.

The reader should understand that these are general observations, not hard and fast rules. The imposition of the accumulated earnings tax turns largely on the facts of each individual case. The best defense in such situations usually is a good offense.

Planning considerations. If a taxpayer can prove by the preponderance of evidence that the accumulation of earnings is attributable to a valid business reason, other than tax avoidance, he can avoid this penalty tax. Courts have found that the following constitute valid reasons for accumulating corporate earnings: the desire to expand a business or a plant without the dilution of the present owners' interest and without borrowing; the desire to acquire a new business, especially if that business is directly related to the existing business of the accumulating corporation; the desire to increase inventories; the desire to retire outstanding debt; the need to provide loans to suppliers or customers; the desire to fund pension plans; and the desire to substitute a self-insurance reserve for commercial coverage. Each of these needs and desires must be adequately documented in the corporate records if it is to be given much weight by an examining agent or the court. If a taxpayer anticipates a potentially dangerous accumulated earnings tax problem in sufficient time, it usually is not terribly difficult for him to find and document some valid reason for the accumulations made. The greater danger of this statutory tax trap seems to be its application in situations that should have been adequately diagnosed and prevented by anticipatory actions.

The personal holding company tax

The accumulated earnings tax proved to be an inadequate weapon for the IRS against the use of the corporate rate shelter by wealthy individuals. In 1934, therefore, Congress enacted a second penalty tax in a further attempt to eliminate the use of this tax shelter. The new provisions were worded to provide somewhat more objective standards than the "unreasonable accumulation" criterion of prior law. Specific provisions were included to snare "incorporated pocketbooks" (that is, corporations whose only business consisted of buying, selling, and holding other stocks and securities); "incorporated talents" (that is, corporations whose only business consisted of the disposition of the owner's peculiar talent as an actor, athlete, or other star performer); and "incorporated pleasure facilities" (that is, corporations whose only business consisted of the leasing of a hunting lodge, island estate, or yacht to its owners). In each of these common situations, the owner was trying to achieve through the corporate entity tax savings that he could not achieve directly as an individual. The incorporated pocketbooks provided the major advantage of the corporate dividend-received deduction plus the lower corporate tax rate. The incorporated talent provided an opportunity to accumulate and reinvest personal compensation beyond consumption needs at a minimum tax cost. The incorporated pleasure facility provided a way to convert a nondeductible personal (pleasure) expenditure into a tax-deductible business.

Basic provisions. The present statutory provisions, contained in Sections 541 through 547, impose a special 70 percent penalty tax on any personal holding company that has undistributed personal holding company income at the end of a year. Thus, this penalty tax may be avoided in either of two ways. First, a corporation can make certain that it is not classified as a personal holding company. Second, the corporation can make certain that it does not retain personal holding company income at the end of the year. The objective of this penalty tax is to force distributions and to make the retention of certain kinds of income in a corporate entity an impractical alternative, not to collect revenues for the government. Thus, the Code authorizes a taxpayer to make a retroactive dividend distribution any time that the personal holding company tax would otherwise apply. If such a distribution is made, the tax base automatically disappears. Since the penalty tax rate is so high (70 percent), the individual owner virtually always will prefer a dividend distribution, even if it is taxed at the highest marginal rate for individual taxpayers, to a retention coupled with this penalty tax.

Before a corporation is deemed to be a personal holding company, it must "fail" two tests. They are (1) a stock ownership test and (2) an income test. A corporation will not be considered a personal holding company if the five largest stockholders own less than 50 percent of the value of the corporation's outstanding stock. This means that any corporation with ten or fewer owners automatically fails the ownership test since some five of those owners would have to own no less than 50 percent of the stock. On the other hand, 11 or more unrelated and *equal* owners would automatically avoid any danger of this statutory tax trap.

If less than 60 percent of any corporation's "adjusted ordinary gross income" is "personal holding company income," that corporation will not be deemed to be a personal holding company. For purposes of this book, we can define personal holding company income as either (1) passive income or (2) income from personal talent. Passive income includes income from dividends, interest, rents (under specified conditions), royalties, annuities, and payments by shareholders for their use of corporate properties. In general "passive" income is to be distinguished from "active" income—that is, income collected automatically through ownership is distinguished from income earned by entrepreneurial effort.

Planning considerations. The shrewd manager will realize that the use of the corporate rate shelter has not been eliminated by either the accumulated earnings tax or the personal holding company tax. His task is to combine active and passive income streams in such a way as to avoid the personal holding company tax and then to prepare a record that will substantiate a finding that all accumulations of earnings have been reasonable. To illustrate this possibility, let us assume that a taxpayer commands an annual income stream of $100,000 from an active business venture and another $50,000 from dividends.

If this taxpayer requires an annual income of about $50,000 before taxes for personal consumption needs, he has $100,000 before taxes remaining for reinvestment. If the taxpayer did not incorporate his two income streams in a single business his tax liability would be in the vicinity of $75,000 per year. If he does incorporate and then pays himself a salary of $50,000, his annual tax liability would drop to something like $38,000, determined as follows:

Corporate income tax		
Gross corporate income	$150,000	
Less salary paid to owner	(50,000)	
Less dividend received deduction	(42,500)	
Corporate taxable income	$ 57,500	
Corporate income tax on $57,500		$21,100
Individual income tax on salary (approximate)		17,000
Total annual tax liability		$38,100

The mixing of dividend-producing stocks with an active business serves to avoid the danger of a personal holding company tax as long as the income from the active business exceeds 40 percent of the total corporate income. The problem of unreasonable accumulations of earnings can best be handled by well-documented plans for corporate expansion, debt retirement, pension plans, and similar programs.

Individuals with nothing but passive income sources might consider the creation of a personal holding company owned equally by 11 taxpayers. The group can enjoy the major benefits of the corporate rate shelter and the corporate dividend-received deduction, even though the owners can not achieve the same tax advantage individually, because such a corporation would pass the ownership test and thus be ineligible for the personal holding company tax.

Collapsible corporations

Code Section 341 was enacted in 1950 to stop the wholesale conversion of ordinary income into capital gain through an unintended tax loophole in the corporate liquidation provisions. The basic scheme, which the courts seemed unwilling to end by judicial authority alone, usually involved four steps: (1) the creation of a property within a corporate shell; (2) either the sale of that corporation's stock or the liquidation of the corporation after the completion of the property but before the increase in the property's value had been realized by the corporate entity (a liquidation would involve the distribution of the newly created property to the corporate stockholders); and (3) the subsequent sale of the appreciated property to a third party. The collapsible corporation notion was most suited to such ventures as the production of a movie, a copyright, a building or other construction object, or an aged whiskey.

The tax law generally provides that any assets received by a stockholder in a corporate liquidation are to be taxed as a capital gain. The measure of the gain is equal to the difference between the fair market value of the property received and the basis of the stock surrendered in the liquidation. In the collapsible corporation, this difference usually is equal to the value of the service rendered by the stockholder in the creation of the property prior to the collapse of the corporation. In other words, this difference in value represents the value of the service rendered by the actor and/or the producer in the making of the movie; the value of the author or composer in the preparation of the copyright; the value of the construction engineer or builder in the erection of a building; or the value of the distiller in the preparation of an aged whiskey. By starting the operation in a corporate shell the owner could withdraw his profit as a capital gain so long as he could defer the realization of any increment in value until after the corporation's liquidation.

The net effect of Section 341 is to require that the stockholder recognize ordinary income, rather than capital gain, on the sale or the liquidation of a collapsible corporation's stock. The technical definition of a collapsible corporation is much too involved for our consideration. Suffice it to observe that any corporation that does not realize a "substantial part" of the income on any property which it produces runs the risk of being classified as a collapsible corporation. More importantly, perhaps, the statutory presumption of collapsibility will not apply if either the shareholder owns less than a 5 percent interest in the corporation's stock or more than 30 percent of his gain can be attributed to noncollapsible property. A taxpayer with sufficient nerve and a good advisor might still convert some ordinary income into capital gain if he can properly mix some limited gain in noncollapsible property with other gains in collapsible property each year. Any mixing solution is always dangerous because the reported incomes are subject to some readjustment by the IRS and the courts. If the taxpayer does not cut his objectives too thinly, however, he may still find that tax-saving opportunities that initially seemed to be closed by statutory measures may in fact be made somewhat safer by statutory presumptions. While sailing these somewhat hazardous seas, the taxpayer should always keep one eye on the judicial clouds that can make havoc of even the best-charted waters.

The preferred stock bailout

Taxpayers' attempts to convert ordinary income into capital gain have not been restricted to any single device such as the collapsible corporation. During the early 1950's a wave of preferred stock bailouts were used rather successfully to this same end. The idea was simple. The corporation would declare a preferred stock dividend, which, under the existing tax rules, could be received tax-free by the shareholders. The shareholders would sell the preferred stock received as a stock dividend to a third party in an arm's length transaction taxed as a capital gain. Shortly thereafter, the corporation would redeem all of its outstanding preferred stock at a small premium. The net economic effect of the several transactions was equivalent to the distribution of a dividend by the corporation. The tax effect, however, was quite different: it produced a capital gain for the stockholders rather than an ordinary dividend. Incidentally, the reason for using preferred stock in this plan was to minimize any risk of dilution of voting control for the old stockholders. If the third party who purchased the dividend shares had refused to allow the corporation to redeem its newly acquired stock, the former owners' problems were minimized so long as the new owners held only nonvoting preferred shares.

IRS attempts to fight this tax plan with only judicial authority were unsuccessful. Therefore, Congress included Section 306 with the Internal Revenue Code of 1954. That section in effect stipulates that any gain realized on the sale of preferred stock received as a tax-free stock dividend will be taxed as ordinary income rather than as capital gain. This statutory provision has a few remaining loopholes that may be useful in planning the disposition of a large estate consisting primarily of stock of a single corporation, and in making a bootstrap sale of a corporation to a new owner. On balance, however, the remaining tax-saving potential is relatively limited and the greater danger may be the inadvertent disposition of "tainted" Section 306 stock and the need to recognize ordinary income. This statutory tax trap is well understood by most tax advisors, and business managers would be wise to consult them before disposing of any preferred stock that was not purchased directly in an open market.

Constructive ownership

Many tax consequences can be determined only after one knows what percent of the corporation's outstanding stock is owned by the shareholder who is involved in that particular transaction. For some purposes, it is desirable for the owner to reach as large a percentage ownership as possible; in other circumstances, the taxpayer may desire to minimize this percentage interest. A taxpayer, for example, must own more than 80 percent of a corporation's stock if his individual transfer of property to a corporation is to pass as a nontaxable transaction under Section 351. On the other hand, we just noted why a taxpayer might desire to be deemed to own as little stock as possible when a question of the personal holding company tax or a collapsible corporation's stock is in question.

In order to achieve a smaller percentage ownership, a taxpayer may be tempted to give or to sell some of his shares to a related person. As a practical matter, such evasive tactics are seldom of any use because of the constructive ownership rules. The Code contains several slightly different sets of constructive ownership rules for different purposes. For example, Section 318 contains one set of rules for use in most questions arising under Subchapter C of the Code; Section 544 contains another set of constructive ownership rules for use in connection with personal holding company problems. Although there are important differences in each of these several sets of constructive ownership rules, we need only observe that their common result is to find that a taxpayer is deemed to own many shares in addition to those he owns personally and directly when determining his own tax consequences. Usually, a stockholder must include as his own shares any shares owned by his spouse, his parents, his children and grandchildren, as well as those shares owned by partnerships, corporations, and trusts in which he has a beneficial interest. Finally, the stockholder must also include as shares he owns any shares which he has an option to acquire. The net result of these imputations is, of course, to give many taxpayers a larger interest than they would prefer to have for many tax determinations.

Allocation of income and deductions

The explicit rules of the statutory tax traps that we have examined thus far tend to be aimed at specific abuses which derived from prior practical experience. The only exception is that relating to the accumulated earnings tax, and, in that instance, Congress needed no prior experience to predict accurately what would happen in the absence of a statutory prohibition. Although Section 482 has a similar specific history, this provision has recently been applied in several ways never contemplated when Congress first enacted the section. For this reason it is more difficult to determine the limits of this potential statutory tax trap.

Section 482 in general gives the IRS the authority to distribute, apportion, or allocate any item of gross income, any deduction, or any tax credit between or among two or more controlled businesses if it determines that such an adjustment is necessary to prevent the evasion of income taxes or to reflect income clearly. It is this Code section that the IRS has cited as authority for its enforcement of more realistic pricing policies in sales transactions between related persons, especially between domestic parent corporations and their foreign subsidiaries. The same section has been cited as the authority for requiring interest on loans made between related taxpayers and for charging-out managerial services rendered by one corporation's employees for a related corporation.

Although we do not yet know the limits of the Commissioner's authority under this statutory provision, we do know that business managers must give more careful consideration in the future than they have in the past to the tax consequences that might attach to transactions between related taxpayers. If a taxpayer desires to keep all of these transactions free of any tax consequences he usually can do so either by merging the two businesses or by filing consolidated corporate tax returns. If he does not desire either of these alternatives, the business manager should become more aware of the potential tax implications of Section 482. The danger of this tax trap is that it may trigger the recognition of taxable income at an undesirable time and that it may allocate that income to the least desirable entity.

In summary, a taxpayer should always be aware of the fact that the Commissioner of the Internal Revenue Service has at his disposal an arsenal of weapons to defeat a taxpayer's desire to capitalize on a questionable tax privilege. Tax-saving provisions deliberately written into the Code by Congress are not at issue here. For example, the tax advantages that attach to routine capital gains, to rapid depreciation allowances, to viable corporate business ventures, and to percentage depletion are well established and beyond question by the IRS. When the taxpayer or his adviser extends these special provisions to a new or unusual case, however, he may discover that his objective will be challenged by the IRS on the authority of an elusive judicial doctrine or on the basis of prior statutory action of Congress in somewhat analogous situations. In taxation as in love, however, it often is better to try and to fail than never to have tried at all.

14

The taxing process

ACTUAL PARTICIPATION in the taxing process is quite different from reading about the myriad existing tax rules. Books usually proceed to describe taxation as a series of apparently sterile rules of the "if-A-then-B" variety. The reader is tempted to conclude that taxation consists only of learning and impartially applying all of the many rules. Any reasonable exposure to the real process of taxation will quickly dispel that notion. Taxation is in fact a very dynamic process of interaction between people. *Tax rules are made, interpreted, and administered in minutely different situations by unique humans who work with a very imprecise language.* Because the taxing process is an entirely human one, distinct opportunities and problems are created. First, it means that the tax rules are constantly in a state of flux, and that, under the proper circumstances, they actually can be rewritten or reinterpreted to the distinct advantage (or disadvantage) of one or a few taxpayers. Second, it means that a knowledgeable taxpayer can often prearrange events so that only the most favorable tax result will actually be applicable to his situation. Third, it means that even when a taxpayer fails to exercise any preliminary caution he may be able to argue successfully that his particular situation is (or is not) within the meaning of certain statutory words and that, therefore, rule "A" rather than rule "B" ought to apply.

Our income, estate, and gift taxes are all self-compliance taxes. The individual, theoretically, must determine his own tax liability and report that determination with the proper remittance to the government on a timely basis. As a practical matter, the tax rules have become so complex that a majority of the taxpayers believe that they are individually incapable of self-compliance, and, therefore, they turn to apparent tax experts for assistance. Although an expert can help the taxpayer meet his obligations, the taxpayer alone bears the brunt of the liability for complying with the law.

In practice, the taxing process seems to take place at three different levels: first, at the legislative level, where the initial rules are hammered out in a political process called government; second, at the planning and compliance levels, where the taxpayer works with an advisor and the two attempt to satisfy the legal and financial requirements placed upon the taxpayer; and, third, at the level where disagreements are resolved between the government and the taxpayer. In the latter process especially, the taxpayer tends to stand on the sidelines watching the experts spar over his own fate. He plays the role of an innocent bystander who must ultimately pay the consequence of battle.

In this chapter, we shall consider only the second and third levels of the taxing process. The first level can be dismissed because so very few taxpayers ever attempt to influence tax legislation directly for their individual benefit. Those few who take this narrow route to legal tax avoidance usually have a sophistication ranking far beyond that envisioned for the readers of this book. Virtually every taxpayer, on the other hand, is faced with problems of planning and compliance. A lesser but still significant number face the problems of resolving disagreements with the IRS. The chapter is divided into three major sections. The first section contains a description of tax compliance procedure from the filing of a tax return through the litigation of potential differences of opinion. The second section consists of a brief discussion of the tax experts who offer their assistance on a commercial basis to taxpayers seeking help. The third and final portion of this chapter consists of a very brief forecast of what may lie ahead in the area of federal taxation.

COMPLIANCE CONSIDERATIONS

The first official step in the compliance process generally consists of the filing of a tax return on a timely basis. Long before the reporting date arrives, of course, the taxpayer may have made an investigation into the alternatives available to him and so arranged his affairs that a given result is almost certain. This preparation for the filing of a return may even have included a request for an advance ruling on a technical point by the IRS. Regardless of whether or not preliminary tax planning has taken place, every taxpayer eventually must report the taxable events that have actually transpired to the IRS. The date on which any tax return is due will depend upon many different considerations including the tax involved (for example, the income, estate, or gift tax) and the kind of taxpayer involved (for example, individual, corporation, or fiduciary). Several hundred forms and instructional booklets have been prepared and distributed by the IRS to facilitate this reporting process. In unusual circumstances, the IRS may accept as a satisfactory tax return the taxpayer's computer tapes and individual computer programs in lieu of the more typical forms. However it may be accomplished, the act of reporting is the first common step in the taxing process.

Filing tax returns

In a recent year, approximately 90 million income tax returns were filed with the IRS by individual, corporate, and fiduciary taxpayers. An additional 22 million employment tax returns and 1.5 million estate and gift tax returns were also filed in that year. On the whole, the income, estate, and gift tax returns represent the greatest challenge in terms of compliance considerations. Most tax returns are presently filed with one of the nine IRS service centers located in various sections of the country. These service centers are largely information processing facilities. They do perform a simple check of the arithmetic accuracy of virtually all returns received, but this check should not be confused with an actual audit which will be discussed shortly. Having confirmed the arithmetic, a service center clerk will prepare a computer record of the documents received. The computer record will be forwarded to Martinsburg, West Virginia, for storage and further reference. If the return indicates that a refund is due the taxpayer, the service center personnel will also initiate the action required for the preparation of a refund check. If a remittance is included with a return, service center personnel will separate the check from the tax return and deposit the tax paid to the government's account.

Many taxpayers place unjustified significance upon the fact that they receive a refund check from the government or that the government cashed their check as submitted. As just explained, this means only that their return has passed a simple check of arithmetic accuracy and that it has been logged into the government computer file for possible retrieval at a later date. It says nothing about the general acceptance of the tax return as filed. For most purposes, the IRS has at least three years during which it may raise questions concerning the accuracy of any tax return filed. If a return contains a material error—for example, an omission of more than 25 percent of the gross income—the assessment period extends from three to six years; if fraud is involved, the assessment period remains open indefinitely. As a practical matter, much of the routine work being done by IRS agents involves tax returns that are two to three years old. Thus every taxpayer should keep all of his supporting records for at least three years; certain records are best retained for a lifetime.

Returns selected for audit

The actual audit selection process was, until a few years ago, a special task assigned to some of the most experienced employees of the IRS. Recently that task has been largely delegated to the computer. Based upon a highly classified discriminate function analysis, the computer scores each tax return received by the IRS. The return with the highest score is supposedly the one most deserving of an audit; the return with the second highest score, the next most deserving of audit; and so on. Although the computer program utilized by the IRS must remain secret for obvious reasons, it seems reasonable to speculate that it gives special attention to, among other things, deductions which are larger than normal for a taxpayer in any given income bracket; deductions which are especially prone to abuse (travel and entertainment expenses, for example); returns reporting a substantial gross income but little or no taxable income; and returns reporting very large incomes from any source. Some returns are also selected for audit each year on a purely random basis to determine the general compliance standards of taxpayers as a whole.

The audit of a tax return is conducted by IRS personnel assigned to a district office, not by personnel from the service center. At present there are 58 district offices scattered throughout the United States. To facilitate compliance the IRS maintains resident audit personnel in each of the major cities whether or not there is a district office there. The audit staff is generally divided between revenue agents and special agents who perform rather different functions. The revenue agent conducts more or less routine investigations into the adequacy of the returns selected for audit; the special agent is assigned to more investigatory work in cases where fraud is suspected. Routine audits may be conducted either at an IRS office (which audit is then classified as an "office audit"), or at the taxpayer's place of business (which audit is referred to as a "field audit"). The decision on where the audit should take place is largely a matter of logistics. If a large number of bulky records must be examined, the IRS agents usually will agree to a field audit; otherwise, the taxpayer can expect to report to an IRS facility for completion of an audit.

Settling disputes

A taxpayer receiving his first notice of an IRS examination may panic unnecessarily. Unless the taxpayer has reason to suspect that an audit is something more than a routine investigation, he usually has nothing to fear. The agent will request that substantiating records be produced for his examination. If the taxpayer has maintained good records and the information was reported correctly, the audit may be closed promptly with little or no adjustment. If the records are questionable, or if the agent disagrees with the taxpayer's interpretation of the tax rules, a more detailed administrative review procedure is set into motion. In order to make the contest one between equals, a taxpayer generally would be well advised to be represented in any administrative hearing by a knowledgeable tax expert if the proceeding involves anything other than a simple and direct verification of fact. In other words, it would not be necessary or helpful for a taxpayer to engage a tax expert if all that he is being asked to do is prove the fact that he has ten dependent children or that he gave "x" dollars to his church *and* he has adequate proof of those facts. On the other hand, if the taxpayer is trying to substantiate the conclusion that his aged grandmother really is a dependent, or if he is trying to prove that he made weekly cash contributions to an open church offering, an advisor may be most helpful. In more complicated business situations (involving corporate formations, pension plans, and similar circumstances) a tax advisor is virtually mandatory. Generally speaking, the taxpayer should contact his advisor as soon as he receives a notice of examination, not after he has already met with the IRS representative. The way in which a case is initially presented may have something to do with its ultimate resolution.

Administrative reviews. If the original auditor, his supervisor, and the taxpayer cannot agree upon the correct resolution of a particular issue, the IRS procedure authorizes two additional levels of administrative consultation before the taxpayer needs to consider the possibility of litigating the dispute in a court of law. The administrative review procedure first authorizes a district level conference with a specially trained agent, called a "conferee," who is entirely independent of the agent who conducted the original audit. If the district conferee and the taxpayer still cannot resolve the differences, the case may be moved to the appellate division which is part of the regional office of the IRS. The seven regional offices operate as intermediaries between the district offices and the national office of the IRS in Washington, D.C. Whether or not a taxpayer should utilize either or both of the possible administrative review procedures depends largely upon the question under consideration and the professional opinion of the expert handling the case. A visual presentation of the audit procedure is contained in Figure 14–1.

Judicial reviews. If the taxpayer and the representatives of the IRS simply cannot settle their differences of opinion in any administrative proceeding, the debate can proceed to trial. In tax matters any one of three courts may have initial jurisdiction. A taxpayer will end up in the Tax Court if he refuses to pay a tax deficiency assessed by the IRS and he proceeds to litigate the dispute. If the taxpayer pays the deficiency assessed by the IRS he may then turn around and sue the government in either a Federal District Court or the Court of Claims for a recovery of the money that he thinks was wrongfully collected. The selection of the most appropriate judicial forum should, quite naturally, be heavily influenced by the taxpayer's legal counsel. Each of the courts is quite different in its method of operation and each may be preferred under particular circumstances. Generally, the Tax Court has the better grasp of technical issues because it is a court whose jurisdiction is restricted to tax controversy. The U.S. Federal District Court is expected to try cases in all aspects of the law and, therefore, the judges cannot be equally expert in every technical detail of the tax law. On the other hand, there is no provision for a jury trial in the Tax Court. If the question to be established is one of fact, rather than of law, counsel may prefer the District Court route, believing that a jury may be more sympathetic to a taxpayer's point

FIGURE 14–1

INCOME TAX AUDIT PROCEDURE
Internal Revenue Service

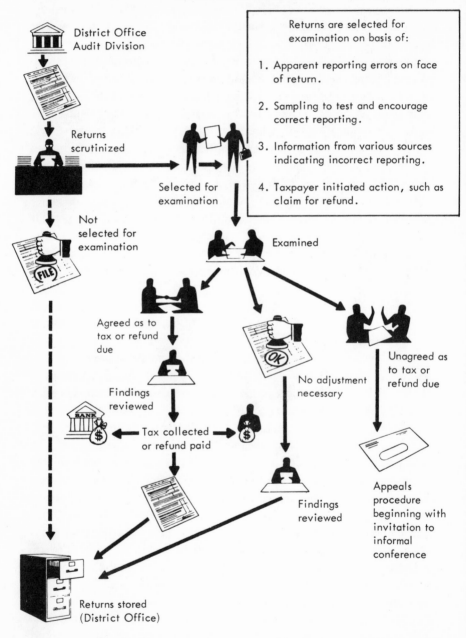

District Office
Audit Division

Returns
scrutinized

Selected for
examination

Not
selected for
examination

Examined

Returns are selected for
examination on basis of:

1. Apparent reporting errors on face
   of return.

2. Sampling to test and encourage
   correct reporting.

3. Information from various sources
   indicating incorrect reporting.

4. Taxpayer initiated action, such as
   claim for refund.

Agreed as to
tax or refund
due

Unagreed as
to tax or
refund due

No adjustment
necessary

Findings
reviewed

Tax collected
or refund paid

Findings
reviewed

Appeals
procedure
beginning with
invitation to
informal
conference

Returns stored
(District Office)

of view. If, for example, a taxpayer is trying to establish the fair market value of a painting that he donated to an art museum, there may be good reason to prefer a Federal District Court to the Tax Court. An appeal from either of these two courts must go to the Circuit Court of Appeals for the taxpayer's place of residence.

An appellate court generally will not review findings of fact. The appellate courts tend to accept the lower court's determination of fact and consider only errors in the application of the law. The losing party can usually force his disagreement before a Circuit Court of Appeals. Once that body has rendered an opinion, however, the only remaining appeal is to the United States Supreme Court. During an average year the Supreme Court will agree to hear no more than five to eight tax cases. These cases are selected either because the court believes that they contain some important tax principle that needs to be clarified or because two or more Circuit Courts of Appeal are in disagreement about how essentially identical questions should be answered. Appeals from the Court of Claims can go only to the Supreme Court. A visual presentation of the income tax appeal procedure, including both administrative and judicial elements, is contained in Figure 14–2, p. 300.

A summary observation

In evaluating the IRS procedures, the reader should understand that any individual taxpayer's chance of having his tax return selected for audit is statistically less than 1 in 20. The reason for this low probability of an audit is the fact that the IRS does not have sufficient manpower to do more, not the fact that all of the remaining returns are deemed to be correct as filed. In one recent year, the IRS audited less than 2 million tax returns. Of the returns audited the vast majority were either accepted as filed or all differences were settled by agreement between the agent and the taxpayer. Only 40,000 cases proceeded beyond the initial auditor to a conference procedure. Nearly two-thirds of those going to conference were settled without judicial proceedings. During that year the IRS conceded about 30 percent of the tax deficiency initially assessed. Considering only the agreed cases which were settled without trial, the IRS conceded an even larger percentage of the initial deficiency assessment. The result of judicial proceedings in tax matters during 1971 can be summarized in Table 14–1, p. 301.

FIGURE 14–2

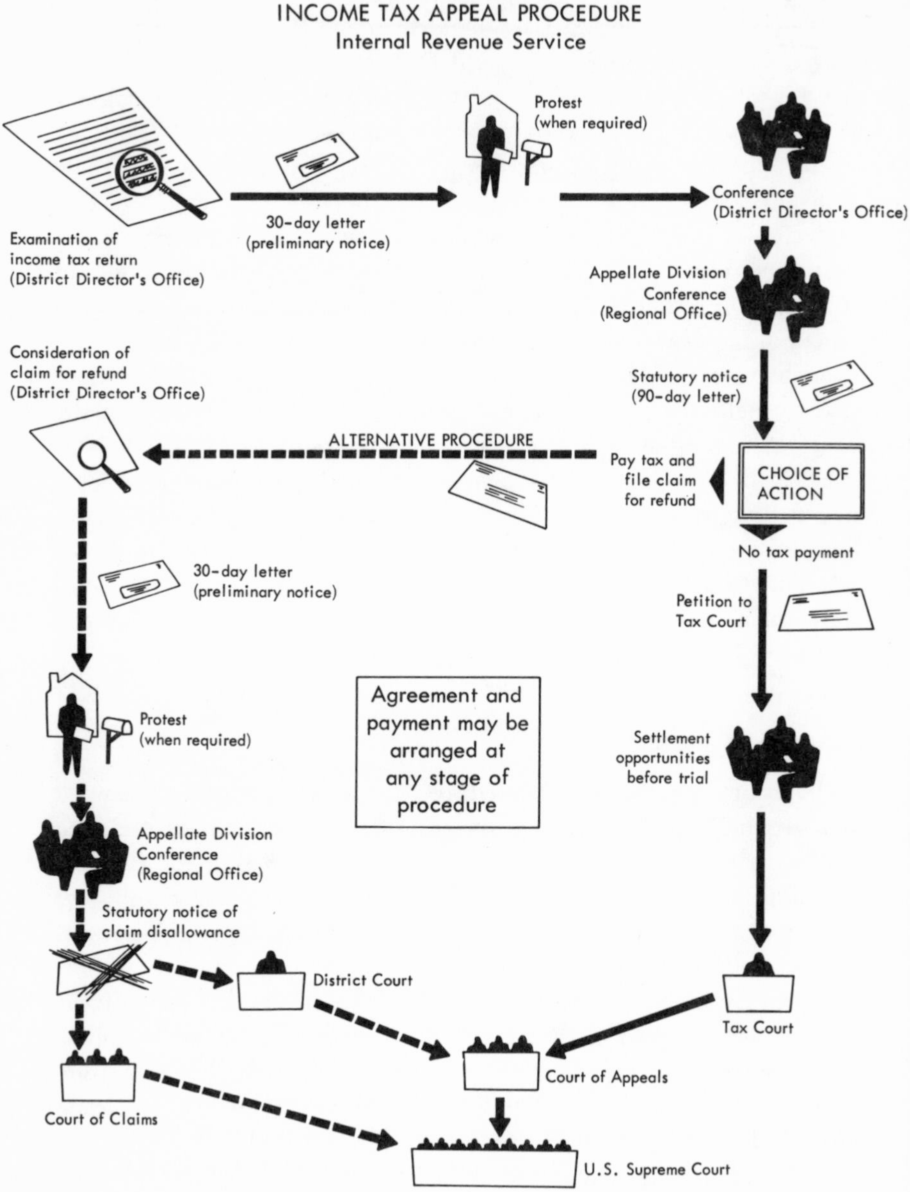

INCOME TAX APPEAL PROCEDURE
Internal Revenue Service

Examination of
income tax return
(District Director's Office)

30-day letter
(preliminary notice)

Protest
(when required)

Conference
(District Director's Office)

Appellate Division
Conference
(Regional Office)

Statutory notice
(90-day letter)

Consideration of
claim for refund
(District Director's Office)

ALTERNATIVE PROCEDURE

Pay tax and
file claim
for refund

CHOICE OF
ACTION

No tax payment

30-day letter
(preliminary notice)

Petition to
Tax Court

Protest
(when required)

Agreement and
payment may be
arranged at
any stage of
procedure

Settlement
opportunities
before trial

Appellate Division
Conference
(Regional Office)

Statutory notice of
claim disallowance

District Court

Tax Court

Court of Appeals

Court of Claims

U.S. Supreme Court

TABLE 14–1
Summary of tax decisions rendered in 1971

Victorious party	Tax Court	Federal District Courts	Court of Claims	Circuit Court of Appeals	Supreme Court
IRS............	407	207	16	172	3
Taxpayer........	100	147	6	72	0
Split	280	70	4	24	0
Total decisions.......	787	424	26	268	3

The point of all these statistics is simply to impress upon the reader the following important conclusions:

1. The chance that any particular tax return will be selected for audit is something like 2 percent.
2. The chance that any error in a tax return will be discovered is even less than 2 percent because the IRS agents obviously cannot detect every error on every return examined.
3. If a return is audited, the overwhelming odds are that the taxpayer and the IRS will be able to settle any dispute without a judicial hearing.
4. If the IRS and the taxpayer do resolve a disputed item without a judicial hearing, the probabilities are that the IRS will agree to accept significantly less than the amount of the initial deficiency assessed.
5. If a dispute proceeds to trial, the chances are about 4 out of 10 that the taxpaper will win at least some portion of his case.

These conclusions are important for several reasons. First, they should explain why a competent tax advisor may not be impressed by the argument that something must be right just because a taxpayer has always done it that way and the IRS has never objected. Second, the statistics should explain why there is no real reason to panic when a taxpayer first learns that he is being audited. Third, the statistics should explain why the level of taxpayer assistance may be substantially less than ideal without ever being noticed by the taxpayer. Critics have often suggested that a surgeon's worst mistakes are buried, undiscovered. There can be little doubt but that that observation holds true for many a tax advisor.

TAXPAYER ASSISTANCE

Taxpayer advisory services have become big business in the United States. It is estimated that there are currently more than 200,000 persons offering their services to the public as tax advisors. Surprising as it may seem to many readers, most of these experts remain almost wholly unregulated. In a world in which those who cut hair and fingernails can operate only by government license and regulation, it is surprising indeed that tax advisory services remain an open frontier.

Questions of competence

Most alleged tax experts can be divided between "regulated agents" and "unenrolled practitioners." The regulated agents can be further subdivided into (a) attorneys, (b) certified public accountants, and (c) "enrolled agents," or persons who are neither attorneys nor CPAs but who have passed a special tax examination given by the Treasury Department. Attorneys and certified public accountants are automatically admitted to practice before the IRS based upon their regular professional examinations and license. Of the 200,000 persons offering tax advisory services, approximately 70,000 are regulated and 130,000 are unenrolled practitioners. The 70,000 are regulated by *Treasury Department Circular No. 230* as well as by the code of ethics of the professions involved; the 130,000 are entirely free to operate without risk of sanction other than the normal risk of civil and criminal liability that everyone has for his own actions. Although the latter group is free to claim almost anything that it wishes, the IRS will not allow an unenrolled practitioner to represent a taxpayer in an administrative conference.

Treasury Circular 230, the Code of Ethics of the American Institute of Certified Public Accountants, and the Canons of the American Bar Association forbid all forms of advertising. Until very recently, professional ethics also forbade the external representation by members of special expertise in tax matters. This meant, of course, that those who were most likely capable of rendering a valid tax advisory service were precluded from claiming their expertness while those who had little or no special knowledge were entirely free to proclaim publicly anything that they wished. Under those conditions, the taxpayer could safely conclude only that anyone who could advertise or who could list himself as a tax expert in the "yellow pages" probably was not highly qualified as a tax expert whereas anyone who could not make such claims just might be so qualified. The necessary "probably" and "might be" in the preceding sentence do little to add to a taxpayer's confidence in selecting a qualified tax advisor. Obviously some few unenrolled agents may have managed to acquire minimal skills in tax matters while others who have proven their right to be licensed as attorneys or as certified public accountants may prove to be inept in matters of taxation. During the past year, a few states have granted attorneys with special expertise in selected areas, including taxation, the right to proclaim their special abilities to the world. Hopefully, the accounting profession will someday soon grant this same opportunity to its members. Until then the buyer of tax advice must be wary of the service he receives.

A common misconception. Most people erroneously believe that the formal education required of an attorney and a CPA includes a heavy background in taxation, especially federal income taxation. As a matter of fact, most colleges and universities offering a major in accounting require only one three-semester-hour course in taxation and most schools of law require no minimal study of taxation. Between 20 and 25 percent of the time devoted to the practice portion of the nationally administered CPA examination is usually devoted to income tax questions. Although some state bar examinations still include tax questions, other states have removed all tax questions from the bar examinations. Notwithstanding the minimal standards for formal tax education, a substantial number of certified public accountants and attorneys have become extremely competent in matters of taxation. Their general education in related subjects has been combined either with special graduate education in taxation or with heavy practical experience in tax problems to produce this high degree of competence. These professionals are, beyond any doubt, those best qualified to advise others on all matters of taxation. The major problem for the taxpayer seeking competent assistance is the fact that he has no easy way to distinguish between the highly qualified advisor and the poorly qualified one. Some day, hopefully in the near future, all of the state and federal professional associations in law and accountancy will recognize the need to certify tax specialists for the benefit of everyone concerned. The first encouraging steps in this direction have just been initiated by the bar association in the State of California.

A controlled study. Recognizing the fact that far too much bad tax advice is being sold to the public under false pretenses, several news media have designed simple experiments to test the comparability of tax advice. The usual experimental design involved a reporter taking a single set of financial records through several different tax return preparation services. The reporter typically would compare the results and conclude that the "best" tax service was the one that gave him the lowest tax liability at a minimum cost. A doctoral student, working under the supervision of the author, decided to expand upon this basic experiment in a more refined study of tax return preparation services. He first obtained the cooperation of ten individuals with one or more interesting tax problems of "medium complexity." Each taxpayer took his records to three different tax return preparation services: one was a nonenrolled practitioner; another was a certified public accountant; and the third was an attorney. The doctoral student prepared a fourth return for the taxpayer which he (the student) deemed to be correct and he paid all of the fees incurred by the taxpayer in this experiment. In exchange, the taxpayer gave the student the right to compare each of the several tax returns as part of his research study.

The results of this study probably are not representative of all non-enrolled practitioners, attorneys, and CPA's for several reasons. First, and most importantly, the sample size is not large enough to permit generalization. (The only reason for restricting the sample size was the cost of the undertaking.) Second, the experiment was conducted in a limited geographical region. Third, the accounting and law firms which were most likely to include the most highly qualified tax experts—that is, the accounting firms which are numbered among the "big eight" and the law firms with partners who were members of the Tax Section of the American Bar Association—were deliberately excluded from the experiment. (Their exclusion was attributable to two factors: one, the need to keep the cost of the study within reason and, two, the attempt to determine taxpayer compliance problems for the *average* individual rather than for the large corporate enterprise or the extremely wealthy individual.) Recognizing these several limitations, we will not review the findings of that study in detail. Suffice it to observe here that the attorneys, the certified public accountants, and the unenrolled practitioners all made a significant and roughly equal number of technical errors in the tax returns they prepared, with one major exception. The unenrolled practitioners distinguished themselves by their tendency to "pad" expenses and to create tax deductions where no legal tax deduction exists. Although attorneys and CPAs made some other technical errors with equal frequency, they did not share the tendency to fabricate. In the author's opinion, none of the groups did an adequate job of explaining difficult problems of interpretation to the taxpayers concerned. Instead, the apparent expert tended to resolve all open tax issues one way or another and to file the tax returns accordingly, without giving the taxpayer an opportunity to influence the way in which questionable items were reported and without even informing him of the doubtful nature of certain items.

Some tax experts guarantee a taxpayer that they will pay for any technical errors made in their preparation of a tax return. The reader should observe that these guarantees extend only to the correct reporting of the facts as they are related to the tax return preparer. If the facts are erroneously reported, the return preparer obviously cannot be held responsible for any additional tax imposed in a subsequent audit. More importantly however, there may be a tendency by the "guaranteed" tax return preparer to resolve all questionable items in favor of the government. To the extent that such a tendency exists, the guarantee becomes less than worthless. The guarantee actually may cost the taxpayer more than it saves him. A real tax expert would explain all questionable issues to the taxpayer and allow him to make the final decision on how those items will be reported. The taxpayer, of course, is entitled to know the expert's opinion of what he would do, were he in the same circumstance, before he makes up his own mind. Given that kind of tax advisory service, a taxpayer cannot hold the expert responsible for an incorrect decision. Nevertheless, this would be the author's preferred way of resolving all doubtful issues. Even though a true tax expert may not be able to guarantee that the IRS and/or the courts will agree with his professional opinion on a difficult tax issue, he is very sensitive to the need to give consistently good tax advice and his charges usually will be governed accordingly.

What is a taxpayer to do? The reader may well wonder how he can find and recognize qualified taxpayer assistance if he cannot trust advertisements and he cannot safely assume that each and every CPA and attorney is knowledgeable in tax matters. The only certain method of locating qualified tax assistance known to the author is through personal reference. In other words, the only safe way to locate your first qualified tax advisor is to ask another taxpayer whom he has found to be satisfactory. Individuals who have been in business for a reasonable period of time have encountered the need for qualified taxpayer assistance on several occasions and they usually are willing to share their experiences with a fellow sufferer. Sometimes, from bitter personal experience, they will tell you who is not qualified as well as suggesting a list of those they deem competent.

Once a taxpayer has made his initial contact with a tax advisor, it is up to him to decide if he is getting the kind of service that he needs and desires. Assuming that the taxpayer is engaged in a continuing business, it is the author's opinion that a taxpayer cannot be getting adequate service unless he and his tax advisor are engaged in frequent communication with each other. The taxpayer must understand that his advisor will have to know *all* of the details of every proposed transaction at the *earliest possible* moment if he is to perform his function satisfactorily. Really qualified tax experts maintain the highest possible ethical standards and keep all client communications and records confidential. Therefore, the taxpayer has nothing to lose and everything to gain by sharing his detailed plans with his tax advisor. A tax advisor who does nothing more than file tax returns on a timely basis is not rendering an adequate service to a continuing business. A good advisor will be making numerous suggestions for change as well as answering all inquiries made by the taxpayer. An expert will also expect to be paid a reasonable fee for the work that he does.

Questions of cost

Most individuals have a natural reluctance to seek the advice of a competent tax advisor until long after the need for his assistance was first observed. The apparent reason for this reluctance is the belief that the fees charged by such advisors are usually exorbitant. Although it is true that good tax advisory service may be expensive, it seldom is exorbitant for several reasons. First, in most instances a competent tax advisor will save his client substantially more in taxes than he charges for his advice. Thus the taxpayer usually comes out ahead, not behind, in dollars. Second, the tax advisor's fees are themselves tax deductible; hence, the cost of that service is shared by the government on a ratio determined by the taxpayer's marginal tax bracket. The higher the marginal tax bracket the lower the real cost of the tax advisor's service. Third, most tax advisors bill their clients on the basis of hourly rates. These rates may range from $20 to $200 per hour for a qualified tax advisor. The taxpayer, however, generally need not fear that the advisor will be anxious to bill him for the largest possible number of hours at the highest possible billing rate. Good tax advisors are so scarce that they cannot begin to handle the work that naturally gravitates to them. Consequently, the more competent the advisor (and, therefore, the higher his billing rate), the more likely it is that he will either refer a problem to another firm or to a less experienced individual within his own firm if your problem really does not warrant his attention. Virtually all of the qualified tax advisors known personally by the author are trying to reduce the number of small clients they advise, not trying to acquire more of them. Some have begun charging a minimum fee just to discourage the taxpayer with a small problem. Fortunately, however, a competent advisor will always advise a client of any minimum fee before he begins to work on a project. In summary, therefore, the author's advice for the reader is to aim too high rather than too low. Taking too simple a problem to an overly qualified tax advisor has a way of correcting itself in most cases; taking too complex a problem to an underqualified tax advisor has a way of becoming very costly in the long run, even though the real cost may not be discovered for several years.

THE TAX FUTURE

No one, including the author, has a particularly clear view of what the future holds taxwise. Successful tax planning must nevertheless take into consideration possible future tax changes. If the tax rates are going to increase significantly next year, we should all accelerate taxable income into this year and defer all possible tax deductions until next year. If the gift and estate taxes are going to be combined into a single donative transfer tax in the near future, wealthy individuals should make major gifts to their children and grandchildren right now. If the investment credit is to be suspended anytime soon, taxpayers should consider the possibility of placing orders for certain equipment earlier than they otherwise might have. The prescriptions come easily if only we know the prognosis.

A few things seem reasonably certain. In absolute terms, the income tax will either remain at its present size or grow; there is little chance for it being substantially reduced anytime soon. In relative terms, the income tax may lose stature with the introduction of new taxes of major importance in the near future. The most likely prospect is the value-added tax, although it appears that the Senate could provide major opposition should the Nixon Administration decide to propose its adoption. Even if defense spending can now be curtailed, the rapidly growing demands for increased health, education, and welfare services at the state and local levels seem destined to increase the aggregate governmental budget. The traditional state and local taxes simply cannot keep pace with these growing demands. Therefore, the federal government is destined to share a larger and larger portion of state and local government expenditures through revenue-sharing measures. Continued inflationary pressures will make federal deficit spending at the present rate an unacceptable alternative in the long run. For all these reasons, we can only anticipate a continuation of the heavy income taxes we have come to know since World War II.

Limited tax reform bills will continue to be introduced into the Congress. Although President Nixon remained relatively silent throughout the campaign of 1972, many other politicians campaigned loudly for the revision of various tax-saving provisions reviewed in this book. The capital gains provisions were attacked more frequently than most others. Whether or not any of the limited tax reform proposals will be enacted into law remains to be seen. Our relatively recent experience with the Tax Reform Act of 1969 tells us that nothing is impossible. On balance, the Treasury Department was better prepared for that round of tax debate than they had been on any prior legislation. To what extent the Treasury Department's preparation resulted in Congressional action, and to what extent that action stemmed from the general political and social unrest of the late 1960s, is still uncertain. The author's best guess is that we will not see tax reforms comparable to those enacted in 1969 for several years. The more likely prospect for the near future is a series of upward revisions of the tax rates, the possible reintroduction of the surtax (a tax on a tax), and a frequent revision of those provisions intended primarily to stimulate critical economic variables, such as rapid depreciation, the investment credit, and rapid write-offs. In short, if the predicted taxpayer revolt is as remote as the author thinks it is, equity considerations will not be given top priority in income tax legislation. A modest value-added tax seems to be a likely prospect.

Most major tax revisions enacted into law during the past few years have been made retroactive to the date on which they were first discussed publicly in a Congressional committee. The reader should, therefore, get accustomed to following proposed tax legislation through daily newspaper accounts and through weekly magazine reports. Any proposal that appears to harbor potential tax consequences for the reader or his business should be called to the immediate attention of a tax advisor. And a really good tax advisor will take it from there.

CASES

Case number one

COMPUTEX INC. (hereafter, CI), a Dallas-based corporation engaged in the computer software business, has four major stockholders:

Name	Title	Percent of common stock owned
Charles Bass (CB)	Chairman of the Board and Chief Executive Officer	25%
Everett Vern Prescot (EVP)	Executive Vice President	20%
Samuel Treadeau (ST)	Secretary-Treasurer	15%
Paul Masson (PM)	Plant Manager	10%

The remaining 30 percent of the outstanding stock of CI is owned by about 300 members of the general public, including 8 percent which is owned by an employees' (profit-sharing) trust fund. CI has been modestly successful since its inception in 1956. During the past 16 years CI has accumulated corporate profits of nearly $1 million; it has reported a profit for each of the last nine years. Unfortunately, however, the reported profit has been getting smaller each year for the past four years and the CI management has little basis for anticipating a sudden change in this trend. In fact, operating losses seem to be a real possibility in the short run due to intense competition and high costs in the industry.

PM, a camera buff (B.S.M.E., Rice, '56; M.B.A., U.T., '58) has spent much of his spare time at night and on week ends developing a new photographic paper and a photographic process which is much cheaper, provides a more accurate color reproduction, and retains true color for much longer than does the paper and the process presently utilized by film-developing companies. During the past few months PM has finally obtained patents on his new photographic paper and process. Except for his substantial investment of spare time, PM has relatively little capital invested in his new patents; they appear, however, to have substantial commercial value.

PM has determined that further commercial development of his patents will require additional skills and a substantial capital investment. He sees essentially two alternative ways to achieve the real potential of his patents: Plan I—PM could resign from CI and devote his entire energies to a new, wholly owned corporation dedicated to the development and exploitation of his discoveries. Plan II: PM could transfer the new patents to CI and allow it to develop the patents directly (Plan II–A) or indirectly, through a new subsidiary corporation (Plan II–B).

If PM were to proceed with Plan I he would be able to withdraw his accumulated benefits from the CI employee (profit-sharing) trust and he could sell his 10 percent interest in CI stock to raise additional capital for his new corporate venture. Additional capital would have to come from external sources because PM has few other assets. PM's share of the employee trust approximates $60,000; his 10 percent interest in CI has appreciated from his initial investment of $30,000 to approximately $180,000. PM hopes that any additional capital needed could be obtained from borrowing or by selling corporate bonds. He would prefer to keep the entire equity interest in any new corporation wholly within his immediate family if he decides to follow Plan I.

The CI Board of Directors has agreed (under Plan II-A) to transfer previously authorized but unissued shares sufficient to increase PM's ownership from 10 percent to 30 percent of the outstanding stock in exchange for his new patents. In addition the CI Board agreed that PM would concurrently be promoted from "Plant Manager" (at a salary of $35,000 per year) to "Vice President–Operations" (at a salary of $60,000 per year) and that it would grant him a five–year contract in this new position.

Finally, under Plan II-B PM would transfer his patents to CI which, in turn, would transfer them to a new subsidiary corporation, P.U. (Patents Unlimited). P.U. would be 100 percent owned by CI.

In exchange for his transfer of the patents PM would be named the Chief Executive Officer of P.U. and be granted an annual salary equal to 50 percent of the profits of P.U. for a period of ten years. In addition, PM would receive a 1 percent increase in the outstanding shares of CI for each $100,000 in after-tax profits accumulated by P.U. within the next ten years, to a maximum of an additional 20 percent ownership in CI. In other words, PM conceivably could, over the next 10 years, increase his present 10 percent interest in CI to a maximum 30 percent interest under Plan II-B.

Suggest any potential tax problems or opportunities which you think should be investigated by a tax advisor before the interested parties proceed to a final resolution of this proposal. State briefly why you think that each item should be investigated (i.e., suggest the general nature of the potential "problem" or "opportunity"). Consider both PM individually and the acquiring corporation in each of the three plans (Plan I; Plan II-A; Plan II-B).

Case number two

Patrick Andrew Willey (PAW), age 47, and Marjorie Ann (MAW), age 45, are the parents of two children, Patrick Junior (JR), age 24, and Mary Sue (MS.), age 21. JR has at least temporarily left society and joined a farm commune where he seems—much to his parents' disbelief—to be very happy. MS, to her parents' great delight, is finishing pre-med studies and will enroll as a freshman medical student at Johns Hopkins next fall. Although PAW and MAW have not disowned JR, they have agreed not to support him any longer (believing and hoping that this will "bring him back" sooner). They fully expect to support MS for the next four years to the tune of approximately $5,000 per year. If MS pursues a graduate specialty they probably will finance her for another three or four years.

PAW has had a rather checkered business career over the past 25 years. At the moment he is the Executive Vice President and General Sales Manager of Playperson Theaters, a chain of 3 dinner-theaters located in Kansas City, St. Louis, and Little Rock. His annual salary is partially dependent upon the financial success of the theaters. For the past few years they have been rather successful and PAW has earned a salary of between $38,000 and $44,000 per year. PAW owns a 40 percent interest in PPT Corporation which owns these three theaters. PPT has been operating for five years and has yet to pay a dividend. The stockholders are not complaining, however, because they are all employees of the firm and they all draw adequate salaries. In addition, a small accumulation of profits (approximately $40,000 over the past five years) has been retained within the corporation to allow for some expansion and any emergencies.

Prior to joining PPT, PAW had worked for several organizations including two which he helped to create and in which he still owns some stock. His last previous venture was with ZINC (Zero, Inc.) which never was financially successful. For the first few years ZINC incurred small losses; then, for a few years, it reported small profits; of the past year it returned to the loss column and the new management of ZINC is predicting that these losses will continue for at least the next two or three years. After that they hope that a new product which they are now developing will turn the company into a tremendous financial success. PAW still owns 10 percent of the common stock of ZINC and thinks that he will retain that interest even though there is a substantial risk that ZINC may never succeed. If it does succeed, PAW and all others agree that it will mean a tremendous financial profit.

Following the receipt of a sizeable inheritance from his parents' estate in 1951, PAW made one of his first investments, in INCO (Inland Nail Company). INCO proved to be a very sound outfit and has paid dividends of about 8 percent every year. This year PAW's dividends from INCO amounted to just under $6,000. Although the market value of INCO stock has not increased significantly, PAW considers it to be a very sound investment because of the generous dividend policy.

PAW and a hunting buddy, HERM, are on the verge of creating yet another new business, AIRRENTS (AR). AR will lease Winnabego campers, Honda cycles, and Glastron boats at carefully selected airports in the U.S. and Canada. PAW and HERM are of the opinion that many people like to take out-of-doors vacations in far-away places but that they spend too much time getting there. Therefore they plan to advertise and to help arrange group fares through cooperating airlines to encourage people to fly the longer distances and then rent from AR the kind of travel vehicle most suited to the perfect vacation in the unspoiled, hinterland portions of North America. They anticipate heavy losses in the first few years due to excessive advertising costs and limited usage. However they believe that they can finance most of the equipment purchases which they must make and thus their initial capital investment can be expended in set-up and advertising costs. They have already done some investigatory work and hope to be in operation within the next six months at four locations (Denver, Seattle, Atlanta, and Boston.) PAW and HERM look forward to inspecting their operations from time to time and, while doing so, engaging in a bit of hunting and sightseeing themselves.

MAW's mother died a few years ago and left MAW and her only sister, Sarah Ina Size (SIS), her entire but limited estate in rural Arkansas. MAW's father had passed away several years earlier. Until this fall MAW and SIS did relatively little with their mother's estate which consisted of a small acreage, a home, and furnishings. They had leased the acreage to a neighboring farmer and had simply locked up most of the furniture in the old home believing that they and their families might use it as an occasional summer retreat. They each used it briefly the first summer but for the past two years the old home has remained vacant and the vagaries of time are beginning to take their toll. Thus MAW and SIS have begun to sell (mostly through the neighboring farmer's wife) pieces of the family furniture to antique buffs who have hounded the place for years. In fact, some of the sales have been sufficiently rewarding that MAW and SIS occasionally take other bits and pieces they have collected to the old home place to sell it. The paint-peeled home with its creaking doors and sagging porch seem to provide an ideal setting for selling such items and the city buyers appear to pay a premium when they can "discover" these gems in their natural habitat.

PAW and MAW seldom have any excess cash lying around. As they approach 50, they increasingly think about their need to accumulate sufficient assets for a comfortable retirement. They have at present no financial interest in a pension fund or any other systematic saving program and, therefore, they must anticipate retirement on social security plus whatever they can accumulate between now and "that day." Although they do have several investments now, only the investment in INCO is of low risk. Nevertheless neither PAW nor MAW are inclined to switch any of their investments for good reason: not PPT (because that would almost certainly mean that PAW would lose his high-paying job and, at 47, jobs like that are hard to find); not ZINC (because they have that investor's hunch that ZINC just may pay off handsomely); not AR (because PAW and HERM have this new dream and no amount of persuasion could divert them at this point.) In short, PAW and MAW are happy with their present investments but their taxes are killing them.

Suppose that you are PAW, MAW, or their financial advisor. What things might you have investigated by a tax advisor which could help alleviate your present tax problem? What potential problems should he also investigate? Describe the tax opportunities and pitfalls.

Case number three

DR. JERIMIAH T. BEA—a cash-basis, calendar-year taxpayer who is widely known by his initials, "J.T."—has been actively engaged in a general practice of medicine in Plano, Texas, for over 40 years. His practice has been financially rewarding; in the past several years his taxable income has averaged between $120,000 and $150,000 per year. On July 1, 1973 Doc announced that he was going to sell his practice to Dr. Ed D. Youngblood, a recent Baylor graduate. The two physicians agreed to share the work and the income from the practice between July 1 and December 31, 1973. On the latter date J.T. would retire completely.

J.T. and E.D. have discussed three possible sales-purchase agreements for the transfer of the practice. Plan A calls for a payment of $450,000 cash on January 2, 1974, by E.D. to J.T., and an immediate transfer by J.T. to E.D. of *all* assets—including the office building and equipment, and uncollected accounts receivable, the supplies inventory, and a covenant not to compete. Plan B calls for a series of six annual payments of $100,000 each by E.D. for a similar transfer of assets by J.T. These payments would begin on January 2, 1974 and continue on the same day each year for six years. Plan C calls for a payment of $300,000 cash on January 2, 1974 and a transfer of all of the same assets *except for the accounts receivable* which total about $225,000 gross. Both parties realize that not more than $125,000 to $175,000 of the receivables ever will be collected. Under Plan C it would be up to J.T. to collect as many of these as he could.

J.T. is presently inclined to accept Plan C believing that most of the $300,000 he received from E.D. in 1974 would constitute either a return of capital or a capital gain since it would represent the gain on the sale of the building and the equipment and the value of his covenant not to compete in the future with E.D. This, he believes, would result in a tax of 25 percent at worst. To further reduce his taxes, J.T. plans to give, in lieu of a latter inheritance, about $100,000 of the older and more difficult accounts receivable to his only child, Lochinvar, who has been a sore disappointment to his father. In this way J.T. hopes to get Lochinvar out of his commune existence and into "work"—the work of collecting the old accounts receivable. Additionally J.T. feels that the tax benefit would be significant since he will still be in a significant tax bracket for several years whereas the son has no other source of income, at least at the present time.

During retirement J.T. and his wife plan to live and travel on the income which will derive from investments made during the years of medical practice. Additionally, J.T. is *not* adverse to spending his accumulated capital since leaving any more than the $100,000-or-so in receivables to Lochinvar seems, at this time, to be unwise. Most of J.T.'s investments are in ranch lands and securities. The current fair market value of these investments is somewhere between $400,000 and $500,000. They produce about $30,000 net income each year. Unrealized (i.e., "paper") capital gains on these investments amount to nearly $300,000.

By late November, 1973 J.T. had traded a few securities which had netted him a $5,000 long-term capital loss and a $2,500 short-term capital gain. He has a limited amount of current investments in all tax categories; i.e., long-term gain, long-term loss, short-term gain, short-term loss. Thus some reshuffling of these "current" investments is possible if that were deemed advisable.

Finally, J.T. has about decided to invest $100,000 of the proceeds from the sale of his medical practice in a new venture-capital deal called V.A.C. The V.A.C. group is a spin-off of a small pharmaceutical firm. Their plans call for development of an innoculation which could prevent dental cavities for a period of three to five years following each shot. Early experimentation with animals suggests that the venture has a chance for success although all of the parties concerned realize it is a high-risk proposition. J.T. does not plan to play an active role in the research or the management of the firm; his participation would be strictly that of an investor.

Assume that you and your family have been close personal friends of Dr. and Mrs. J.T. Bee for many years and that you learned of Doc's plans through a dinner conversation at your parents' home. You feel it appropriate to make a few observations to Doc about the tax aspects of his pending plans. What items would you suggest

he have investigated before he acts, and why? (Incidentally, you may assume that J.T. has charged most of the cost of his office building and equipment to depreciation in prior years.) As part of your comments include some observations about dispositions A and B as well as C—the plan he is currently favoring.

Case number four

RIVER CITY CORPORATION (RCC) is primarily engaged in the manufacture of "Redsuz," a commercial laundry detergent, in Junction, Texas. RCC is a closely held corporation of the Willie Oat family—a family well known in the Junction area for the number of lawyers and politicians it has produced. Although RCC is predominantly a manufacturing company, the Oat brothers occasionally invest excess corporate cash in real estate in and around Travor County, which is growing like the proverbial rabbit hutch. Exclusive of their earnings from RCC, the majority of the RCC stockholders, i.e., the Oat brothers, have a taxable income of between $50,000 and $100,000 per year from their other activities. This means, of course, that their individual marginal tax rate is somewhere in the 62 percent to 70 percent range. RCC typically has a taxable income of between $40,000 and $60,000, excluding any "extraordinary" gains or losses it may realize as a result of real estate investments.

In February 1973 the RCC Board voted to purchase four separate but contiguous parcels of realty just west of State University for a total price of $325,000. Each piece of realty presently included a somewhat oldish building which was being rented to students at the university. With a minimum investment (say $15,000 to $20,000 total) these four old buildings could be made minimally acceptable for continued rent properties, for at least five to ten years. Eventually the Oat brothers anticipate the demolition of the four old buildings, thus making way for another massive apartment project. After purchasing these four parcels of realty the four brothers split two to two on how to proceed. Two recommend the demolition of the buildings as the present leases expire (during June, July, and August) and the immediate preparation of the site for an apartment project to be available by early fall. They estimate that the four properties, offered as a single unit, will be worth nearly $400,000. The other two brothers recommend that RCC make the minimum investment and continue to rent the properties for a few years before proceeding with the demolition. Monthly rents would amount to over $1,500 cash.

Explain in general the tax consequences of each of the two alternatives the Oat brothers are now considering. (Note: do *not* recommend or explain any additional alternatives for utilizing this realty—rather, all you need do is explain the tax consequences of the two alternatives they are presently considering.)

Case number five

THE BOARD OF DIRECTORS of Textax Corporation (TTC) are planning a major expansion in compensation for all salaried personnel. Among the alternatives being considered are:

1. Increase in cash salaries through an annual bonus;
2. Installation of a qualified profit-sharing plan;
3. Installation of a restricted stock purchase plan;
4. Issuance of a qualified stock option; and
5. Initiation of a deferred compensation contract.

Among the limited number of salaried personnel of TTC are three representative married men: Al Young, Ben Middle, and Carl Old. Al is a recent UT-MBA graduate earning $14,000 annually. He comes from a family of modest means and has two young children. Ben, a 48-year-old engineer, is earning a $50,000 annual salary. Except for his earning capacity, Ben has little wealth now and very little reason to believe that he will have in the future. Carl, on the other hand, is independently wealthy in addition to drawing his $100,000 annual salary as corporate vice president. Carl's wealth is estimated at in excess of $7 million.

Considering their relative financial and, therefore, tax position, indicate the probable first and second preference of each employee toward the five alternative compensation methods being considered by the TTC Board. You need *not* rank these preferences 1 and 2; simply check (√) which two you think each is most likely to prefer. In making your selection you may assume that long range projections estimate that TTC stock will increase approximately 8 percent in value per year though no one, of course, can guarantee this or any other growth rate. Further, you may assume that the

restricted stock purchase plan would allow the salaried employees to buy a limited number of shares of stock at $4 per share while the stock is currently selling at $6 per share. The restriction provides that the employee can obtain the actual shares only after he completes five years additional service; separation from employment prior to that time will cause these rights to be forfeited and permit the corporation to repurchase the shares requested under this plan at the $4 per share figure, or at the then-market price, should it be less than $4. Thus, the restrictions would lift in 1976 on any restricted stock purchased in 1971; in 1977 on shares purchased in 1972; and so on.

	1 Cash bonus	2 Qualified profit- sharing plan	3 Restricted stock purchase plan	4 Qualified stock option	5 Deferred compen- sation contract
Al					
Ben					
Carl					

Explain your selections for each of these men. An adequate explanation involves not only explaining why you selected the ones you did but why you rejected the others as well.

Give a few factors that would influence TTC's preference for one plan over another.

Case number six

AFTER losing three consecutive political races, Jerry Ervin was financially ruined. Although Jerry's political failure had been notorious, it had provided him with an opportunity to meet many interesting and potentially influential people. To begin to reestablish himself financially, Jerry spent most of 1972 looking around Austin for a good business opportunity.

He first investigated the possibility of acquiring an old theater (Studio X) that was known for its colorful films. Jerry engaged an M.B.A. student to do some marketing research and a law student to review potential censorship and film-lease problems. Meanwhile Jerry discussed his new business plans with several old friends. To make a long story short, Jerry was cautioned by every one of his "advisers" to steer clear of this particular business. By the time this idea had run its course, Jerry found that he had simply increased his financial woes. He paid the M.B.A. student ½ of his $1,000 fee and the law student ½ of his $1,200 fee, and promised that he would pay the remainder as soon as he was financially able.

During his discussion with friends about the theater business, someone suggested to Jerry the need for a new, quiet beer-garden in the capitol-university-stadium area. Jerry agreed with this suggestion and immediately began scouting around for an appropriate site. He located an old home on a corner lot with many trees. The property extended nearly half a block and bordered on Waller Creek. Jerry got an option on the property and began making plans. This time he engaged an architectural student (who demanded his $2,000 fee in advance) to plan the necessary remodeling. Meanwhile Jerry began to locate the financial assistance necessary to open his new spa—"Ervin's Inn on Waller Creek."

While working on this project Jerry invested over 2,000 hours of his personal time and $15,000 that he had been able to borrow from his only sister. Realizing the need for still larger sums of additional capital, Jerry took time out to manage without compensation the political campaign of G. Charley Brown, a wealthy gentleman who was running for a state senate seat. The gamble paid off when G. Charley won the senate seat and agreed to finance a one-half interest in Jerry's new political center (the beer garden) for $70,000 cash. G. Charley asked that his investment in the new business be arranged in "the most judicious manner" and that "some serious attention be given to tax factors." Both Jerry and G. Charley want to get this business opened by no later than April 15, 1974.

Near the end of 1973 Jerry comes to you for some elementary tax and business advice. After relating all of the above events, Jerry tells you that he earned only $1,800 cash during 1973. He earned that sum by working as a lobbyist for the Gibberish Industry Trade Group. During the year he has been living in an apartment paid for by the Anguish Corporation—a firm which Jerry occasionally represents in hearings before the Railroad Commission. During 1973 he had only one request to represent Anguish and that job took less than a week of his time.

Finally, you learn that Jerry is 38 years of age and that he was recently divorced. He and his former wife had no children. He is a cash-basis taxpayer.

1. What items of gross income must be included in the calculation of Jerry's taxable income for 1973? Explain briefly any potential problem areas.
2. To what deductions (*other than* a personal exemption and, perhaps, a standard deduction) is Jerry entitled in determining his 1973 taxable income? Explain briefly any problem areas that should be investigated further by a tax specialist.
3. What business form do you recommend for "Ervin's Inn on Waller Creek?" Remember to consider both G. Charley's wishes and Jerry's financial status. Include a suggestion for the form of the capital invetsment; that is, debt versus outright ownership. Explain your reasons for making whatever recommendations you make—also note any implicit conflicts of interest.

Case number seven

AFTER WORKING hard for nearly 40 years, Dusty Rhoades has built up his contracting business to a very sizable and profitable operation. Dusty has decided that he had better retire now, however, if he is to enjoy life before it is too late. Although Dusty has been somewhat sloppy in separating his personal and business transactions, he has managed to isolate most of his business transactions in two separate operations: Contrax, Inc., and Rhoades Construction. Contrax, Inc., is a closely held family corporation that has been utilized to handle most of his building contracts. Rhoades Construction is a sole proprietorship that has handled the road and bridge building operations. Dusty has had several recent opportunities to sell each business and at the moment he is inclined to do so.

Although the taxable incomes of the two businesses have fluctuated widely, for the past several years Dusty's personal taxable income has been between $80,000 and $120,000 per year. Except for the annual profits from the proprietorship and the salary drawn from the corporation, the Rhoades have relatively little other personal income. During retirement years Dusty would like to receive approximately $35,000 to $50,000 after-tax income per year. The higher amount will be required until his 82-year-old mother passes away. Dusty has been her sole support ($8,000 to $10,000 per year) since she became a semi-invalid four years ago.

Dusty's only son is a successful physician with little or no interest in the contracting business. His only daughter married a devoted high school coach who, though he often works for Dusty in the summer, would not be willing to leave coaching. Mrs. Rhoades is a housewife and quite unprepared to assume Dusty's role in the business venture. Incidentally, the Rhoades have five grandchildren.

Dusty feels fairly certain that he could arrange any of the following business dispositions:

1. Outright cash sale of Contrax, Inc., stock for $2.5 million and Rhoades Construction assets for $1.5 million. Dusty's tax base in the corporate stock is approximately $500,000. Data relative to the three primary assets of Rhoades Construction are as follows:

Assets	Tax basis	Fair market value
Land with large gravel pit	–0– *	$750,000
Heavy construction equipment	$250,000†	450,000
Contracts in process	100,000	300,000

* All cost has been recovered through depletion of the sand and gravel operation.
† Rapid depreciation claimed since 1962 on these assets amounts to $480,000.

2. Merger of Contrax, Inc., with Concrete Supply on the basis of three shares of Contrax for one share of Concrete Supply. The latter firm is a reputable national corporation with a very low dividend policy but a substantial growth rate over the past 15 years.
3. Merger of Contrax, Inc., with American Builders (on a 2½ for 1 basis). Builders is a conservative firm with a reputation for a generous dividend policy and a slow capital growth rate.
4. Installment sale of Rhoades Construction to a group of local investors headed by Dusty's chief foreman. Payments on this contract would call for a $300,000 downpayment plus $80,000 per year for 15 years. In addition, interest at 6 percent would be provided on the unpaid balance.

Assuming that Dusty is 62 years of age; in reasonably good health; planning to leave most of his estate to his family (after making limited charitable contributions to a few organizations); and willing to part with some of his property now if there is a good reason to do so (although he has not done this in the past), what do you recommend that he do and why? To answer this general question, first answer the following question: **What would be the immediate and future tax consequence to Dusty (and his family) of each alternative?**

Case number eight

MRS. FINE CHINA, a 65-year-old grandmother, sold her large ranch and moved into a penthouse suite in capital city. The sale price of the ranch was $300,000; Mrs. C's basis in the ranch was approximately $200,000. The sales agreement called for a $60,000 downpayment and annual installments of $21,000 plus interest.

Mrs. China has accumulated other assets including a block of railroad common stock with a basis of $50,000 and a fair market value of $30,000; a block of oil pipeline shares with a basis of $40,000 and a fair market value of $65,000; and an oil interest which provides an annual income of approximately $12,000.

This lady explains to you that she has one son, a realtor with a substantial income; one daughter, married to a physician with a large practice; four grandchildren under ten years of age; and one elderly sister who requires constant attention and who lives in a retirement home. Mrs. C provides all financing for her sister's care. She goes on to explain that she has a very limited interest in financial matters. She does, however, want to be sure that her annual income will remain approximately $20,000 per year for as long as she may live; she does want to continue to provide for her sister; and she would like to give the university a significant gift, perhaps $50,000.

Provide Mrs. China with a rough outline of a suggested "tax plan" which will achieve her objectives with minimal tax consequences. Explain each recommendation.

Code section index

Topical index

324